3–2–1
BOMB
GONE

3–2–1
BOMB
GONE

Fighting Terrorist Bombers
in Northern Ireland

Steve Smith

SUTTON PUBLISHING

First published in the United Kingdom in 2006 by
Sutton Publishing Limited · Phoenix Mill
Thrupp · Stroud · Gloucestershire · GL5 2BU

British Library Cataloguing in Publication Data
A catalogue record for this book is available from the British Library.

ISBN 0-7509-4205-3

Typeset in 10.5/15pt Photina.
Typesetting and origination by
Sutton Publishing Limited.
Printed and bound in England by
J.H. Haynes & Co. Ltd, Sparkford.

CONTENTS

List of Illustrations

PREFACE

When I first announced to a serving brigadier, who had himself worked as a bomb-disposal operator in Northern Ireland in the 1970s, my intention to produce this history, his initial response was, 'Well, good luck. Many have tried but failed.' He was absolutely right. Trying to piece together the history of the war against the terrorist bombers in Northern Ireland is no easy task. For obvious reasons, the work of the British Army's bomb-disposal experts has been deliberately shielded from the public's gaze. The understandable fear is that any revelation of tactics, techniques and procedures will inevitably highlight vulnerabilities that the terrorist may exploit to his advantage. Added to this, during the early years of the Troubles, the operators themselves were under such pressure that little thought was given to preserving any coherent history. Survival was the name of the game. With around twelve operators being employed in the Province at any one time, and with these changing over every four to six months, it is hardly surprising that events and developments were rarely recorded in anything other than a fragmented fashion.

As well as the lack of coherent records, any researcher in this field is up against the very nature of the operators themselves. While on the face of it they may have performed deeds of quite outstanding courage, their own views are rather more modest. Typical comments are: 'I was only doing the job I was trained to do, and the training was very good', or 'Please don't make me out to be a hero; I only played a small part, and many others were braver than me.'

In producing this book, I have drawn on the reminiscences of some fifty former operators, gained through personal interviews, written submissions, historic archive material and, in some instances, published works. I was fortunate in receiving numerous photographs from the personal collections of many individuals, frequently accompanied by contemporary newspaper clippings. My thanks go to the former Director Royal Logistic Corps, Brigadier Richard Rook CBE, for his encouragement and support in bringing the project to fruition.

Unfortunately, I have been unable to trace a source of permission for the extract that I have quoted from *The British Army in Ulster*, volume 2, by David Barzilay (Century Books, Belfast, 1973) that appears on pages 219–20. This section covers the recollections of former soldier Clive Evans, who witnessed the deaths of a bomb-disposal operator and two other soldiers at an incident near Forkhill in 1975.

Although a purely chronological account of the history of the unit's fight against the terrorist bombers would seem an obvious approach, I found that this risked becoming a depressing litany of death and destruction. Accordingly, I chose to structure this book in three parts. Part One charts the development of the bombing campaign in Northern Ireland in the early years of the Troubles, between 1969 and 1972, and the Army's response to it. In just over three years the bombers from both sides of the sectarian divide rapidly expanded their skills. In the process, they became increasingly cunning and depraved. Meanwhile, the Army tried to meet the growing threat, initially in an amateurishly enthusiastic, almost haphazard manner, learning constantly from its mistakes, and sometimes losing lives in the process. By the end of 1972, nobody was safe; everybody was a target – whether they had any connection with the Security Forces or not. Part Two therefore examines the enduring nature of the threat, which staggeringly persisted in the Province for more than thirty-five years. It examines the terrorists' strategy of waging war against the civilian population, creating a climate of fear, shattering Northern Ireland's infrastructure and causing a spiral of inter-sectarian violence. It also looks at the ongoing war against the Security Forces, using a mixture of booby traps, ambushes and home-made weapons. Part Three turns to the Army's response to the persistent and increasingly sophisticated threat. It covers the selection and training of bomb-disposal operators, the part played by the back-room boys in devising effective equipment and countermeasures, the experiences of operators on tour and a review of the occasions when the ultimate sacrifice has been paid.

Throughout the book, I have tried to abide by three guiding rules. First, I have scrupulously avoided any detailed explanation of our tactics that might be likely to give the terrorist the edge. Secondly, for the same reason, I have refrained from describing the precise technical capabilities of current equipment. And, finally, I have tried as far as possible to avoid recounting situations that might cause unnecessary distress or embarrassment. As the reader will imagine, the last point is not always easy when dealing with a subject that has caused so much suffering over more than three decades. Not surprisingly, it has therefore been necessary to leave out certain elements of the history, which, even now, cannot be revealed to the public at large.

The bottom line is that this is not just the history of those who are quoted in the book. Every single operator who has taken the 'long walk' has contributed to the preservation of life and property in Northern Ireland, and to the immense esteem that has been accorded to 321 EOD Squadron as a result. This is their story, and I salute all of them for their courage in shaping it.

Steve Smith
30 June 2005

ABBREVIATIONS

16PF	16 Personality Factor Questionnaire
ANFO	a home-made explosive, consisting of ammonium nitrate mixed with fuel oil
AOC	Army Ordnance Corps
AOD	Army Ordnance Department
APC	Armoured Personnel Carrier
AS of A	Army School of Ammunition
ASU	Active Service Unit
AT	Ammunition Technician
ATO	Ammunition Technical Officer
AVRE	Armoured Vehicle Royal Engineers – a tank fitted with a bulldozer and other mechanical plant tools
BAOR	British Army of the Rhine
BI	blast incendiary
CAQ	Clinical Analysis Questionnaire
CATO	Chief Ammunition Technical Officer
CILSA	Chief Inspector Land Service Ammunition – head of the Army's ammunition trade in the early 1970s
CIRA	Continuity Irish Republican Army
CLF	Commander Land Forces
CO	Commanding Officer (usually a lieutenant-colonel)
COP	Close Observation Platoon
CSM	Company Sergeant Major
DLSA	Director Land Service Ammunition
DPI	Dynamic Personality Inventory
DUP	Democratic Unionist Party – the Protestant political party headed by Ian Paisley
EOD	explosive ordnance disposal

EOKA	*Ethniki Organosis Kyprion Agoniston* (in English: National Organisation of Cypriot Fighters) – a Greek Cypriot guerrilla movement that campaigned against British colonial rule and aimed for union with Greece
FARC	Revolutionary Armed Forces of Colombia
FVRDE	Fighting Vehicles Research and Development Establishment
GC	George Cross
GM	George Medal
GOC	General Officer Commanding
GPMG	General Purpose Machine Gun
HMTD	hexamethylene triperoxide diamine – an organic peroxide home-made explosive
HQNI	Headquarters Northern Ireland
IAAG	Improvised Anti-Armour Grenade
ICP	Incident Control Point
IED	improvised explosive device – a terrorist bomb
IEDD	improvised explosive device disposal
INLA	Irish National Liberation Army – a breakaway, extremist, Republican paramilitary group
IPG	improvised projected grenade
IPLO	Irish People's Liberation Organisation – an offshoot of INLA, which split during a feud in 1986
IRA	Irish Republican Army
JNCO	junior non-commissioned officer
MOD	Ministry of Defence
MVEE	Military Vehicles Experimental Establishment
NATO	North Atlantic Treaty Organisation
NCO	non-commissioned officer
NICRA	Northern Ireland Civil Rights Association
NIFSL	Northern Ireland Forensic Science Laboratories
O Group	orders group – meeting of key commanders and personnel at which operational orders are given out
OC	Officer Commanding (usually a major)
OIRA	Official Irish Republican Army
OP	Observation Post
PAF	Protestant Action Force
PARA	Parachute Regiment

PATO	Principal Ammunition Technical Officer
PIRA	Provisional Irish Republican Army
PRIG	projected recoilless improvised grenade
R&R	rest and recuperation – the military expression for mid-tour leave
RAOC	Royal Army Ordnance Corps
RCIED	radio-controlled improvised explosive device
RE	Royal Engineers
REME	Royal Electrical and Mechanical Engineers
REST	Royal Engineers Search Team
RGJ	Royal Green Jackets
RHF	Royal Highland Fusiliers
RIRA	Real Irish Republican Army
RLC	Royal Logistic Corps
RM	Royal Marines
RPG-7	shoulder-fired, rocket-propelled grenade, used to defeat armoured vehicles
RSM	Regimental Sergeant Major
RSP	render-safe procedure – the act of making a bomb safe
RTE	Radio Telefís Eireann – Eire's public-service radio and television broadcaster
RTU	return to unit
RUC	Royal Ulster Constabulary
RWF	Royal Welch Fusiliers
SAS	Special Air Service
SAT	Senior Ammunition Technician
SATO	Senior Ammunition Technical Officer
SDLP	Social Democratic Labour Party
SF	Security Forces/Special Forces (e.g. SAS)
Sinn Fein	political wing of the IRA
SLR	7.62mm Self Loading Rifle – the standard Army rifle
SMG	sub-machine gun
SNCO	senior non-commissioned officer
SOCO	Scenes of Crime Officer
SOPs	standing operating procedures
TAOR	Tactical Area of Responsibility
TATP	triacetone triperoxide – an organic peroxide home-made explosive
TPU	timing and power unit

UDA	Ulster Defence Association – the principal Loyalist paramilitary organisation
UDR	Ulster Defence Regiment – a British Army regiment, locally recruited within Northern Ireland, made up of full-time and part-time members
UFF	Ulster Freedom Fighters – a cover name used by the UDA
UUP	Ulster Unionist Party – the principal Unionist party in Northern Ireland
UUUC	United Ulster Unionist Council
UVF	Ulster Volunteer Force – a Loyalist paramilitary group
UVIED	under vehicle improvised explosive device
VCP	vehicle checkpoint
WO1	Warrant Officer Class 1
WO2	Warrant Officer Class 2

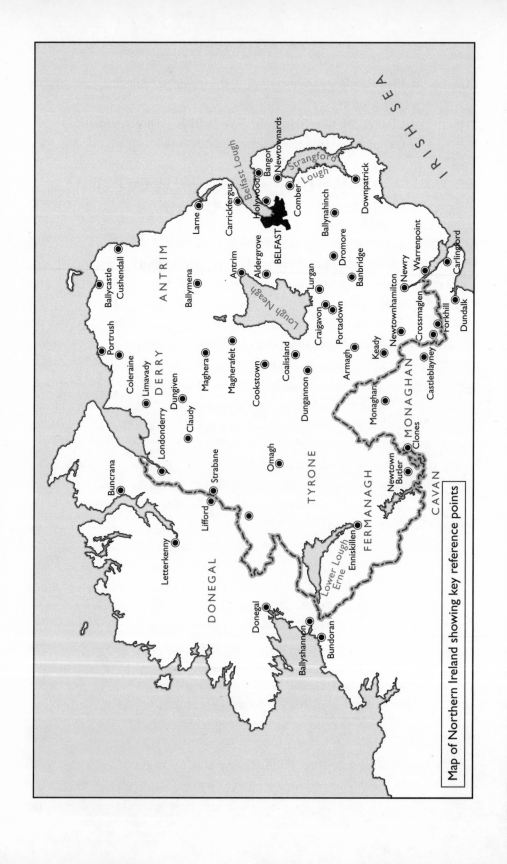

Map of Northern Ireland showing key reference points

PROLOGUE

SETTING THE SCENE

It had been daylight when we started. Now it had moved on into dusk. On a November evening, in a cold, bleak, austere factory complex, Wheelbarrow, the tracked robot, was edging its way along the corridors of the single-storey, on-site office building, hunting out its sinister prey. We thought we knew where the device was; the witness had been calm, almost matter-of-fact, as he recounted his tale. They weren't always like that. Often, we would find witnesses had been reduced to a state of unintelligible gibbering by the shock of what had happened to them. This was rarely helpful. Anyone would think that we were going to ask *them* to go and take the device apart for *us*. But this one was OK.

He could tell us exactly what had happened. The car, a Cortina, had entered the factory area, travelling fast, and had pulled up outside the offices. Two men had got out and entered reception. Both were wearing masks. One had covered the reception staff with a handgun, barking out his commands with fierce authority. Nobody had dared move. The other had been carrying something. He had disappeared down one of the corridors for no more than a minute. When he returned, he had deposited whatever he had been carrying, and now he too held a pistol. Shouting 'This is the IRA. There is a bomb in the building. You have five minutes to get out!', the terrorists had extracted rapidly through the front door, firing a succession of shots into the ceiling as they went. Linda, the 22-year-old blonde receptionist, had immediately lapsed into hysteria. By the time we arrived, we were told that she was being comforted in the back of a nearby police Land Rover – one of the big, grey, RUC Hotspurs – and there was no point trying to get anything out of her. But Mike was OK.

It had been Mike who had sounded the alarm and cleared the building. He had also seen the device – standing upright against the centre of the far wall at the end of a corridor. Quiet, menacing and, no doubt, ticking. The outline description was enough to tell me all I needed to know. It was a BI – a blast incendiary. Simple in concept; deadly in effect. A plastic container of petrol, with an explosive charge strapped to it, along with a TPU – a timing and power unit – which would count down the seconds to detonation. Just like the one that had immolated the diners at the La Mon restaurant in February 1978. That had killed twelve partygoers when the blast had propelled a huge ball of flame across the room, burning everything in its path – tables, chairs, furnishings . . . people.

As it happens, operators can find blast incendiaries quite easy to deal with – when they are outside. Evacuate the area. Keep the crowds back. Drive the Wheelbarrow down. Shoot the device. Simple. But this was inside. A whole different ballgame. If my No. 2, my assistant operator driving the robot, could not get Wheelbarrow up close and personal with the device, I would be into a manual approach. The long walk, which might be a one-way ticket. My friend Mark had done that with a BI. No matter how they had tried, Wheelbarrow just could not find a way through. So Mark had decided to go in by the quickest route – via the window – straight in; straight out. Except that the window had been a tight fit, so he'd left his helmet behind. When the device functioned, his face was the only part of him that burnt. Now he was married to the nurse who had treated him – the ultimate love story. The standing joke among operators though was that we knew where the skin grafts had come from. He was one of the few people who could pucker up and say 'Kiss my butt' without intending any offence.

The last thing I wanted to do was get the big green suit on and go wandering down to look into the mouth of the dragon when it could still wake up and breathe fire all over me. So the No. 2 had persevered. Mike, the witness, had given us a reasonable diagram, so we stood a better than average chance of finding the evil contraption. He had even helped by watching the CCTV monitor built into the back of the van, which was displaying Wheelbarrow's progress from its onboard cameras. That way he could relate the TV picture to the sketch map for us. Then we found it. Picked out in the gloom by Wheelbarrow's twin beams. The reflection off a metal canister, taped to the side of the petrol container, indicated that the terrorist had kindly presented us with a fragmentation hazard as well as blast and flame. Oh great!

But Wheelbarrow was there. The saviour of the hour, and possibly the saviour of my bacon as well. The No. 2 set the controls to 'creep forward', and we could see the robot easing towards its target – not unlike a docking manœuvre. The TPU was the target. Hit the plastic petrol container instead, and we would certainly remove the threat of a fireball, but there was every chance that we would set light to the fuel at the same time. And the last thing anyone needed – us, the fire brigade, or the factory-owners – was a burning pool of petrol, inside an office complex, with an explosive charge still ticking away next to it. So we had our plan: take out the battery, take out the timer, and render the monster dead.

This was where the No. 2 would earn his pay. Get this wrong, and 'Plan B', the unpleasant chore of donning armour for the long walk, would once again become the only option. Wheelbarrow nudged forward until the blast incendiary filled the entire screen. The TPU was quite clear now. In theory, unless the device was booby-trapped, this plywood box, not much bigger than a hardback book, contained everything that could set it off. Get a good hit with one of Wheelbarrow's disrupters, and we would be left with just so many inert components. Then it would be a simple case of declaring the area clear, taking the police Scenes of Crimes Officer down to sweep up the forensic evidence, and back to base in time for tea and medals.

The weapon was lined up now. We could see how close it was because of an ingenious, effective, but extraordinarily cheap and simple aiming mechanism. Projecting some 3 inches from the front of the weapon was a loop of masking tape. As soon as the masking tape touched the device, it would start to bend, without causing any disturbance whatsoever. Back at the Incident Control Point (ICP), this would be relayed back to us from Wheelbarrow's 'attack camera'. That slight distortion of the tape seen on the TV monitor gave us the signal that we were on target and ready to fire.

I turned to the Incident Commander – the major commanding the infantry who were providing the cordon and security for my team – and told him to warn his men to expect a controlled explosion in two minutes. This was important. The last thing we wanted was for the cordon troops to think they were under attack when they heard the sharp crack of one of our weapons firing. Equally, there was always a small chance that our so-called controlled explosion might become rather less controlled if we got it wrong, resulting in what was technically known as 'complete detonation'. This meant that everyone should take cover – just in case.

Another of my colleagues, Bryan, had experienced an unexpected complete detonation. He had tried to open up a van packed with explosives using a

'Maxi Candle'. A Maxi Candle is a plastic container, about the size of a can of baked beans, stuffed with a low explosive. If you are in a hurry, and you think a car might be booby-trapped, it is a useful way of opening it up remotely, fast, from a distance. Drop it in, set it off, and it opens the doors, the bonnet, the boot and, if you're lucky, the roof. On a good day, it will also give any device inside such a good wallop that it gives up the ghost.

The problem is, you really do not want to be putting a Maxi Candle in close proximity to a massive explosive charge. And Bryan had inadvertently done just that. With spectacular results. The aerial photographs of Springfield Avenue, taken shortly afterwards, just showed complete devastation where five houses had stood only moments before. I had been on my basic course at the time, and Bryan was the talk of the course. He came home on mid-tour R&R (rest and recuperation) a week later, and popped into the Officers' Mess bar. We flocked around him, keen to hear the latest 'war story' from the front line. But our celebrity chum was in less than talkative mood. His error had been treated with rather more gravity by Headquarters Northern Ireland, where he had tapped the boards in front of the General Officer Commanding, having to explain this act of professional ineptitude. Indeed, he had come within an ace of being drummed out of the Province. But everyone knew it was a difficult job. And we could all make mistakes – better to lose property than lives.

I checked my watch. Two minutes were almost up: 'Five, four, three, two, one – OK No. 2, hit it.' My No. 2 looked up momentarily to shout the standard warning: 'Standby, firing!' Then he pressed the button. Despite being over 100 yards away, inside a building, the sharp crack of the disrupter could be heard, as it drove a slug of water and gas into the target at lightning speed, tearing the electric circuit to pieces before it could react. On the CCTV screen, the picture momentarily blacked out with the sudden flash of light. As it started to gather, I peered hard, trying to make sense of what I was seeing. The camera was now staring at a blank wall, where the BI had stood. The No. 2 pulled Wheelbarrow back slightly and tilted the camera downwards. Everything looked good. The petrol container, still intact, had been thrown into the corner at the end of the corridor. Even though I was looking at a black-and-white picture, I thought I could pick out at least one nine-volt battery lying among the shattered remains of the plywood box. The metal canister had also been blown off in the blast, and, although still in one piece, should no longer present a threat.

The No. 2 looked up, justifiably proud of his handiwork. 'All right, Boss?' he asked, grinning. 'Yeah, not bad,' I replied. 'Guess that's a beer I owe you later. Now let's get the suit out.'

Even though we were now pretty sure the immediate threat had been dealt with, the job was still not over. Before anyone else could be allowed near the scene, it was down to me to check that the area was 'clear' – that is, absolutely safe. Some operators had got this wrong in the past, and people, generally policemen, had died as a result. Policemen such as 43-year-old Constable Arthur McKay of the Royal Ulster Constabulary Reserve. On 8 October 1976 he had been about to steer a suspect stolen car as it was towed back to the local police station from Gortnacrene, near Kilrea, Northern Ireland. An operator had already examined the vehicle. He had even set off a controlled explosion. But he had missed the booby trap, linked to a pressure switch under one of the wheels. Constable McKay died instantly in the ensuing explosion.

Declaring the area clear still meant undertaking the long walk, but it never seemed quite so long when you knew that most of the contents of the device were now scattered harmlessly across the floor. But our standing operating procedures, or SOPs, contain certain 'mandatory actions', and one of those mandatory actions is that an operator *will* wear the big, heavy, green, protective suit every time he walks up to a bomb, even if he thinks he has already killed it.

There are six main parts to the suit. First the operator steps into the padded leggings, shaped rather like a set of cowboy's chaps. Then, standing upright, he holds his arms out straight, parallel to the ground, while two members of the team pull the heavy jacket on over him from the front, heaving it over his shoulders, and fastening the long zip that runs up his back. With the jacket on, a further, one-piece, padded back-protector is fitted, giving an appearance not unlike a cockroach's carapace. Two moulded sections of Kevlar armour are then slotted into large pockets on the front of the jacket, one covering the groin and lower stomach, the other acting as a breastplate, the top of which curves upwards and outwards under the chin. Last comes the helmet. Traditionally, this is always the No. 2's job – a last chance to check that the Boss knows what he intends to do when he gets down there, and that they have thought through all the options. Eye-to-eye, just for a moment, both knowing that it could all go wrong. And, more pragmatically, ensuring that the Boss's ears stay flat when the helmet is slid down over his head. When you are walking down to look at a bomb, you really don't want to be worrying about one of your ears being bent over inside the helmet.

With the suit on, the No. 2 handed me the weapons and tools that I had selected for this job. The rule is: never go down empty-handed; you never know what you might find. My principal weapon of choice this time was a hand-carried disrupter – identical to the one with which we had already shot the device from Wheelbarrow. If I got down there and found that the bomb was still 'live', I could set up the disrupter, retire to a safe distance and give it another whack. As well as the disrupter, I would be taking a bag for any forensic evidence, a torch and a 'cee-vee' tool. Nobody knew what 'cee-vee' stood for, but it was essentially a mechanical grab on the end of a 3-foot metal arm, operated by squeezing a lever on the handle. Quite useful for picking up any dodgy-looking remnants of a device (although some old hands would say, 'If you're too worried to pick it up by hand, what are you doing picking it up at all?').

Suitably tooled up, I moved out from behind the vehicles, which had been parked in a V-shape at the front of the ICP to provide extra protection to the team during the task. I knew that I would have to walk forwards about 10 yards, following a factory building wall, then turn left at the corner. The entrance to the office complex would then be some 80 yards in front of me, across the other side of the road. I simply had to follow the coaxial command cable, which Wheelbarrow had unreeled behind it as it had made the first approach to the bomb. It was dark now, and, although some yellow, neon streetlights illuminated the factory's outside areas, the office complex was shrouded in darkness. Taunting, menacing – I was glad that the scattered components revealed by the camera indicated that I was now dealing with a dead device. But you never knew . . .

Constrained by the suit, I started my stiff-legged walk towards the office-building entrance. My torch had been strapped to my forearm, over the padded jacket sleeve, using masking tape. It was already switched on – one less thing to cram into my hands, but also a good target for a sniper. I hoped the cordon was tight. I reached the open door, and mentally kicked myself. Was I absolutely sure that the office workers had come out this way? Was I absolutely sure that they had actually seen the terrorists run out and drive off? Or had the staff raced out of an emergency exit amid the gunfire, and just heard the car screaming away? It could be the latter. I doubted it, but I should have known for sure. If it was, then the terrorists might just have had time to string a tripwire booby trap across the door to catch out the next person coming through. I knew that Wheelbarrow had already come in this way, so, if there was a tripwire, it would have to be at least 4 feet above the ground for the robot to pass underneath it. A quick flash with the torch around the outside of the door frame confirmed that it was safe to step through.

Inside, I scanned the reception area. It already seemed familiar from the pictures relayed back to me from Wheelbarrow's camera. Everyday office furniture was positioned around the open space – a desk, some chairs, a couple of coffee tables and notices fluttering on a board on the wall. Three corridors led away from reception. I took the right-hand one, already starting to relax a little – just the forensic clearance to go. At the far end of the corridor, I could already pick out by torchlight the shattered components strewn on the floor.

Then I saw it. About 5 yards down, on the right-hand side was a small alcove, within which a fire extinguisher was mounted on the wall. As if in silent mockery, a second BI stood underneath it. If the timer ticked down now, I would be right in the centre of the fireball. I halted, momentarily frozen to the spot.

'What are you going to do now, Sir?' The voice of the instructor standing just behind and to one side of me, watching my every move over my shoulder. The same man who, earlier, had played Mike the witness, then the infantry company commander, and who was now my instant judge and jury.

I paused for a moment to gather my thoughts. The instructor looked at the weapon in my hand. It might have been an involuntary glance; it might have been a deliberate prompt. Either way, it spurred me into action. Stepping forward, I placed the disrupter on the floor, on its stand, aiming directly at the TPU of this second blast incendiary, then prepared to beat a hasty retreat. As I turned away, he smiled and gave me the thumbs up: 'Ok, Sir, we'll call it a day there. That's a pass.'

I was a 27-year-old Ammunition Technical Officer – an ATO – one of that small but select band who took their turns as bomb-disposal operators in Northern Ireland. I had already been trained for a year in the science and mechanics of 'things that go bang'. I had studied explosive chemistry, ballistics, electronics, metallurgy and demolitions. I knew every item of ammunition in the British Army's possession, and how it worked – from trip flares to missiles. I had been trained in basic counterterrorist bomb disposal – or explosive ordnance disposal (EOD), as we called it in the military. I had even been sent off to practise my trade in Germany for a year. But this was the big one. The make or break. Four weeks on the 'Pre-Operational EOD Course for Northern Ireland', the last week of which was 'Test Week'.

Test Week saw us broken down into teams, working with other operators, or No. 1s, from the rank of sergeant through to captain, and No. 2s, corporals and below, all destined for the Province – if they passed the course. And passing Test Week was by no means easy. Each operator would be assigned four tasks during the week. He had to pass three. The failure rate for first timers was 60 per cent. Although there were exceptions, most would be given only two attempts at the course. And, while failure might sound an attractive option, it would not be good. We were, after all, volunteers – young, with a zest for living and excitement, each convinced of his own immortality. We *wanted* to go to Northern Ireland. To be where the action was. Whenever anyone saw the red, black and gold flaming grenade badge on our arms, it was the first question they asked: 'Have you done Ireland yet?' We all yearned for the kudos that went with being able to reply, 'Yeah'. Insouciant, understated, never proffered without being asked.

Failure meant being 'RTU'd' – returned to unit. Persistent failure meant having to choose another specialisation within the Army – like accounting for blankets in one of the Army's big stores depots. But, once you had Ireland under your belt, a whole new range of possibilities leapt into view. There was Weapons Intelligence in the Province, snooping around in civilian clothes. Or the Parachute Section, which was trained to deploy onto ships under way at sea to deal with a bomb on board. There was even an ATO with the SAS, in their Counter Revolutionary Warfare Wing, on permanent standby to join an assault force into a terrorist stronghold should intelligence suggest a bomb threat. But first you had to get through 'Ireland'.

By the time I attended the Pre-Ops Course, the organisation, procedures, training and equipment of the Army's counterterrorist bomb-disposal operators were well established. This had not always been the case. Although improvised explosive devices, or IEDs, had been encountered throughout history – ever since the invention of gunpowder – their prolific use in sustained terrorist campaigns really took off only after the Second World War. Over the next twenty years or so, the British Army found itself fighting a variety of terrorist organisations worldwide as the Empire began to collapse.

During the blitz of Britain's cities in the Second World War, bomb disposal had been largely the province of the Royal Engineers, who were trained in demolitions and the handling of explosives. They also possessed the necessary skills required to dig down to unexploded aircraft bombs, which had become buried on impact. From a standing start at the outbreak of the war, by the middle of 1940, the Royal Engineers had managed to establish over 200 bomb-disposal sections. Even these were barely enough. The constant Luftwaffe raids generated an almost overwhelming quantity of unexploded bombs, which, if not dealt with smartly, threatened to bring paralysis to London, and to Britain's other heavily bombed cities. In order to make the teams' task more difficult, the Germans frequently tried to 'wrong foot' them by introducing new fuses, anti-handling mechanisms and delayed timers. Each lesson learnt might be at the expense of an operator's life. However, the constraints of mass production meant that, once a particular threat had been identified, it could be dissected and analysed and appropriate counter-measures drawn up.

Improvised explosive devices presented a different challenge. Individually constructed by the terrorist, each had the potential to be unique, incorporating a variety of traps to catch out the unwary operator. They might be triggered by a burning fuse, or a timer, by the victim's own actions – opening a door, tripping a wire, lifting an everyday object – or by the terrorist simply pressing a button. They might contain commercial explosives, home-made explosives, or be constructed from discarded military munitions. In size, they might vary from under 1lb of explosive, right up to over 1,000lb. Lethality might be enhanced by strapping on a container of petrol to provide a searing ball of flame, or adding nails, nuts and bolts to achieve murderous fragmentation. The requirement was to find a body of individuals who had a real understanding of explosives and their associated mechanisms from first principles, and who could take on this challenge.

The task of dealing with terrorist devices therefore fell to the ammunition specialists of the Royal Army Ordnance Corps – the RAOC. This Corps routinely had the unglamorous task of receiving, storing, issuing and accounting for the Army's vast range of stores and materiel. As such, it had developed professional skills appropriate to certain specialist areas of supply, such as fuel, rations and, especially, ammunition. Indeed, the very word 'ordnance' referred to military weapons and munitions, and the Corps' cap badge contained a shield, bearing cannons and cannon balls, as its centrepiece.

Within the RAOC, those who chose to specialise in bombs and bullets were, and still are, known as Ammunition Technical Officers (ATOs), if commissioned, and Ammunition Technicians (ATs), if non-commissioned. It was considered that the substantial degree of technical training that they received in explosives and munitions made them ideally suited to countering this new and deadly type of warfare.

By the time the first bombs of the current Troubles exploded in Northern Ireland, the ATOs and ATs of the RAOC had already been blooded in the war against terror through a number of peacekeeping operations around the globe. When the *EOKA* (National Organisation of Cypriot Fighters) insurgency campaign swept through the island of Cyprus in 1955, it had quickly become apparent that the Cypriot Police were completely unable to deal with terrorist devices, or the subsequent collection of forensic evidence to bring the bombers to justice. An ad hoc unit of ammunition specialists had been thrown together rapidly and assigned to the various Police Divisional Headquarters. The campaign lasted from April 1955 until December 1958. During this time the operators rendered safe 4,688 IEDs, investigated 4,300 explosive incidents and recorded 3,000 recoveries of arms, ammunition and explosives.

Sadly, this was not without cost; two operators lost their lives in the process. Early on 31 July 1955 Staff Sergeant R. Kilby accompanied a police patrol that was following up a report of a number of home-made mines planted in a village known as Sinda. He had already located two and rendered them safe when he was killed by a third, alongside the village well, which detonated as he attempted to disarm it. The subsequent investigation revealed that the design was a new one, which the operators had not previously encountered.

Only two months later, Staff Sergeant J.A. Culkin met his death while dealing with a cache of explosives buried in a hillside cave near Limassol. Precisely what happened remains unclear. The explosives were stored in boxes, which were giving off the trademark smell of almonds. Realising the danger, Staff Sergeant Culkin cleared all other personnel from the cave, and went forward alone to carry out his render-safe procedure. Minutes later, a massive explosion rocked the hillside. He was buried with full military honours the next day.

Less than a decade later, the RAOC's ATOs and ATs found themselves fighting another terrorist campaign, this time in Aden. With the sun setting on the British Empire, and the flame of anti-British feeling being fanned by neighbouring Yemen, the internal security situation had deteriorated rapidly. Initially, the conflict had been confined largely to the Radfan, an inhospitable, barren region of jagged peaks and sheer cliffs, some 60 miles north of the city of Aden itself. Although a British infantry brigade had been successful in regaining control of the Radfan, by early 1965 terrorist attacks had migrated to the urban areas. A promise by Harold Wilson's government to withdraw all British forces from Aden by the end of 1967 did not have the anticipated effect of restoring law and order. On the contrary, the level of violence rose. From just 36 bombings in 1964, the figure increased to 286 in 1965, then 2,000 in 1966, before peaking at over 3,000 in 1967.

Against this backdrop, the ATOs of a new generation were able further to refine their skills. With their woefully inadequate equipment of scissors, wire-cutters, surgical scalpels, string, fishhooks and masking tape, they went into battle against time bombs, anti-handling devices and 'come-on' situations. Men like Major J.F. Elliott, who carried out 309 tasks, including hoaxes and false alarms, of which 184 proved to be 'live'. On one occasion he answered a call to an explosion in the Officers' Mess of Headquarters Middle East Command, to find that the bomber had blown himself up. On further checking the room, he discovered two more time bombs, which he then had to dismantle. Throughout, the dismembered remains of the bomber surrounded him, serving as a grisly reminder of what could happen if he made one wrong move.

Major Elliott was replaced in due course by Major G.C. Brownlee, who went on to conduct 170 tasks, of which just over 100 were real devices. Probably his most nerve-racking job was that in which he had to dispose of a bomb placed in a village well. If it had been allowed to function, the whole village would have been deprived of its water. Having lowered himself into the well, he worked in cramped conditions, in semi-darkness, to render the device safe. It subsequently became apparent that the breaking of a single thread would have been sufficient to set it off. For their outstanding gallantry, both officers were awarded the George Medal.

Perhaps the best preparation for Northern Ireland though had come during the short but intense bombing campaign in Hong Kong during the last seven months of 1967. Determined to destabilise the British colonial government, Maoist terrorists had mounted bomb attacks on an unprecedented scale. By the time the campaign fizzled out, 8,960 incidents had been reported. The aim had been total saturation in order completely to fragment the day-to-day running of the colony. On one single day, 280 devices were reported. Luckily for the administration, the vast majority of live bombs used low, rather than high, explosive. This often limited their effects to little more than that of a giant firecracker. Even so, 15 people were killed, and 340 injured. The dead included one AT, Sergeant Charlie Workman, who was killed in a 200-foot fall while working on a device on the Lion Rock mountain.

With only two years to go before having to confront the savage excesses of Northern Ireland's paramilitaries, the RAOC's operators found Hong Kong a useful testing ground. Equipment improved, with the introduction of specially equipped vehicles, armoured vests and helmets, anti-mine goggles and the development of explosive opening techniques – the so-called controlled explosion. The technology available to the terrorists also improved, with the emergence of small transistor batteries to provide a power source, light-sensitive cells to catch out the unwary ATO and the incorporation of various time-delay mechanisms and relays.

The stage was set.

PART ONE
THE EARLY YEARS

ONE

1969–1970: STUMBLING FROM BOMB TO BOMB

In 1969, the year that man first landed on the moon, British TV screens brought the rising sectarian violence of Northern Ireland into the home. As families sat down to tea, the six o'clock news displayed the horrifying images from the night before. Stark black-and-white pictures. Stone-throwing mobs, illuminated by burning rows of terraces. Sobbing families driven from their homes. Policemen in long black coats and cork 'moped' helmets, truncheons out, seeming to beat anyone within reach. Politicians and protestors, faces twisted in hatred, spitting venomous outrage and condemnation at the other side.

But what other side? 'Surely they're all Irish, aren't they?' I asked my father. Except that some were Protestant Irish and others were Catholic Irish. But why should that matter? I had a Catholic boy in my class. What difference did it make? Sometimes he had to stay for an extra hour after school when the priest came round. But he was still my friend.

For the majority of the population of the United Kingdom, the Troubles in Northern Ireland were ancient history, in the same league as the English Civil War and the Jacobite Rebellion. The stuff of musty schoolbooks. This was the era of 'Flower Power'. The spirit of 'Peace and Love' had made its way across the Atlantic from the United States. It had even crossed the Solent for the 1969 Isle of Wight Pop Festival. But, somehow, it had been brought up short at the Irish Sea.

Few on the British mainland understood where the Troubles had sprung from. With the established Church losing its influence, few could see why one would even care whether one's neighbour was Protestant or Catholic. But, of course, it went deeper than that. Hundreds of years of mutual distrust, bigotry and murder had created a tinderbox just waiting to burst into flames.

The spark was the Northern Ireland Civil Rights Association (NICRA), born out of the youthful optimism of the late 1960s. NICRA's aims included the establishment of fairer electoral boundaries, universal adult suffrage in local government elections, and the removal of anti-Catholic discrimination in employment and the allocation of public housing.

On New Year's Day 1969 civil-rights protestors set out to march from Belfast to Londonderry. Almost exclusively Catholics, they had an escort from the Royal Ulster Constabulary (RUC), itself almost exclusively Protestant. As it transpired, this was about as useful as having no escort at all. At Burntollet Bridge, on the outskirts of Londonderry, the marchers were ambushed by a Loyalist mob of approximately 200. Thirteen marchers required hospital treatment. The RUC was blamed for making little, if any, effort to prevent this and the other harassment and attacks that took place throughout the four-day march.

The Catholic community, outraged as news film of the incident showed the Loyalists apparently being allowed to conduct their rampage with impunity, rioted in Londonderry. Northern Ireland's independent Stormont Government, led by Prime Minister Captain Terrence O'Neill, came under pressure from Westminster to bring in reforms as a matter of urgency. As O'Neill continued to dither, the Protestants, sensing weakness, accused him of bending towards appeasement.

And then the bombs started to appear. They were initially laid by the Ulster Volunteer Force (UVF) against utilities, the intention being to undermine Terrence O'Neill by giving the impression that they were the work of the Irish Republican Army (IRA). The hope was that this would put paid to any further concessions towards the Catholics. On 31 March the electricity substation at Castlereagh was the first target, suffering a number of blasts. More attacks followed in rapid succession. On 20 April both the electricity pylon at Kilmore, County Armagh, and the Silent Valley reservoir in County Down were hit. Four days later, the target was the water pipeline at Templepatrick, which was fractured, and a similar attack occurred the next day on another pipeline at Annalong. Overlaid on these explosions were a number of petrol-bomb attacks against post offices in Belfast.

O'Neill's position was becoming increasingly tenuous, undermining any ability he might have to effect change. On 10 May 1969 the *Belfast Telegraph* published an interview with him, in which he explained how difficult it was to gain support from among his fellow Protestants for his 'moderate policies'.

Over thirty years later, his comments come across as patronising and prejudiced:

> It is frightfully hard to explain to Protestants that if you give Roman Catholics a good job and a good house, they will live like Protestants, because they will see neighbours with cars and television sets. They will refuse to have eighteen children, but if a Roman Catholic is jobless, and lives in the most ghastly hovel, he will rear eighteen children on National Assistance. If you treat Roman Catholics with due consideration and kindness, they will live like Protestants in spite of the authoritative nature of their Church.

The UVF's clandestine bombing strategy worked. The authorities did indeed lay the blame at the door of the IRA, although it was still, at that stage, a dormant organisation. O'Neill was forced to resign, and his place was taken by his cousin, Major James Chichester-Clark. In his memoirs, O'Neill said that the bombings 'quite literally blew me out of office'.

It was several months – months too late – before the truth about who was behind the bombings became apparent. On 19 October 1969 a 45-year-old quarry foreman, Thomas McDowell, met his death in an 'own goal' – the first of the current Troubles. He was attempting to place a bomb at the Ballyshannon Power Station in County Donegal, Southern Ireland, when it functioned. Seriously injured in the blast, he did not die immediately, but clung on till the next day, suffering from severe burns. Although he made no confession before he died, his coat was found to have the initials UVF inscribed on the lining. His death led to the round-up of a number of Protestants, one of whom implicated McDowell in all the previous explosions. This individual was jailed for twelve years.

By the summer of 1969, emotions on both sides had reached fever pitch. The traditional Loyalist marches provided the catalyst. Banners waving, drums and pipes playing, the Protestant working class showed its antipathy towards its Catholic neighbours. The 'Glorious Twelfth of July', to celebrate the Battle of the Boyne, brought rioting to Belfast and Londonderry. Then, on 12 August, the Apprentice Boys' March, along the walls of Londonderry, sparked further riots of such ferocity that they earned the title 'The Battle of the Bogside'. The rioting spread, first to Belfast, then to other towns, with hundreds of families being burnt out of their homes. The Stormont

Government was forced to mobilise the reserve police force, known as the 'B Specials', but this was itself a wholly Protestant organisation, and therefore served only to inflame the situation further. With Belfast and Londonderry in flames, 10 people dead, and 154 suffering from gunshot wounds, British troops were called in.

On 14 August 1969, after several days of rioting in Londonderry and Belfast, it became apparent that the RUC, assisted by the B Specials, could no longer contain the mounting violence. The 1st Battalion, The Prince of Wales's Own Regiment of Yorkshire, moved into Londonderry. Other units moved into Belfast shortly thereafter. At first, they were welcomed with open arms by the Catholic community, which saw them as an unbiased force whose only aim was to offer protection from the nightly assaults from the Loyalist mobs. However, the imposition of military curfews and searches throughout late 1969 and early 1970 soon soured relations between the Army and the Catholics, allowing the slumbering IRA to reawaken. And with the IRA came the bombs.

The bombing campaign itself was slow to take off. Only ten explosions were recorded in 1969, mostly the work of the UVF. This was just as well, as the Army initially failed to identify the developing threat. In traditional style, it tried to muddle along by diverting ATOs to the task in an ad hoc, virtually random, manner.

Before the Troubles, Northern Ireland had become something of a sleepy hollow as far as military postings were concerned. In West Germany, the British Army of the Rhine took its place shoulder-to-shoulder with its NATO allies, ready and waiting for the ever-impending attack by the Soviets' Third Shock Army across the East German border. On the British mainland, many ATOs and ATs were busy tending the Army's vast stockpile of ammunition that would be outloaded to Germany as soon as the attack came. Others manned a specialist company, known as No. 1 Ammunition Inspection and Disposal Unit, with small detachments spread throughout the country. In their blue-light vans, they would answer calls to items of stray ammunition, often dating as far back as the First World War, which turned up in farmers' fields, building sites or attics, or which were handed in to police stations.

But Northern Ireland was removed from all this. It was a military backwater, and those garrisoned in the Province welcomed the serene out-door pleasures offered by the beaches of the North Antrim coast and the Mourne Mountains. Ammunition specialists were thin on the ground. At

Headquarters Northern Ireland (HQNI), on the outskirts of the quiet town of Lisburn, there was one ATO. This was Captain Bob Willcox, in his twenties, straight off the course, and charged with looking after the safe storage, maintenance and inspection of the Army's ammunition in the Province. He was supposed to be assisted by a Warrant Officer Class 2 (WO2), but the post was gapped because of manning pressures elsewhere. After all, nothing much happened in Northern Ireland!

Down on the south-east coast, whipped by the winds coming up off the Irish Sea, stood the small ammunition depot at Ballykinler. This would have made the ideal setting for a black-and-white Ealing comedy film of the 1950s – the sort of place where the staff might all be 'excused boots', running their own chicken farm and trying to distil the illegal local brew, *poteen* (pronounced 'potcheen'). This was manned by a captain ATO, Ken England, who had come up through the ranks, a staff sergeant, Jack Day, and a small group of soldiers.

On the rare occasions that an explosive device turned up, Bob Willcox would be called away from his desk at HQNI to deal with it. He recalls:

> Actual explosive ordnance disposal [EOD] operations, that is, making safe terrorist-laid, or made, unexploded objects, were going on in Northern Ireland long before 1969. For example, during my take-over in February 1968, a 'blind' grenade of US origin was demolished in situ in Belfast, having bounced off a police car!

However, as the rioting increased in intensity, and British troops poured into the Province, dealing with bombs was the last thing on anyone's mind. Suddenly, the Ammunition Depot found itself under severe pressure as large quantities of rubber bullets, CS gas canisters and small-arms ammunition were flown into theatre for issue to the deploying units. Luckily, by this time, the vacant WO2's slot at HQNI had been filled, as Captain Willcox had suddenly found himself on call twenty-four hours a day, seven days a week.

> We were inundated with work, servicing the reinforcing battalions, motoring anti-riot ammunition around – straight off planes to unit locations, and coping with bombing incidents, which always seemed an annoying interference to our normal supply role. Eventually, we became exhausted, and all pleas via and around official channels fell on deaf ears.

The Chief Inspector Land Service Ammunition [CILSA] did not rate Northern Ireland in those days. One major even visited on behalf of CILSA, and reported back that we were coping! When the RUC were disarmed for political reasons, and their ammo had to have a safety inspection before being sent back to the depot at Ballykinler, my estimate of it being an 80 man/day job was 'pooh-poohed' at CILSA.

In the early days when bombs turned up, the incidents were overseen almost exclusively by the police. Initially, in the absence of an Operations Room at HQNI to coordinate the military response, the call would generally come through to Captain Willcox's married quarter in Lisburn.

During silent hours, my wife was the unofficial 'EOD Report Centre', in effect, and I always rang back to see if it was OK to come home, or was there another job? A duty policeman once rang her from a small village: 'Two sticks of gelignite have just been thrown out of a car, and they're lying here in the gutter. Could the Captain come please?' She knew that the village was near Lough Erne, so she asked which side of the Lough it was on. The reply was as quick and accurate as it was unhelpful: 'Why, it's this side,' followed by the click of the handset being put down.

However, all this was about to change. With the military on the verge of assuming primacy for security matters, Captain Willcox suddenly found himself in unexpected conflict with the General Officer Commanding (GOC) Northern Ireland, Lieutenant-General Sir Ian Freeland. Willcox recalls:

Just before the Army went to the aid of the Civil Power, my WO2, Mel Mason, was on duty and attending a call from an RUC station in Belfast. He couldn't get through because of riots, and went to sit it out in Holywood Barracks (North Belfast). The Duty Officer there reported his presence to Headquarters Northern Ireland. The then GOC (Freeland) was furious at the news. I was summoned from my married quarter, not knowing anything other than 'the General wants to see you'. Freeland was new, and I had not yet met him. So, when I walked into the Operations Office, where the General was with Major Tony Wilson, the Operations Officer, I held out my hand in greeting. When he found out who I was, he roared: 'Pack your bags and leave my command now!'

Tony Wilson was taken aback, and tactfully asked if he could be given a reason. Freeland explained that under *my* authority, as a mere captain, a WO2 was on the streets of Belfast in support of the Civil Power before *he*, the General, had received any authority from Harold Wilson. I indicated that I understood and left, shortly to return with 'Home Office Circular No. 5', which embodied the agreement between the Police and Army for EOD. It was now my turn to explain to the GOC that, although he had not yet had *his* authority, I certainly had *mine*, as had all of my predecessors. It was a standing authority, and this Circular was it. He said he hoped to see me in the Officers' Mess on Sunday. No apology. Just this polite dismissal. Flap over! I didn't explain to him that the writ of the British Home Office did not extend to Northern Ireland, as that wouldn't have suited my purposes. But within 24 hours, General Freeland had his authority, and a new political ball game had begun.

Military speak is littered with jargon and acronyms. It is, therefore, hardly surprising that the simple term 'bomb' would not suffice, being replaced by 'improvised explosive device', abbreviated to 'IED' to describe the terrorist's deadly home-made weapons. The majority of IEDs encountered at this early stage were comparatively primitive. Many of the first bombs were little more than improvised grenades. The 'nail bomb' was especially popular, consisting of several sticks of commercial explosive, with nails embedded in the surface to provide a lacerating shrapnel effect. When the terrorist wished to throw the bomb, he would light one end of a length of 'safety fuse', in true cowboy film style. This would then burn down to a detonator – a small metal tube, usually no thicker than a pencil, containing a highly sensitive explosive, buried in the main charge. Once the flame reached the detonator, it would explode, immediately setting off the bomb. The only time delay was provided by the length of time that it would take for the fuse to burn down. This meant that the bomber had scant opportunity to distance himself from the scene of the explosion. Clearly, the explosive charge could be as large as required, but the larger the charge, the longer the safety fuse.

However, even this comparatively simple means of creating an explosion did not always go to plan. Captain Bob Willcox was called out in the aftermath of one botched attempt:

My largest ever device was 55lb of gelignite, laced with Cordtex, connected to two separate detonators, which were to be initiated by a particular type of burning fuse known as 'blue sump'. The whole bomb was buried under quarry dust on the back of a stolen lorry. What happened was that an IRA gang made an armed attack on Crossmaglen RUC Station. It was the first of many. The RUC slammed shut their steel window shutters – with some difficulty, as the painters had been in and they were stuck. In those days, the shutters were all that protected Crossmaglen, in line with all RUC stations. Having closed the shutters, they tried to open the rifle slits in them, but the flaps shielding them were also stuck fast with paint. So they banged off their pistols and rifles into the wooden stairs inside the building. At this, the raiders fled. When the RUC emerged, they found the lorry parked against the walls. I attended, as the lorry was suspect. Sticking out of the pile of quarry dust were two ends of safety fuse, each surrounded by a pile of spent matches. The gang had run out of matches, not knowing that an ordinary naked match flame doesn't light blue sump fuse.

The first attempts at providing a degree of time delay were crude and very high risk. The IRA took to inserting clothes pegs into their circuits. Each jaw of the peg would have a drawing pin pushed through it, and the pins would then be wired into the circuit. Once the jaws snapped shut, the pins would touch, the circuit would be completed and the device would explode. Keeping the jaws apart might be either an elastic band, or a length of soldering wire. As the spring on the peg overcame the resistance provided by the wire or elastic, the jaws would start to close. Without any other safety mechanisms built into the device, this was clearly enormously dangerous for the bomb layer, as he had no idea how strong the soldering wire or elastic band was in relation to the peg. Even the operators feared such devices. In Willcox's words: 'The IEDs I hated most were the clothes peg type – very prevalent then. I hated the uncertainty they created.'

In July 1969, before the first troops were on the streets, Captain Ken Nash took over from Captain Ken England at the Ballykinler Ammunition Depot. He continued to provide a back-up, unofficial bomb-disposal service whenever Captain Willcox happened to be busy on another task. His memories of the early days are very similar to Willcox's:

1969–70 was mainly a case of clothes peg, alarm clock and safety fuse devices. Car bombs made their first appearance in 1970. I only had to deal with one car – it was abandoned in the Mourne Mountains, and I checked it out as free from explosives. It was later reported that the owner was found elsewhere, having committed suicide.

At that time, Captain Bob Willcox and myself were kept busy doing lectures on dealing with terrorist device situations to the RUC and infantry. The Ammunition Depot was working seven days a week, all hours, to cover routine servicing of ammunition and EOD duties. Activity was cyclic, and Murphy's Law dictated that any reinforcements were on their way back home when trouble flared again.

Most of the incidents I dealt with were routine, run-of-the-mill occurrences. One might be worthy of mention. The ATO at HQNI was advised of a suspected device in mail being sorted in the Belfast General Post Office. The mail in question was packed into a 10-ton Post Office lorry, which was driven by Bob Willcox to the Ammunition Depot. I was given the task of checking the contents – opening and examining all the packets. It took six full working days – nothing untoward was found.

Although the typically modest Nash might describe most of his encounters as 'routine' and 'run of the mill', a yellowing scrap from an unidentifiable newspaper, which turned up during the research for this book, gives a truer picture of an ordinary 'day at the office'. The article's author had obviously got word that there was a bomb ticking away in a house in the Donegall Road, Belfast, in the early hours of the morning. By chance, this happened to be one of Captain Nash's tasks. The story opens at 2 a.m. as the security cordon of troops goes firm. The journalist describes the tension in the air, with the soldiers not knowing whether they are in hostile territory. Graffiti is on the outside wall of the house, reputed to be the headquarters of a group calling itself the 'Freelance Defenders', and this does not bode well:

VIGILANTES GHQ

WE WILL GET YOU BERNIE

This is not a nice area, and there is an air of menace. Groups of local residents are described lurking on the outskirts of the cordon, and the troops, uncertain of the various tribal loyalties, wonder if they are friendly. The nervous doubt starts to lift when some Protestant girls appear with mugs of tea for the soldiers, but it is over an hour before the bomb-disposal team arrives.

Suddenly, a speeding red-and-tan jeep with brilliant blue flasher slopes in from the nearby M1 motorway. And a severe-looking bespectacled captain, who might be a schoolteacher if you took his cap and belt away, goes briskly in to inspect our 'bomb'. He's out again straight away though, and leaning on his jeep with its impressive sign 'RAOC Explosive Disposal'. Waiting again, this time for 'heavy equipment'.

Eventually, the so-called heavy equipment arrives. It is the portable X-ray kit – the best of its day – clumsy, heavy and not particularly effective. Captain Nash enters the building three times to try to get a decent shot of the internal workings of the device. The first two attempts draw complete blanks, and the third is only a little better – but deemed good enough. At around 6 a.m. the incident draws to a close, with the ATO emerging from the building 'gingerly carrying the object in a cloth', intending to take it away and blow it up. Nash himself recalls:

> The 'cobalt bomb' source – our name for the original X-ray system – was at the end of its life, as I only discovered during this task. Eventually, the plates seemed to indicate that no detonator was present. I took the suspect item to a deserted building site and blew the bottom off, using Cordtex, to reveal inert, harmless, powder filling, a clock mechanism and loose wiring.

The press article concludes: 'At ten the next morning a sleepy phone call to the Army headquarters at Lisburn brings a deflating response. "Oh, that was a hoax," said the Press Officer airily. An elaborate one? "Not really – our experts soon found it out."'

Of course, what lies unspoken is the immense stress that must have been imposed on Nash as, on five occasions, he approached the potential source of his own instant oblivion. Every time his X-ray equipment failed to produce the required result, it condemned him to yet another 'long walk'. For all the supporting cast of cordon troops, policemen, firemen, journalists, spectators and other members of the bomb team, ultimately this boils down to a game of one-on-one. One man, one bomb. A game demanding the highest stake a man can play – his own life.

As 1970 dawned, the pace of terrorist bombing activity increased exponentially. The Protestant UVF started to attack Catholic-owned pubs, and planted small IEDs at the homes of politicians seen to be in favour of reform.

As the IRA awoke from its slumber, and the 'honeymoon period' between troops and Catholics ended, Republican terror attacks commenced against both innocent civilians and Security Forces alike.

Into this worsening situation arrived 28-year-old Captain Kevin Goad. He had come straight from the ATO course in March 1970 as the routine replacement for Captain Bob Willcox at HQNI. Young, fresh-faced and totally inexperienced, he was, not surprisingly, nervous about the daunting task ahead of him. Instead of facing the anticipated routine existence as a staff officer looking after ammunition inspections, storage and maintenance, here he was being thrown into one of the bloodiest terrorist campaigns ever conducted – at the deep end. Goad's attitude on arrival in the Province is described by Lieutenant-Colonel George Styles GC in his book *Bombs Have No Pity*. Styles, an ATO himself, was at that time serving as a major on the HQNI staff, charged with looking after the Army's in-theatre fleet of vehicles. Only a short time later, he was to take over command of the nascent bomb-disposal organisation in Northern Ireland. Styles recalls a conversation with Captain Goad over a beer in the HQNI Officers' Mess Bar within days of the new ATO's arrival: 'Sir, I think you should know I'm a ruddy coward . . . I think you should know, Sir, that I don't like this job: I don't like it at all. If I get to a bomb situation, I don't know what I'll do.'

Frankly, Kevin Goad's concerns mirror those of pretty well every ATO entering a hostile, high-threat theatre for the first time. No matter how calm one might appear on the surface, it is difficult to override that ever-present, nagging sense of dread. A not-untypical experience was described to me by one former operator, who was sent to Northern Ireland as a sergeant in 1972 – the worst year for operator deaths. He arrived in the Province with the usual feelings of apprehension, until he met the Officer Commanding 321 EOD Unit. Rather than being dressed in the warlike camouflage combat suit and boots, which might be expected in an operational theatre, the Major was wearing standard office uniform of cream shirt, smart khaki trousers and highly polished brown shoes. He conveyed such an air of normality that the sergeant was immediately put at his ease. Had he known that the operator arriving with him on the same day would soon be killed, as would his own successor, that sense of ease might not have lasted very long.

The challenge is to manage the fear until the first task is under the belt. Then the relief kicks in and one realises that the training really works. To quote Styles: 'Who could face the ultimate test of bomb disposal without feeling fear? If you won, you lived. If you failed, you died.' As with most other operators, Kevin Goad quickly overcame his apprehension, and went on to become a highly competent operator, eventually retiring as a brigadier. Indeed, within weeks, one of his exploits was appearing in a newspaper article under the headline 'Army hero wins death race with "delicate" bomb':

> Army explosives expert Captain Kevin Goad had to make a life-or-death decision yesterday when he faced a 20lb gelignite bomb. The bomb – crudely made with an electric timing device – could have gone off at any moment. And 28-year-old Kevin had to decide if he had enough time to get protective clothing. He tackled it dressed as he was. It took him only three seconds to make it safe, and 45 minutes to dismantle it.

But, heroics aside, it is glaringly apparent that, for the first year of the Troubles, the control of the Army's entire bomb-disposal effort in Northern Ireland was passing through the hands of very inexperienced, 'green' young captains (Willcox and Goad), both of whom had been sent out immediately after their respective ATO courses. And this did not please Captain Sydney Brazier of 321 EOD Unit. As we shall see, it did not please him at all.

By February 1970 the chain of command had woken up to the fact that ATO resources were spread so thin in Northern Ireland that permanent reinforcement was both vital and unavoidable. In Willcox's words: 'Chief Inspector Land Ammunition did eventually twig that people do need sleep.' The decision was therefore made to activate 321 EOD Unit. 321 existed only on paper, having been formed a few years earlier as a so-called shadow unit. That is, its members were identified and earmarked against posts within the unit, but they actually performed other duties within the Army on a day-to-day basis. The understanding was that they could be called to man their alternative 'shadow' posts at any time. In the case of 321, the unit was principally made up of ATOs and ATs who routinely worked in the Central Ammunition Depot in Bramley, Hampshire. 321 EOD Unit was to form the basis of the long-term bomb-disposal organisation in Northern Ireland, and still exists today as 321 EOD Squadron. The deployment date was set for 7 February 1970. Leading the first elements into the Province was Captain Sydney Brazier GM, a veteran ATO, who had come up through the ranks, and who had considerable experience of front-line bomb-disposal work. Brazier recalls:

321 EOD Unit deployed to Northern Ireland for the first time in February 1970. I was in command of the lead detachment. The Major in overall command of the unit remained behind in Bramley Ammunition Depot. I went by sea, with a vehicle, X-ray equipment, and armoured suits, accompanied by Staff Sergeant Hill. Until my arrival, Captain Willcox had handled all EOD (counter terrorist) activity, along with his normal ammunition duties.

After three days in Northern Ireland, the Commander RAOC, Lieutenant-Colonel Farrelly, asked Captain Willcox and myself to prepare a plan, should the threat spread across the Province. This plan, based on my experience in Cyprus (1956–60) was accepted, and became the EOD organisation during the next ten years. In mid-February, I was appointed EOD Staff Officer, responsible for all EOD activities across Northern Ireland.

It is clear from Captain Brazier's assessment that he did not like the way things were being done. At all. Although Captain Willcox had been making valiant efforts to cope with the increasingly desperate situation, he had been hampered by his own inexperience and the lack of manpower to assist him. As a seasoned bomb-disposal operator, who had received the George Medal for heroism in the field, the newly arrived Brazier was quick to spot flaws in the existing set-up. The accommodation, the records (or lack of them), the manning, the means of responding to incidents, the equipment and the quality of the staff were all submitted to his probing scrutiny:

The accommodation was an office in Headquarters Northern Ireland, occupied by the ATO captain, a warrant officer, a staff sergeant and the Fire Adviser. Office equipment consisted of three large lockers full of largely out-of-date paperwork. No filing cabinets were present. With the influx of 321 EOD Unit there was insufficient space in the office, and suitable alternative accommodation was found for the Fire Adviser. The absence of filing cabinets made the task of finding EOD files difficult.

One series of file numbers had been allocated to EOD incidents (stray munitions and political incidents). *Some* attempt had been made to separate files for some of the political incidents. Standing operating procedures had been prepared and distributed, but were not being adhered to with regard to maps, etc. No map was available showing details of incidents or

explosions. This made it difficult to realise the extent of incidents. No index
was available of the initiating methods of the various terrorist devices. No
intelligence data was readily available.

By the time Brazier arrived with his new broom, a worthy attempt was
already being made to provide three EOD teams on constant, immediate call –
one based permanently in Belfast and the other two at Army Headquarters in
Lisburn. Of the Lisburn-based teams, one would be constantly on standby to
react to incidents in Belfast. With routine ammunition duties still impinging
on EOD activity, trying to maintain this level of cover was clearly proving
difficult. Captain Brazier's tone implies that he simply did not believe that it
was working.

The Team 1 task was being carried out by WO2 Glover in Girdwood Park
Barracks, Belfast, the Tactical Headquarters of 2nd Battalion, The Queen's
Regiment. When we went to visit Glover, the ATO had great difficulty in
finding the location. Sleeping accommodation for Glover was bad (sleeping
in a room with eight to ten other senior NCOs, all of whom were on duty
at intervals during the night). Glover had been in location, unrelieved, for
five days.

   Team 2 *appeared* to be Captain Willcox, based in Lisburn, with a phone in
his married quarter. Team 3 *appeared* to be Staff Sergeant Barry, based at
Lisburn, with a phone in his billet. The Ammunition Depot personnel from
Ballykinler were being used on EOD activity whenever possible. Royal Navy
personnel were being used on stray munitions in the Londonderry area.

At that stage, the military base at Londonderry, which was later to become
Ebrington Barracks, was still a Royal Navy shore establishment, known as
HMS *Sea Eagle*.

Brazier was appalled to discover how the ATOs were being tasked to
incidents. The casual way in which the police simply rang up Captain Willcox
at home did not gel with his concept of an efficient, properly manned
operations room. If the police had the slightest sniff of a bomb, they had got
into the habit of asking for an ATO, who would be despatched, regardless of
whether a device had actually been found or not. The effect was that
operators could find themselves racing around Belfast simply responding to
one false alarm after another, as was demonstrated on Brazier's first night in

the Province: 'A phone call was received by the ATO, saying a bomb had been placed in the City Hall. The caller asked for Captain Willcox by name. The ATO informed the Ops Room, contacted WO2 Glover, and sent him to the scene.'

Brazier immediately realised that the call-out procedure needed to be revised as a matter of urgency. The ATOs had to be able to operate at the very highest level of alertness. They were not going to be able to do this if they were constantly being called upon to respond to false alarms on the basis of scant and inaccurate information. Later the same evening, after WO2 Glover had been deployed, a further episode occurred that reinforced this message:

On the first night, I was summoned from my bed to the ATO office, where I found Captains Willcox and Goad and Staff Sergeant Hill. I was told there had been an explosion in Belfast and that we were to stand by, as information was available that there were to be four more explosions. Willcox was having a third, ad hoc, EOD kit made up in the office. He further suggested we make up lengths of safety fuse, with detonators in position, along with lengths of Cordtex on cardboard [pre-formed in preparation for conducting controlled explosives]. I objected to this, and said that I could see no point in sitting in an office in Lisburn all night. Five people, including Glover in Belfast, were being committed on one single night without justification. Willcox agreed, and we all retired to bed and were not called. No further explosions occurred that night.

This turned out to be one of the very first hoax calls to be received during the Troubles. Thousands more were to follow over successive years. Based on his experience in Cyprus, Brazier directed that a proper drill should be drawn up for such occurrences. In short, no ATO should be tasked until a suspicious object had actually been found. On digging deeper it became apparent that other elements of the call-out procedure also needed to be addressed quickly. Duty rosters were not being applied effectively, nor was any record being maintained of the number of hours worked by individual operators. With so few operators, and a rapidly increasing workload, it would not have been long before individuals stared to fall over from sheer exhaustion if these details were not taken in hand.

On looking at the equipment, Brazier discovered that some of the kit that had been cobbled together was simply not good enough for the task:

The 4×2 (short wheelbase) Land Rover from the Central Vehicle Depot, taken by me to Northern Ireland, was not suitable for Number 1 Section of 321 EOD Unit. Even with only two in the team, it had proved too small to carry personnel, kit and EOD equipment. There were three armoured suits available. All three were of one size, and certain operators had great difficulty in wearing the vests due to the tightness under the arms.

Brazier pulled no punches when describing the operators. One senses that he was appalled that such young, amateurishly enthusiastic, but dreadfully inexperienced, ATO captains had been appointed to deal with the unravelling situation:

Captain R. Willcox had arrived in Northern Ireland direct from the ATO course. He had no knowledge or experience in EOD organisation and administration. He had worked long hours for some considerable time, but had, on his own admission, stumbled from bomb to bomb. Captain K. Goad had been sent to Northern Ireland at a time of political upheaval and direct from an ATO course. He lacked confidence and frankly admitted that the task frightened him. He was completely overawed by the situation. WO2 Glover appeared competent and had worked hard and unstintingly on EOD work. Staff Sergeant Barry had arrived from the Southern Command Ammunition Inspectorate [in England] as a member of 321 EOD Unit and was being used as a general factotum, to his disgruntlement. He felt his main task should have been EOD. All three drivers seemed competent, but were unsure of their duties or hours of duty.

Brazier took immediate action. He started by drawing up a duty roster for the coming month, with the operators reporting to him at the start and end of their duties. He extracted all incidents deemed to be of 'political significance' – in other words, terrorist related – and made a separate file for each. He obtained a desk with a single filing cabinet drawer – little realising that the bombing attacks would soon number thousands. Incidents already on file were categorised by 'means of initiation'. For example, devices being set off by clockwork timer would be filed separately from those using clothes pegs or safety fuse. A map of Belfast was displayed, showing the location and type of each EOD incident by means of coloured pins. Standard forms were created for reporting incident details. All these measures would contribute to the intelligence picture, making it easier to spot patterns, and helping operators to avoid making fatal mistakes.

New procedures were also put in place for handling bomb calls. Captain Willcox's married quarter ceased to be the unofficial EOD Tasking Centre. In future, all calls would be routed through the HQNI Operations Room. Before an ATO was tasked, searches were to be carried out by police or troops. Only then, when a suspicious or unrecognised object was found, was the ATO to be called. The improvements came just in time, as Brazier notes:

EOD activity intensified in early April. The activity was confined to Belfast, and thus I arranged to sleep in Girdwood Park Barracks [a former TA barracks in Belfast], and was able to control the work of the EOD team direct. During the day, when EOD activity was quiet, I worked at Lisburn on reports and advising the staff. As a result of this upsurge in activity, I was now in a position to give more concrete advice on the likely position of bombs. I prepared charts, indicating the nights on which explosions took place, and also the times of explosions. All this intelligence was fed into the General Staff. Hence, greater emphasis was placed on searching for bombs, and certain critical areas were flooded with troops.

As a result of Brazier's critical analysis, the new EOD organisation in Northern Ireland began to take shape. The next few months would see more operators drafted into 321 EOD Unit and rushed out to the Province. This would allow the establishment of ATO cover in each of the three brigade areas across Northern Ireland, including the remote country areas, where activity gradually started to rise. Two teams would be permanently located close to Belfast city centre, and a major would be appointed to Headquarters Northern Ireland to act as the Senior ATO (SATO).

Within two months of Captain Brazier's arrival, the IRA carried out its first daylight bomb attack. At around 9.30 a.m. on 5 April 1970 the terrorists planted a time bomb in an estate agent's office in Donegall Street, Belfast. The ensuing explosion wrecked the office and smashed plate-glass windows all along the street. One of the office girls was blown through a window and out into the street, where she stood screaming, the blood running down her face. Three other people in the office amazingly escaped with just shock and relatively minor cuts from the flying glass. A blue Mini car outside was peppered by flying metal and glass splinters. There had been two other explosions during the night, one in a tailor's shop in Royal Avenue, and the other at Alderman Joseph Cairn's furniture shop off the Shankill Road.

Amazingly, despite the steep rise in the overall number of bomb attacks, by the middle of 1970 the only fatalities had been caused by 'own goals'. The death of UVF member Thomas McDowell, as he tried to blow up the Ballyshannon Power Station in October 1969, has already been mentioned. Eight months later, more deaths followed. As would so often be the case throughout the Troubles, the explosion took innocent victims as well.

Thomas McCool, Thomas Carlin and Joe Coyle were all senior members of the IRA. Indeed, McCool had been arrested in 1957 and sentenced to eight years in prison for gun possession. On 26 June 1970 they would earn their places on the Republican 'Roll of Honour' as the first IRA men in the modern Troubles to be killed by their own bomb. Sometime after midnight, an explosion was heard coming from McCool's house at Drumcree Gardens, on Londonderry's Creggan estate. A fierce blaze started in the kitchen and quickly swept through the building. When the fire crews arrived shortly after 1 a.m., they found Thomas McCool and Joseph Coyle lying on the kitchen floor. Both were dead and very badly burnt. Littered among the debris in the room were several bottles containing paraffin or petrol, a small filter funnel and crystals of sodium chlorate, a chemical used for bomb making. Thomas Carlin had managed to stagger as far as a neighbour's back garden, but had collapsed, writhing in pain. He was to survive for a further eleven days before succumbing to his terrible injuries. Tragically, McCool's two young daughters, Carol, 4, and Bernadette, 9, were discovered in bed upstairs, and were passed out, wrapped in blankets, to an ambulance. One died on the way to hospital, and the other some hours after arrival.

It was to be another two months before the IRA finally managed to target and kill members of the Security Forces using an IED. On 7 August 1970 a red Ford Cortina was stolen from outside the Ardmore Hotel near Newry. By 11 August it had reappeared, apparently abandoned at random on the Lisseraw Road, off the main Crossmaglen-to-Dundalk road. Local people thought that it had been there for about two days. The police were informed, and two constables, Samuel Donaldson and Robert Millar, were despatched from Crossmaglen RUC Station, with orders to tow it away.

By the time the policemen arrived, the car had already attracted a certain amount of attention. A farmer had noticed it, as he had driven home for his tea on his tractor. Some time later, at around 7.30 p.m., he had walked back down to the car, and tried all four doors, which were locked. Another man, a labourer, had stopped to have a look inside while driving by with his son. He saw nothing to arouse suspicion. This was at about 8.30 p.m. Only minutes after he had driven away, the police arrived at the scene. The labourer was still driving towards Crossmaglen when he heard the thud of an explosion from behind him.

A local parish priest and a district nurse were among the first on the scene, where they discovered Constables Donaldson and Millar, both badly wounded and lying in an adjacent field, having been blown over a hedge. Donaldson had received terrible injuries to his face from flying glass and, although disoriented, was trying to stand up. Millar was conscious, lying on his back, having lost one of his legs. They died in Daisy Hill Hospital the next day. It appeared that they had been trying to open one of the doors when the device functioned. The bomb was later assessed by an ATO to have contained 15–20lb of gelignite, and had been wired into the electrical circuit that illuminated the car's interior courtesy light.

Bomb attacks were now becoming commonplace, but, surprisingly, there were to be only two more deaths from IEDs that year, both of them own goals. Captain Kevin Goad was called out to the first of these. He had daily put his life on the line to counter the terrorists' murderous acts, so one can sympathise with his grimly humorous description of events:

Late on 4 September 1970, the IRA blew up an electricity transformer on the Malone Road. An RUC mobile patrol was in the vicinity, and arrived just after the explosion. They reported seeing a figure limping away. I then proceeded to approach the seat of the explosion in ever decreasing circles to check against booby traps, when I came across what was obviously a hand and lower arm. I asked police whether the man they'd seen was noticeably missing an arm. They replied that it had only been a glimpse, and they couldn't confirm one way or the other. I went back to my task and then found the body – really just a torso with head. I called the police over to report the 'own goal'. The first thing one of them said to me was: 'Sor, the man we saw limping away definitely had a head on him!'

The body belonged to 35-year-old IRA man Michael Kane, from the hardline Republican area of the Ballymurphy in West Belfast. He came from an IRA family, his grandfather, Jack Coogan, who was also an IRA man, having been killed in Valentine Street in the 1920s. In his book *Bombs Have No Pity*, Lieutenant-Colonel George Styles attributes the premature explosion to an unreliable clothes-peg mechanism.

The last own goal of 1970 came on 6 November. After a threat was made to burn down his mother's home, 21-year-old Catholic Derek Lagan decided to make a pre-emptive strike on an Orange Hall near Carrickfergus. With an accomplice keeping guard outside, Lagan took a makeshift incendiary device, consisting of two cans of petrol, upstairs. Shortly afterwards, there was a 'whoosh', as the device functioned with Lagan still alongside it. He was engulfed in the fireball. He managed to drag himself to a back room, where firemen found him lying naked and badly charred. He died within hours. Although the attack had sectarian motives, it is not thought that Lagan was an IRA member.

And so 1970 drew to a close. The number of explosions for the year totalled 170 – seventeen times the figure for the year before. The IRA had succeeded in killing two members of the Security Forces, but had lost four of its number in own goals. It had also succeeded in killing two innocent civilians, the first of many more to come, in this case the two young daughters of one of the bombers. The naive and misguided Derek Lagan had also managed to kill himself. Despite the dramatic increase in bomb attacks, no ATOs had yet been killed. This would soon change.

Two

1971: The Year of the Castlerobin

The year 1971 marked a step-change in terrorist activity, with the IRA actively trying to kill members of the Security Forces. On 6 February a burst of automatic fire in the New Lodge Road, Belfast, killed Gunner Robert Curtis, the first soldier to die in the Troubles.

Three days after Gunner Curtis's death, five BBC technicians lost their lives when their Land Rover triggered a booby-trap device, intended for an Army patrol, as they drove up Brougher Mountain in County Tyrone to inspect a transmitter. The actual device was hidden under rocks at the side of the track. It was a simple booby trap. A fishing line had been stretched across the track at knee height. In the early morning darkness, it would have been invisible. The circuit of the IED was wired in to the traditional clothes peg, with drawing-pin contacts. The drawing pins were kept apart by some form of insulating material, which was tied to one end of the fishing line. The other end of the line was secured on the far side of the track. As the Land Rover drove into the line, it tightened, snatching the insulator from between the jaws of the peg. The jaws snapped shut and the pins came into contact, completing the circuit, and allowing the device to explode. Simple, effective, deadly . . . and the wrong target.

By this time, the new EOD organisation for the Province was starting to bed in. A major had been appointed as the Senior Ammunition Technical Officer, or SATO, to run the show from HQNI in Lisburn. Initially, this was Major John Fitzsimmons, as a short-term stop-gap measure, which lasted only three months from August to November 1970.

And then George Styles took over. Styles – bluff, hearty, direct, avuncular, cigar smoking and a stickler for military form – was a true major of the old school, and, under the circumstances, exactly the right man for the job. Passionately interested in what he was doing and seemingly without fear, he set the standard for EOD in the Province by leading from the front in every sense. A comment from one of the ATOs who arrived in the unit in March 1971, Captain Alan Clouter, sums up Styles perfectly: 'I remember George Styles arriving most upset from a job on which he'd been shot at. His complaint was not the shooting, but that they'd used a mere .22 inch [small bore] calibre against the Army *Full Bore* Rifle Association Secretary!'

In spite of the improvements in organisation and procedures, life was still far from comfortable for the ATOs arriving in Northern Ireland for their bomb-disposal tours. Frank Steer recalls arriving in Lurgan as a young captain:

> I went to Northern Ireland on 9 February 1971, at 24 hours' notice, to move in with the Headquarters of 16 Parachute Brigade, as the Brigade ATO, in the shirt factory at Lurgan. We were the first headquarters to move into Lurgan and, for the first few weeks we were there, whilst all the internal works services were being done, we slept on laboratory benches, and on the floors in manufacturing rooms, in what was still a factory as opposed to a headquarters. As the Brigade ATO, I shared the dormitory with the Parachute Brigade Chaplains, known as the 'Leaping Deacons'. I often wondered whether or not there was any significance in this arrangement.
>
> After seven weeks or so in Lurgan, we moved into Belfast, to replace the section led by Captain Murray Stewart. It was George Styles' idea to switch the two teams round from the high pressure existence of seven or eight jobs a day in Belfast, as against the low pressure existence of one or two a week out in the country. In those days 'country bombs' hadn't reached the level of sophistication that they have now, and the greatest danger was probably the drive to get to the job.

In *Bombs Have No Pity*, Styles comments on this switch:

> With the Brougher Mountain explosion a great deal of bomb activity moved into the countryside. This was somewhat tough for one of the RAOC Ammunition Technical Officers, Captain Murray Stewart, because I'd just moved him into the country as he'd been having a busy time in Belfast. But he was equal to the challenge, later being awarded the MBE for gallantry.

Certainly, the ATOs operating in the rural areas had to adapt their procedures rapidly to counter the developing threat. Initially, bombs in the countryside were treated no differently from those in the cities, although some of the environmental hazards might be different, as former Captain Kevin Goad recalls:

In January 1971 I attended an incident near Rosstrevor. An ex-B Specials hut had been bombed. It was about 2.30 a.m. when I met up with three burly RUC officers, and proceeded in single file, with flash lights, through a field and up a gentle hill towards the burning hut. As an aside, I shudder at our naivety at walking straight into what could have been an ambush or booby-trap situation. Halfway up the hill, my flashlight illuminated an extremely large goat, which, having recovered from the shock of the nearby explosion, decided to hold me personally responsible for disturbing its peace. After the first charge and butt, I fled down the hill, followed by the three policemen. We all dived into the front seat of my Land Rover, waking up my gently dozing driver, Lance Corporal Stewart. Space was limited, as you can imagine! Over the next fifteen minutes or so, the goat proceeded to butt hell out of the side door and panels of my Land Rover (the wings were still painted red in those days).

Eventually, Lance Corporal Stewart, a man of Devon, who in his youth had worked on a farm, got out and pacified the goat by stroking it like a dog. All it wanted, obviously, was a bit of love and comfort. Goats, however, smell strongly and, hence, so did Lance Corporal Stewart, and then me, and then the RUC policemen. On my return to HQNI, I noticed how everyone paled and kept their distance from both me and the policemen during our debriefing. The all-pervading smell of goat will live with me forever! Oh yes – and the REME [Royal Electrical and Mechanical Engineers] subsequently raised a 'Negligence, Misuse and Damage Report' for the battered Land Rover!

It did not take long for the ATOs to realise that they could not simply go blundering about in the countryside at night looking for a bomb. The Brougher Mountain incident showed how very easy it would be to lure the Security Forces into a trap. Although the frequency of incidents was never to match that encountered in the cities, the rural environment allowed the IRA much greater freedom of action. Operating among the fields, hedgerows and country roads by night, they could take their time to set up massive, remotely detonated IEDs and ingenious, victim-operated, booby traps. In South Armagh and Fermanagh, the proximity of the border with Southern Ireland presented a safe base from which to mount attacks, and a quick escape route in the aftermath. Indeed, despite the huge number of devices appearing daily in the cities, one of the IRA's earliest successes against the Army was in the countryside. On 6 September 1971 terrorists detonated a roadside bomb, as a Land Rover passed by, in the rural area of Derryberg, near Bessbrook. Trooper John Warnock of the 16th/5th Lancers was blown off the tailboard to lie, bleeding profusely, in the road. He died shortly afterwards at the Daisy Hill Hospital, Newry, the first military casualty to a roadside ambush bomb. Eventually, the IRA's consistent successes with rural culvert bombs and so-called landmines throughout the early 1970s was to have the effect of making some areas off limits for military road transport, with helicopters being used instead. As early as 1971 the ATOs started to adapt their own tactics to suit, as Frank Steer remembers:

We were the first RAOC EOD section to undertake joint operations with the Royal Engineers in the country on the approach to a device. We didn't have a Royal Engineers Search Adviser and all the good bits of kit that exist today. I went out with a Sapper section, commanded by a corporal, using old-fashioned mine search techniques – looking for trip wires, pressure pads and the like, on the way up a mountain track to a radio mast at the top of a hill, which had been blown up. It was an incident that occurred shortly after the Brougher Mountain murders. We were of the view that the explosion on the radio mast which *I* went to could have been a 'come on'. So we took the precaution of searching the road on the way up so that we could get the vehicle to it. I meanwhile took an unorthodox approach across the fields to get to the scene of the incident. This type of operation was carried out on a number of occasions after that, but much more informally than is now the case.

The downward spiral of events in Northern Ireland hit a new low with the murder in cold blood of three young Scottish soldiers, Dougald McCaughey (23), and brothers Joseph McCaig (18) and John McCaig (17), at Squire's Hill, in the Ligoniel area on the outskirts of Belfast on 10 March 1971. The three had been drinking at a bar in the centre of Belfast while off duty. It is believed that they had fallen in with some Republican girls, who invited them on to a party. Having been lured to a car, they were driven to a quiet area where they were each assassinated with a shot to the back of the head. Condemnation was widespread, and thousands, many of them shop stewards and shipyard workers, marched through Belfast demanding a tougher stance on security. The Northern Irish Prime Minister, Major James Chichester-Clark, asked for more British troops, but his request was turned down. He resigned shortly afterwards, being replaced by Brian Faulkner. As violence and public disorder on a massive scale continued to escalate, the bombers stepped up their attacks, wreaking carnage throughout the Province. Whereas the early bombings had been against public utilities after dark, now, crowded bars, police stations, shopping centres and military installations all became 'legitimate targets'.

The bombing of the Springfield Road RUC Station, in Belfast, on 25 May 1971, was typical of the new, indiscriminate style of attack, which was just as likely to kill or maim innocent bystanders as members of the Security Forces. A car had pulled up outside the police station, and a man had jumped out to hurl a suitcase through the front doors and into the reception area. As the car sped away, the suitcase exploded, killing one soldier. Two other soldiers, seven policemen and eighteen civilians were also injured in the blast. The death toll would undoubtedly have been far higher had it not been for the heroic actions of the soldier who lost his life, Sergeant Michael Willets of the 3rd Battalion, The Parachute Regiment. Frank Steer was the ATO captain who was called to the scene of the explosion:

I investigated the explosion in the Springfield Road Police Station, which killed Sergeant Michael Willets of the Parachute Regiment, and for which he was posthumously awarded the George Cross. Terrorists driving past in a car threw a small suitcase packed with explosives into the front door of the police station. Sergeant Willets took under his wing a woman and her two children, who were standing alongside him in the foyer. He ushered them down a passageway, shielding them from the bomb with his own body. When it went off, he took the full force of the explosion, but they were saved. He lived for a couple of hours afterwards, but died that night in the Royal Victoria Hospital.

It was a pretty emotional experience, but it wasn't helped when the women of the Springfield Road attempted to spit on the stretcher as he was being carried away. I had to employ physical restraint to stop my escorts from the Royal Highland Fusiliers [RHF] doing something to assist their Parachute Regiment colleagues in the dispersal of these women. Already during that tour, three young soldiers from the RHF had been murdered – all shot in the back of the head – on the outskirts of Belfast, at a place called Ligoniel.

On the 'Glorious Twelfth of July', the IRA attacked the Protestants' Orange bands and marchers by setting off several bombs along the traditional route. At the request of the new Northern Irish Prime Minister, Brian Faulkner, Westminster agreed to the introduction of internment – detention without evidential proof or trial. Viewed by many as an act of desperation, the process was not handled well. On 9 August 1971, 342 men, described as 'Republican suspects' were picked up in swoops by the Security Forces. In many instances, the wrong individuals were arrested through a combination of poor intelligence and mistaken identity. The Army's robust methods left a perpetual legacy of ill feeling simmering throughout the Catholic estates. Although a third of those interned were soon released, the arrests continued. Gunfights and bombings quickly became everyday events.

The level of activity now facing the ATOs and ATs on the streets was overwhelming. D.H. Green was then a WO2 operator stationed in Belfast, traditionally the busiest area for IEDs. His words convey the mixture of apprehension and exhaustion that operators would have to contend with on a daily basis:

All days became as one, day and date immaterial. During this period, all IED disposal work was carried out manually. Operators relied on conventional explosives and equipment, mainly the Stanley knife, wire-cutters and Cordtex. Knowledge was sparse, but we learnt – the hard way, perhaps. Mid-tour R&Rs had been introduced, but many were loath to take these as it disrupted their balance and what had become a 'way of life'. Fear and fatigue had also become constant companions. Most of those who took this mid-tour R&R regretted it on their return. One believed the mental switch was too great. There was humour – soldiers always find some, even in adversity. Personally, I have none worthy of mention. Perhaps one could have written up completed tasks better, and forensic recovery was poor (lack of knowledge). The aim of most operators at that time was *survival*.

Amid this rising tide of terrorist attacks, it was only going to be a matter of time before an ATO was killed. That day came on 9 September 1971. At around 8.30 a.m. a postman on his morning rounds had noticed a suspicious package lying up against the wall of the Orange Hall in the small village of Castlerobin. This largely Protestant village, situated along a winding country road, skirting the slope of Colin Mountain, was not far from Lisburn. It was also close to the edge of the IRA heartland of Catholic West Belfast. The package appeared to be a wooden box, similar in size to a shoebox. Choosing to make the luckiest decision of his life, instead of picking the box up, the postman informed the local policeman.

The policeman arrived on the scene. He too must have been sorely tempted to move the box, even if only to confirm his suspicions before getting the Army involved. After all, nobody likes to make a fuss. What if he dragged a whole lot of people out onto the ground, only to discover it really was just a wooden box? But luck was also on his side that day. The box stayed where it was and the call was made to a higher authority.

Probably at about the time the box was discovered, Captain David Stewardson would have been settling down behind his desk at Headquarters Northern Ireland, preparing to fight the paperwork war. Twenty-nine years old, married and an ATO, he had been in the Province for just over a week. He had been flown out as a reinforcement at the end of August, as the violent backlash continued against internment. Now he found himself held in reserve at the Headquarters in Lisburn, working in the office with the Officer Commanding 321 EOD Unit, Major George Styles. Although Styles had already sent the young officer up to Belfast for three nights to get 'blooded', he had yet to tackle his first bomb. In the meantime, he found himself assigned to the worthy but tedious task of drafting a paper advising government departments and commercial firms how to guard against bomb attacks.

At around 10 a.m. the phone rang. Stewardson answered, with Styles listening in on the linked extension. It was the EOD team from Lurgan. They had just been tasked to deal with the suspicious box at Castlerobin, but were already busy with another job. They therefore wondered whether a team might be sent out from Lisburn instead. With Major Styles nodding his assent to the Lurgan team's request, Captain Stewardson took his chance and asked if he could be the operator tasked to deal with it. So far, two individuals had made lucky decisions that morning, but luck was now starting to run out.

Minutes later, the ATO was heading eagerly for the door. His team's vehicle was ready, still fully kitted out from his recent stint up in Belfast.

By the time Captain Stewardson arrived at Castlerobin, a small crowd had gathered. Keen to see the spectacle, the onlookers were lingering much too close to the device. The ATO ordered his infantry escort to move them back, then set about planning his render-safe procedure. We know from subsequent timings that he did not take long over this. Within minutes, he had walked up to the box, tied a line around it, then retired to pull it from a distance. We do not know the extent to which he managed to disturb the box at this stage, but he obviously thought that he had done enough to trigger any anti-handling mechanism.

Witnesses relate that Captain Stewardson then paused for a couple of minutes. Perhaps by this stage he had convinced himself that this was just a simple wooden box. Jolting it had not set it off. He could see no obvious means of causing fragmentation or fire – no nails or petrol container. There were no telltale signs, such as a length of fuse sticking out or a battery pack. Was the outside wall of an Orange Hall in this quiet country village really a terrorist target? Whatever his thoughts during those two minutes, he quickly made up his mind to look into the mouth of the dragon one more time. Taking his tool bag with him, he knelt down next to the box and began to cut into it.

A short while later, the phone rang again in Styles's office. It was a staff officer from Headquarters 39th Infantry Brigade, the Formation HQ that had tactical responsibility for the Belfast and Lisburn region. Details were sketchy, but it was already clear that an ATO had been killed in an explosion – the first to die in the Troubles.

In *Bombs Have No Pity*, Styles recalls being called to see the GOC Northern Ireland, Lieutenant-General Sir Harry Tuzo:

'What the hell's happening, George?'
    'Right now, Sir, we don't know. But we will. The point is they're after us. They're not going to do too much damage because the bombs don't have too much power. They don't have power because they only want to take us out. Don't worry, we'll find the secret soon enough. We'll be on top soon.'

The new device, specifically designed to target ATOs, was christened the 'Castlerobin'. Work immediately commenced to determine how to kill it before it killed again. And there were plenty of opportunities to practise. The IRA, keen to exploit its initial success, followed up with several more Castlerobins in quick succession. On the very night of Captain Stewardson's death, a second device turned up in a garage outside Belfast. On Major Styles's instructions, it was X-rayed, sandbagged and then pulled from a distance. It detonated immediately. It soon became apparent that Stewardson had been particularly unlucky, in that the device had not gone off as soon as he had tried to pull it. Subsequent bombs invariably exploded at the slightest movement, but the X-ray pictures that were always taken first allowed the operators to start building up a picture of the secrets that lay inside the wooden boxes.

Much of the credit for the breakthrough must go to Captain Derek Markham, an ATO running one of the Belfast teams, who was nearing the end of his four-month tour. Over the period of the tour, he and the two other operators in the Belfast Section were successfully to disarm a total of 150 bombs. By 2 October, when he encountered several Castlerobins over a period of just a few hours, he had already experienced one narrow escape – only one week after David Stewardson's death. On 16 September, while walking back from a device, he had come under such heavy terrorist rifle fire that one of his infantry escorts, Lance-Corporal Peter Herrington of the Green Howards, had been killed and two others wounded. After the tour, Markham was awarded the George Medal, the citation for which pays particular attention to his role in defeating the Castlerobins:

> On 2 October 1971, in central Belfast, he encountered a concentrated attack by the terrorists, using bombs so designed that each could kill the EOD operator. One of a similar design was believed to have been responsible for the death of one of his brother officers on 9 September 1971.
>
> In full knowledge of the danger and uncertainty concerning this particular type of bomb, he safely, over a period of three hours, disposed of four of these sinister devices. He also obtained photographic and radiographic information that subsequently allowed another team to safely dismantle two more the following evening. By his meticulous care, and with the risk of immediate death always present, he minimised the effects of exploding the four devices concerned.

Markham's efforts led directly to the capture of two Castlerobins, by another operator (Sergeant Chris Carrier), relatively intact, in the space of one night. This was a major step forward. When the knowledge gleaned from the dismantled Castlerobins was combined with the X-rays already taken, it was possible to re-create an exact replica from scratch. Styles ordered one of his ATO captains to put one together, with a bulb to replace the detonator, then took it home and practised late into the night in his kitchen. Whenever he made a mistake, the bulb would illuminate. The box was fitted with micro-switches at the top and bottom. If it was lifted or tilted, or if the lid was opened, a real device would explode. The problem was to isolate the switches so that the rest of the circuit could be dismantled without setting the bomb off. By the next morning Styles was confident that he had mastered the technique, and lost no time in explaining it to his operators.

Along with Styles, two young ATO captains were to be in the forefront of the fight against the Castlerobins. Captain Alan Clouter had been sent out straight from his ATO course to replace Captain Kevin Goad at HQNI at the beginning of March 1971. He had also experienced a very near miss, on the same day that Derek Markham's escorts were shot. On 16 September 1971 Lisburn RUC Station came under small-arms fire. In the immediate follow-up to the incident, a partly opened holdall was discovered on the steps leading to the front door. Captain Clouter was called to the scene, to find that the holdall held a ticking 10lb time bomb, which might possibly be booby-trapped. At this point, the police station was still occupied by duty staff, so Clouter decided to try to drag the device clear to minimise both casualties and structural damage. Having attached a hook and line, he had managed to pull the holdall only a couple of feet when it snagged and the line broke. Without a moment's thought, he dashed out, repaired the line, then, taking cover again, continued to pull. The holdall had been dragged only a further 10 feet before the bomb exploded, causing no casualties and only superficial damage to the police station.

The other captain was Roger Mendham. Only 24 years old, he had attended the same ATO course as David Stewardson, and the two had been close friends. On 1 October 1971, only three weeks after Stewardson's death, he found himself deploying right into the thick of the action.

Styles was now convinced that the operators had the upper hand. So long as they took it slowly and carefully, they could defeat the Castlerobin with relative ease. On 20 October 1971 the time came to put theory into practice. At about four o'clock in the afternoon, a wooden box was discovered in the telephone booth of the Whip and Saddle Bar of the Europa Hotel, Belfast. Completed as recently as July of the same year, the Europa was a smart, modern hotel, boasting twelve storeys of bedrooms, and situated on Great Victoria Street, one of the main thoroughfares leading into the city centre. The sort of place where businessmen from the UK mainland and journalists would stay, this was a prestige target for the IRA.

The Belfast team, led by Roger Mendham, was first on the scene. It immediately became apparent that the device was a Castlerobin, and that X-ray equipment would be required. Major Styles despatched Captain Clouter from Lisburn straight away with the kit, then followed on close behind. By the time he arrived at about 5.30 p.m., Clouter already had an X-ray picture.

The image had not been obtained without some difficulty. Alan Clouter had discovered that the box was pushed tight into the corner of the telephone booth. Two of its sides were therefore hard up against the walls. In order to take an X-ray, the machine needed to be on one side of the target, and the film cassette on the other. The size of the film cassette – around half an inch thick – meant that it was impossible to achieve the correct configuration without disturbing the device. The ATO therefore came up with a method of using the paper-thin film without its cassette, and very carefully slid it between the telephone booth wall and the box. It was just as well that the positioning of the film plate was carried out with extreme caution, because, when it was developed, it showed a perfect picture of a micro-switch. The switch, which had been resting against the wall, had been just slightly depressed when the plate had been slid in. When Captain Clouter removed the plate, the switch had come out again to rest back against the wall. The slightest clumsiness would have caused the device to function.

With infinite care and patience, and using the X-ray picture for guidance, the operators now began the intricate and time-consuming task of dismantling the booby-trap mechanisms. Only when it was finally safe to move the IED did they attach a line to drag it outside, into the adjacent railway station car park. Here, amid a protective wall of pre-positioned sandbags, two small and precise controlled explosions were used to deliver the *coup de grâce*. The theory had worked. It had taken seven hours from start to finish, but the job was done. No one had been hurt and no damage had been caused. The hotel manager had promised the operators half a crate of champagne if the device was a hoax, and a whole crate if real. They got their whole crate.

It had been a resounding victory against the terrorists, who clearly did not like it, because two days later, on 22 October, they were back – at the same venue. On this occasion, three hooded and armed men burst into the reception area of the Europa. While they covered shocked customers and staff with sub-machine guns, a fourth man brought in a large and heavy box, which he placed on the floor in front of the reception desk. Styles, Clouter and Mendham were soon on the scene, and were somewhat surprised to see the hotel manager stop at the desk on his way out to answer the telephone and accept a booking for that night!

Luckily, the exposed position of the box in the hotel foyer meant that obtaining detailed X-ray pictures was not quite so problematic this time. The device was very similar to previous examples, but much bigger, being some 2 feet high by 18 inches deep and 18 inches wide. At first, the circuit, as revealed by the X-rays, also seemed rather more complex, with additional wiring and micro-switches, but, after the picture had been analysed, it became apparent that the terrorist was deliberately trying to mislead the operators. The bomb-maker had also thrown in some taunts; scribbled on the outside of the box were the words: 'Tee-hee, He-hee, Ho-Ho, Ha-Ha'. Just enough to give the operation an extra edge.

Despite the extra wiring, the fundamental make-up of the device was unchanged. Slowly but surely, the anti-handling mechanisms were identified, isolated and defeated. For the second time in two days, the Royal Engineers built their beehive of sandbags in the station car park, and the long, slow drag commenced as, for two hours, the bomb was hauled carefully outside on an improvised sled. Once it was safely contained, Captain Mendham went forward to place the disruptive charges that would ensure that the device was finally dead. This time, it had taken nine hours of tense work, and the team enjoyed their second champagne party.

Up to this point, the ATOs had been granted the luxury of being able to take their time to defeat a Castlerobin. The terrorist was about to take that luxury away. During the very long disposal operations on 20 and 22 October, the IRA had observed and taken note. The BBC had even been kind enough to televise the second event (prompting the operators to take the plug off their X-ray equipment, and put it onto a spare hotel television set, so that they could see themselves at work!). Indeed, Major Styles had counted down the last few seconds before the disruptive charges were fired in the railway station car park, to ensure that the cameras obtained the best shot. The fact that the procedures had stretched to many hours would not have gone unnoticed. So the IRA decided to see how successful the operators might be if they had to work against the clock: they built in a time bomb.

On the evening of Sunday 24 October, two teenagers, one male, one female, entered the hallway of the Celebrity Club in Donegall Place, Belfast. Stairs led up from the hallway to the club itself, which was situated over the city centre's C&A store. It was packed at the time. Despite their youth, both teenagers were members of 'C Company, 1st Battalion', of the IRA's 'Belfast Brigade', and both were armed with revolvers. Unwittingly, they could not have chosen a worse time. As they came in through the door, they encountered two armed RUC officers in plain clothes, who had popped in to check the club and were just leaving.

Before they reached the door, the policemen found themselves being held at gunpoint. The male gunman, 19-year-old Martin Forsythe, pointed to one of them, saying: 'Hey you, big fella, don't you move.' While the officers remained motionless, a third terrorist then entered, carrying a large box, which he put down on the floor. Shouting a warning, the bombers ran out of the door. They did not get far. As soon as the terrorists had bolted, the policemen drew their own weapons and set off in pursuit. In a flurry of shots, Martin Forsythe was hit at least five times, spinning and falling dead on the pavement. The girl with him was also shot and critically injured. Back at the club, rather than descend the stairs and exit past the bomb, the members sensibly decided to knock down part of the wall to escape into an adjacent shop.

But the bomb was still ticking, and it was Captain Roger Mendham who was tasked to deal with it. On arrival, he carried out the usual drills of learning as much as he could about the situation: 'What is it? Where is it? What does it look like? How long has it been there? Has anybody touched it?' The answers must have pointed towards this being yet another Castlerobin, and Captain Mendham set off on his initial reconnaissance to gain a glimpse of the sinister object lying inside the Celebrity Club. And there it was. Another box. But, unlike the others, and unknown to him, this one was ticking. As Captain Mendham walked back towards the Incident Control Point, the seconds counted down to zero, the contacts closed, and the device functioned. The explosion caused complete devastation, blowing out the downstairs entrance to the club, and showering Donegall Place with fragments of glass, masonry and wood. Captain Mendham survived unscathed, but it had been a lucky escape.

The terrorists had now presented the ATOs with a new challenge. Styles's original method had been fine, but it had relied on having the time to take X-rays and then plan and execute a painstaking render-safe procedure. The presence of a timer put a whole new complexion on things. An ATO faced with a timer must spend the minimum possible time at the device. It is a gamble. Will it tick down as he is actually leaning over it? Luckily, the scientists were about to come to the rescue; they invented the first disrupter – 'Pigstick'.

Up until the invention of Pigstick, EOD operators essentially had three methods of disposal available to them. First, they might employ scalpels, wire-cutters and Stanley knives to cut into the IED, diagnose the circuit and disarm it. Clearly, this involved a high degree of risk. The terrorist might have incorporated anti-tilt or anti-movement switches, light-sensitive sensors, anti-intrusion screens or a collapsing circuit (whereby the cutting of the wrong wire would set the device off) to catch out the unwary operator. Alternatively, explosive charges of varying sizes might be employed to effect a 'controlled explosion', hopefully shattering the bomb's mechanism in the process. The third option was the 'hook and line kit' – an assortment of lines, hooks and pulleys, which could be used to jolt and move the bomb. While the primary purpose of the hook and line kit was to discount the presence of anti-handling mechanisms, on a good day the device might fall apart completely if it was given a sufficiently vigorous tug. Sometimes a combination of all three methods might be used in the same job – as was the case with the Castlerobins ('stun, drag and bang').

The problem with all these options was the huge degree of uncertainty involved. An ATO cutting into an IED could not be completely certain that he would not trigger a booby trap. The tumbling effect of the hook and line might rupture the circuit, but there was no guarantee. And, although an explosive charge could be put in place rapidly, it was hardly a precision weapon, and there was every danger that it would cause the bomb to detonate completely. What was required was something that could be deployed quickly, accurately and effectively, minimising the ATO's exposure time. Pigstick provided the answer.

For some considerable time, the technology behind Pigstick was shrouded in secrecy. Over the years, though, repeated exposure, on the streets, in technical publications, through international defence sales and in media articles and documentaries, has put it very much in the public domain. In simple terms, Pigstick is like a miniature cannon, which fires a mixture of water and gas into a device, with the intention of disrupting it. It consists of a steel tube, about 45 centimetres long, with a breech at one end. A precise quantity of water is poured into the muzzle of the tube, and the open end is sealed with a plastic cap. A specially designed cartridge is then loaded into the breech. The weapon is fired remotely, using an electrical firing cable. It can therefore be delivered right up to the device, either by robot or by hand, and then set off, with the operator hiding behind cover a safe distance away. The effect was once described to me as 'like putting an angry little gnome inside a device, and letting him kick the hell out of it'. When it is fired, the cartridge propels the water out of the tube at very high velocity. The water emerges in a formed slug and smashes its way into the device, where it dissipates rapidly, shattering components, breaking connections and short-circuiting the electrics. Although not an infallible method, it will generally cause complete disruption before any in-built anti-disturbance mechanism can operate. The propellant gases given off by the cartridge when it fires follow up behind and add to the bursting effect. Although Pigstick will completely shatter the bomb's working parts, it will not set it off. The scattered pieces can therefore be recovered intact and used for later forensic analysis and evidence.

Since 1972 Pigstick has been a fundamental weapon in the ATO's armoury, but initial trials were unconvincing. Geoff Thomas, the captain at Lurgan from August to December 1971, recalls: 'The first theatre demonstration of Pigstick, held at a quarry just outside Lisburn, was attended by George Styles, Alan Clouter, Roger Mendham and myself. I was unconvinced, disliked big bangs and, when invited to fire Pigstick, was a little concerned. A high order [complete detonation of the device] ensued, showering us all with debris.'

Captain Alan Clouter was also sceptical of the trial model. The test firing in the quarry had shown that there was clearly a chance that the weapon might set a device off. Moreover, the original version, officially known as the 'Injector XL1E1' (and assigned the temporary nickname 'Jack Horner'), weighed 45lb and, to preserve its secrecy, was disguised as a piece of X-ray equipment. An operator trying to stay alert in a high-threat environment would hardly relish being so heavily encumbered. Discussions between George Styles and Queen's University resulted in the production of a lighter-weight version, which became the basis of future production models. The final version consisted of a corrosion-resistant steel tube, some 18 inches long and

1.5 inches in diameter, weighing just under 6lb. By sheer good fortune, the issue of the first operational Pigsticks came within days of Captain Mendham's narrow escape.

Simon Scourfield-Evans, an ATO captain serving in 3 Brigade's rural patch around Lurgan, remembers the first Pigsticks turning up:

Pigstick was introduced, which became the main means of disrupting packages, but this still meant a manual approach. I had a trial run in the garages of the 'Knitwear Factory', which was being used as Brigade HQ. I didn't bother to notify the Ops Room. They began to initiate the appropriate responses when muffled explosions were heard in the immediate area of the Headquarters. This all came to light the next day, when I suggested that it might have been me playing with a new toy.

Pigstick could not have arrived too soon. With the IRA building a timing mechanism into devices modelled on the original Castlerobin, the operators could no longer afford the time-consuming render-safe procedures that had been used so successfully at the Europa Hotel. Captain Mendham's own lucky escape at the Celebrity Club had proved this. Luckily, the first prototype weapon arrived in Northern Ireland in time to be used against a similar bomb placed in the Midland Hotel in Belfast on 18 November. On this occasion, the operator was WO2 Ian Pennington, who had earlier assisted in the initial reconnaissance of the second bomb at the Europa Hotel. A controlled explosion using the new disrupter resulted in complete disruption of the device, thereafter known as the 'Midlander', and its secrets were laid bare.

Pigstick gave the ATOs the edge they needed. The new weapon allowed them to spend just seconds at the device. So long as it was accurately positioned, it would achieve complete disruption, leaving the vital components of a bomb scattered harmlessly on the ground. But, they still had to get to the device before it went off. The easiest way for the IRA to prevent that happening was simply to ensure that little or no warning was given. Throughout the final quarter of 1971, therefore, the IEDs that caused most death and destruction were those that came without warning.

Army and police posts were obvious targets for blast-bomb attacks. On 4 October the Scots Guards lost two soldiers only eight days apart when the IRA twice attacked the observation post in Cupar Street, off the Falls Road in Belfast. On 27 October it was the turn of 45 Medium Regiment, Royal

Artillery, when its post at the Rosemount RUC Station, Londonderry, came under attack. Two 10lb blast bombs were tossed over the wall, killing two soldiers. The next day, a corporal in the 16th/5th Lancers was fatally injured when an ambush device detonated next to his Ferret armoured scout car, as it travelled in convoy along a road near Kinawley, not far from the border. And, on 29 October, a police inspector lost his life when a time bomb on a short fuse was placed in a shop alongside Chichester Road RUC Station in Belfast.

But soldiers and policemen were not the only targets. Bars and shops began to receive the frequent attention of bombers from both sides of the sectarian divide. If warnings were given, they were often so late or garbled that multiple deaths were the inevitable result. Typical of such attacks was that on the Red Lion pub and a drapery shop on the Ormeau Road, Belfast, on 2 November. The buildings were on either side of the Ballynafeigh RUC Station, which was the bombers' intended target. As would so often be the case, the only people to die were innocent civilians. Bombs were planted in both premises by three IRA men shortly after 4.25 p.m. On the way out of the pub door, one of the bombers shouted: 'You have ten seconds to get out.' He overestimated. Within about six seconds, the device had exploded, completely demolishing the bar and killing three of the customers. The other bomb functioned without causing further deaths.

Amid this firestorm of bombs, the loss of another operator was becoming ever more likely. Throughout September and October, near misses had become commonplace. Captain Alan Clouter had been at a device only minutes before it exploded after he had dragged it out of Lisburn RUC Station on 16 September. WO2 Terry Green, a Belfast operator, had been dismantling a bomb at a bonded spirit store on 1 October when he found a second IED nearby. He neutralised it on the spot, only later discovering that it had just four minutes to run down on the timer. Captain Roger Mendham had been walking away from the Midlander when it had functioned on 24 October. Only five days later, the same thing happened again, this time bringing a house down around him. And, on 13 November, yet another bomb went off as he retired after an initial reconnaissance; later that same day, he was to attend six further incidents without displaying any qualms. This run of good luck could only hold out for so long.

On 24 November WO2 Colin 'Taff' Davies was tasked to a bomb in a car showroom in Lurgan. Gunmen had entered the building and ordered the staff to leave. They had then placed a large box somewhere inside, although the staff did not see where. The incident was reported to the police, who alerted the Army, and the Lurgan team was despatched to the scene.

Unlike Captain Stewardson, who had been in theatre for only a little over a week, WO2 Davies had ninety-three days' experience under his belt. Indeed, so far was he into his tour that his replacement, WO2 Bob Harvey, had already been nominated and had passed the training course. Harvey remembers speaking to Davies on several occasions up to the night before 24 November:

> The course finished and we all returned to our respective units to await our summons and our fate. Once I knew where we were going to I began to make arrangements to ensure that we, the team, would be well fed and watered on our arrival and comfortably billeted. I spoke with Taff Davies, the incumbent WO2 of the Lurgan detachment. I had known Taff on and off for years; we always seemed to meet up at Bramley [the Army School of Ammunition]. We had several long conversations, and he was looking forward to coming home. He wasn't too much fussed about the situation; as he said, he was too much of an old sweat to take risks out there.

WO2 Davies had deployed to the Province on 23 August. Based at Lurgan, he had notched up eighty-eight tasks since his arrival, many of them conducted in small towns, such as Newtownhamilton and Craigavon, or out in the countryside. He had dealt with nine live IEDs and attended the scene of thirty-two explosions. In addition, he had been tasked to ten hoax devices, fourteen false alarms, fourteen clearances of suspect cars, and two searches. He had also attended seven 'finds' of weapons and explosives. Most of the explosions were against commercial premises, government buildings and public utilities. The targets had included a car showroom, a garage, a telephone exchange, several pylons, the Beleek Customs Post and Newtownhamilton Court House. Records show that he had not been called out in the four days prior to 24 November. Furthermore, he was not tasked at all over the period 2–9 November, nor over 11–19 November. It is, therefore, probable that he had returned to the mainland for R&R at some time during one of those periods. It would appear that none of the IEDs that he had disposed of were particularly complex: there were no time bombs or anti-handling mechanisms; rather, they tended to be failed blast bombs with burnt-out fuses.

Although we cannot be certain, this limited information allows us to build up a picture of WO2 Davies's possible state of mind by 24 November. He had survived most of his tour unscathed. He had completed his R&R, and his replacement had already been in touch. He was busy, but things were not as bad as he had expected. Although he was called out frequently, most of the devices had already functioned by the time he got there. Those that had not had invariably already failed for one reason or another, and over a quarter of his call-outs had been to hoaxes or false alarms. Lurgan was apparently proving to be far less risky than Belfast with its Castlerobins and Midlanders. Play it safe and he would soon be home in one piece.

It was late afternoon when the team arrived at the car showroom. Because the gunmen had ordered the staff to leave, none of the witnesses could pinpoint precisely where the box had been placed. Having checked that his safety cordon was in place, and that people were being kept well back, WO2 Davies entered the building, followed closely by his No. 2, who remained near the door. At last he found it. The box was sitting on an office desk at the back of the building – ticking. As he retreated towards the door, Davies called out to his assistant: 'We're going to leave this one a bit. It's ticking.'

Those were his last words. The heat and overpressure from the blast swept through the building, blowing out walls, sending masonry flying and causing it to collapse on top of him. His injuries proved fatal. His assistant was also injured. Bob Harvey comments: 'His death the day after my last conversation with him came as a great shock. It just did not seem possible that Taff could have been killed by this bunch of bungling amateurs, but unfortunately it was all too true.'

It *was* true, and it reinforced the message that an operator would always be at risk when approaching a ticking time bomb. Even if his time at the device was counted in seconds, those could still be the crucial seconds when time ran out.

At this stage of the campaign, the Army had yet to develop any form of remotely controlled robot, which would allow the ATO to dispose of a ticking device quickly from a safe distance. Certainly, the need for such a machine had already been recognised, and George Styles had prevailed upon Queen's University, Belfast, to knock up a prototype. The original model was known as 'Little Willie', having been based on an electric wheelchair obtained from a Belfast hospital, which had the patient's name, 'Willie', painted on the back of the seat. Captain Alan Clouter was to use it successfully, shortly after Taff Davies's death, to deploy one of the new disrupters against a 30lb gelignite time bomb in the main Belfast GPO sorting office. But it was an unwieldy contraption, with no rough terrain capability, unable to climb stairs or surmount small obstacles, such as kerbstones, and no camera to track its progress. In short, probably more trouble than it was worth. That particular prototype was never further developed, but it laid the germ of an idea that was to come to full fruition in the following year.

In the meantime, the operators were still in the business of walking up to ticking time bombs, with the risk that they might explode at any moment. Very early on, the maxim had been established that lives were more important than property – and that included the life of the operator. The impact of this was that, so long as an area had been evacuated, there was no need for an operator to rush down immediately to deal with the device. Therefore, in the case of a likely time bomb, an ATO might wait for a reasonable period, to allow the timer to run down, before he approached it. Clearly, there had to be some reasonable limit on his waiting time, or the terrorist would simply cause a city to grind to a halt by planting several simultaneous hoax IEDs. Also, in hostile areas, the longer that a protective cordon had to stay in place keeping people away from the bomb, the more vulnerable would be the troops to some other form of attack, be it shooting, blast bombs, grenades, petrol bombs, or simply bricks. The application of a 'waiting-out' period had been experimented with as early as 1970. It was later to become a 'mandatory action' to be observed by all operators, and would become known officially as the 'soak time'.

Unfortunately, it would appear that WO2 Davies had simply not allowed sufficient soak time. In the formal investigation that followed his death, the Senior Ammunition Technical Officer (SATO) for Northern Ireland concluded that two important operational rules had been broken: namely, that the soak time had not been observed and that the 'one-man-risk' rule had been contravened (two individuals had approached the device simultaneously), allowing the No. 2 to be injured. There are all sorts of pressures that might cause an operator to break the soak time, and we do not know which of these affected WO2 Davies in his plan of action. Did he think this was yet another false alarm or failed device? Was he being asked to hurry along by the Army incident commander or by the police? Was he keen to wind the job up before dark? We simply do not know.

As Davies's nominated replacement, WO2 Bob Harvey was then despatched to the Province to join the section at Lurgan just before Christmas, arriving on 15 December. He was initially taken to HQNI at Lisburn for his 'induction' to theatre. There he met Major Styles:

I was interested in the details of Taff's death, but this was a taboo subject with Styles and company, and, after a cursory briefing on the lines of: 'You ain't seen nothing yet, mate,' we left for Lurgan.

The attitude of the Brigade to the EOD teams was really splendid. Taff Davies had been a really popular man, and his death was keenly felt by the whole of the Brigade HQ. His escort had insisted on staying on as our escort and, in consequence, we, the new boys, inherited an enormous amount of goodwill. I would rather that it had not been at such expense.

Although the Brigade might have welcomed the new intake with open arms, the facilities hardly provided a home from home. Harvey goes on:

Lurgan was the Headquarters of 3 Infantry Brigade, commanded by Brigadier Plunkett. His idea of a negotiated settlement was three brigades of British infantry keeping the peace in Dublin. The Headquarters' accommodation was in an old factory, and was primitive, dark and dank. It was never discovered whether the factory had been operational prior to the troops' takeover, but, if it had been, it must have been a prime target for shutdown by the Factories Inspector.

Harvey had been met and taken to Lurgan by Sergeant Tony Dedman, who was halfway though his tour, having arrived in October. Initially posted to the Belfast Section, he had been transferred to Lurgan as the immediate, on-the-spot, replacement for WO2 Davies after the fatal explosion. Harvey again:

Tony took me to our quarters, which were shared by three of us. 'Fingers' Lewis was an inanimate hulk of rubbish, lying in his pit fully clothed. 'Just come off duty,' Tony explained. A portable gas heater pumped a gallon or so of water vapour into the atmosphere daily. The windows were blacked out with the ubiquitous army blankets, never to be opened. The atmosphere, to say the least, was heady. Surprising how one became acclimatised so quickly.

I was paired with Tony and, as he was on standby, I changed into uniform and donned the flak jacket which, stink and all, was to be my constant companion for the next four months.

Lurgan had three teams: 'immediate', 'standby', and the 'stood-down' team. This, in theory, gave us two days on and one day off. The teams covered an enormous area, and to transport us we had two Safari Land Rovers, not of the most recent vintage, but serviceable, fitted with a Pye communications system. Safaris did not have the necessary 24-volt system to run standard radio sets.

The outgoing team had removed all their incident pins from the operations map, possibly thinking that we should like to start with a clean sheet. I spent some time putting them all back in again. At least we should have some information of those areas of greatest activity and, consequently, danger.

Lurgan at that time was extremely busy. Border incidents and investigations kept the duty team out for a full twenty-four hours. The opposition did not neglect the standby team, keeping us on the hop by placing suspect parcels on the window ledge of a nearby factory. Tony, alias the 'Cordtex Kid', had evolved his own technique for dealing with this. It was always the same ledge, always the same type of box. It had been going on for all of his tour. 'It's a come-on to let the yobs have a go at us, but I always treat it as the real thing.' These confrontations, known as 'aggro', were frightening when first encountered. Luckily, Brigadier Plunkett had a secret weapon, which he only unleashed at night. Within the factory was an old vehicle shed – a large building, ensconced within which was a detachment of the Royal Artillery, equipped with Saracens [six-wheeled armoured cars]. They were only deployed at night, enjoying their role, which was to stir up the bad guys, bust a few heads and generally keep the peace. It was most comforting when facing the nightly aggro, small beer perhaps by national news standards, that one heard the distinctive whine of a Saracen. The mob used to visibly flinch, and their enthusiasm to depart was positively heartening to a beleaguered ATO and escort.

The time came when I did my first job. It was nothing too technical, just a simple case of removing a Gelamex [commercial explosive] sausage from a JCB digger. I had no idea where we were; it was definitely in the middle of nowhere. I spent a long time over it, to the bored attention of my escort and the Royal Marines.

The teams were continually working in the Newry/Bessbrook area, and it was here that my team had a brush with the opposition. We had been tasked to a suspect car just over [our side of] the border. The Marines were very suspicious, and we went into the area mob handed – two sections of Marines, two escort scout cars from the Queen's Dragoons, plus us. The car was cleared. It turned out to be a poteen smugglers' car, fitted with two fuel tanks; the normal tank took the poteen, and another tank in the engine compartment provided fuel to the engine. It was this latter tank that caused a lot of time wasting. It had all the characteristics of a device. The loud ticking noise was eventually explained when the battery ran flat – it was an electric fuel pump.

Whilst working on this car, we were tasked to another car at Narrow Water Ferry. This entailed looping back through Newry and driving down the other side of the loch. As we came opposite our previous site, we came under fire from two automatic weapons and a rifle. My driver, Lance Corporal Tiplady, took immediate evasive action. I urgently admonished him to stop messing about and get us out of there. I could hear our escort firing back with their SLRs (Self Loading Rifles), but the scout car did not open up. I felt so useless. The Macralon armour precluded any attempt at having a go back; we had to sit and take it.

We made it to the police station, which had closed down as soon as the shooting was heard. All was excitement and adrenalin, and we gathered our breath back, counted the holes in the vehicles, and I started smoking again. The young subaltern in charge of the scout car asked if we could do it again, as his gun was now working and perhaps he might get a shot at them. He was put very firmly in his place by the crews of the soft-skinned vehicles.

That day, in total we cleared five suspect vehicles and, after this sort of introduction to the day, three of them were given the full benefit of the 'quick run in and hit it' treatment. The last car, the fourth, was given the full treatment. It was a Morris 1100, parked right opposite the area we had been attacked from. I waited until midnight before I approached it, quickly making it safe. They were after me that day.

While WO2 Bob Harvey was settling in as an operator out in the countryside around Lurgan, back in the cities all-out war was under way. As Christmas approached, and 1971 neared its end, Belfast was to experience the worst incident, in terms of civilian casualties, thus far during the Troubles. It was around a quarter to nine on the evening of 4 December, and the Tramore Bar, commonly known as 'McGurk's' after its owner, was doing a reasonable trade. By a quirk of fate, the bar was about to become the target of UVF bombers, although, according to *Irish Times* journalist David McKittrick, it was chosen only at the last minute. In a 1978 article he wrote: 'The car carrying the bomb had been occupied by four loyalists, most of them members of the UVF. Their target was not McGurk's but another pub further along North Queen Street, the Glen Bar . . . the bombers had miscalculated, and found they could not get to their original target. They chose McGurk's instead.'

The device detonated at 8.47 p.m. 321 EOD Unit's log shows Captain Roger Mendham's team being tasked to attend seven minutes later. At the inquest, held in June 1972, a boy who lived in the neighbourhood gave a description of the events leading up to the explosion. He had been about to go into the bar, when he saw a big man dressed in a long coat enter and place a large square parcel, covered in plastic, in the hallway. He watched the man first use matches to light the parcel, then run down the street to a car that was waiting for him. The boy approached the parcel, realised that it was a bomb, and just had time to warn a man standing on the street corner before the device exploded, throwing him to the ground.

The bar was completely demolished and began to burn. Locals, firemen, policemen and soldiers used their bare hands to pull aside the rubble that buried the victims. The death toll mounted as bodies were located throughout the night, finally reaching fifteen, over half of whom had been crushed by the collapsing building. They included the owner's 14-year-old daughter and a 13-year-old schoolboy, who had been in the living quarters of the building.

At the time, the explosion, caused by an estimated 30–40lb IED, was attributed to the IRA. On the face of it, this was a plausible theory. The IRA was, by this stage, producing more bombs than the UVF. It was also experiencing a considerable number of own goals (three since the beginning of September), and there was every possibility that this had been a bomb factory that had gone wrong. As recently as 23 September, two teenaged IRA members, Gerard O'Hare and Rose Curry, had been blown apart as they tried to assemble a bomb in a house in the lower Falls Road area. Certainly, George Styles believed the bomb-factory explanation. In *Bombs Have No Pity*, he wrote:

From an examination of the wreckage, we worked out the area where the explosion happened, and it seemed to be well into the pub. Normally if a pub is attacked, the explosion occurs fairly near the entrance. We estimated the size of the bomb at around 50lbs of explosive and this would have been a fair weight to carry into a pub undetected. Thus, I reckoned it was another own goal.

My theory was that a terrorist was instructing some IRA volunteers in bomb-making . . . certainly the examination of human debris found in the wreckage suggested three or four men were right over the bomb when it went off. I pictured the scene as the terrorist and his pupils sat around a table with the device on the floor between them . . . we could never be certain that this is what happened but it is the theory that fits all the known facts.

Unfortunately, it does not fit all the known facts at all. But that is with the benefit of additional knowledge and hindsight. From the inquest, we have both the testimony of the young boy who saw the bombers, and that of the adult to whom he shouted a warning. Furthermore, when one considers the victims, they look an unlikely band of hardened terrorists. Out of the fifteen killed, two were children, and only one other was under 30, the next youngest being 38. Four were in their fifties, two in their sixties and one in his seventies. The remaining four were in their mid- to late forties. These were mostly middle-aged to elderly customers, some married, some with their friends, who had simply gone out for a quiet drink. In 1978 a UVF man was arrested and tried for the bombing, receiving fifteen life sentences, which amounted to ten years in prison.

Possibly in a revenge attack, a week later the IRA hit the Shankill Road, Belfast, with a no-warning attack at lunchtime on a busy furniture showroom. There were four deaths, including a 2-year-old child and a 19-month-old baby, and nineteen innocent people, out enjoying their Christmas shopping, were injured.

So this was the scene as 1971 drew to a close. Terrorist activity had continued at a relentless pace, numerous innocent civilians had lost their lives and two ATOs had been killed in the course of their duties. But worse was to come. The year 1972 was to prove to be the deadliest in the history of the Troubles – for the civilian community, for the Security Forces as a whole and, not least, for the operators of 321 EOD Unit.

THREE

1972: THE WORST YEAR

In the entire history of the Troubles, spanning more than thirty years, no year witnessed more bloodshed than 1972. The statistics tell the story. This was the year in which there were 1,853 explosions and 10,630 shooting attacks. Innocent civilians took the brunt of the terrorists' campaign, with 223 being killed. The Security Forces had the next highest death toll, as 146 soldiers and policemen were cut down. All this was not without cost to the paramilitaries: 95 IRA men and 3 Loyalist terrorists lost their lives.

The previous year had seen the IRA's bombing campaign really take off, with increasing numbers of direct attacks on the Security Forces, and the bombing without warning of soft targets, such as pubs, shops and commercial premises. In 1972 the terrorists further exploited both forms of attack, with a tendency towards much larger and more complex devices. Car bombs, home-made explosives and ambush devices became the order of the day, along with the emergence of the first radio-controlled bombs.

All hope of bridging the widening divide between the Army and the Catholic community disappeared on Sunday 30 January – otherwise known as 'Bloody Sunday'. A proscribed Northern Ireland Civil Rights Association (NICRA) march in Londonderry ran up against a barrier of troops, put in place to prevent the marchers progressing along a banned route. Minor 'aggro' broke out, which soon developed into a full-scale riot of stoning and petrol-bomb throwing. The 1st Battalion, The Parachute Regiment, had been drafted in from Belfast, to back up the Londonderry-based units, to cover just such a contingency. With the level of violence becoming unmanageable, the paratroopers were released, with orders to break up the crowds and arrest the troublemakers. Like a ferocious dog released from its restraining leash, the Paras charged deep into the hostile crowd. Snatch squads, batons in hand, moved forward into the area of the Rossville flats to bring in the ringleaders.

Then the shooting broke out. There is some evidence to indicate that the IRA may have fired first; certainly, IRA gunmen were known to be operating in the area that day. Whatever the rights and wrongs, what there is no doubt about is that thirteen civilians were shot dead, none of whom appears to have been firing weapons at the time. The British Army could not have done anything more to galvanise recruitment into the IRA. The slaughter now spiralled out of control.

Just before Bloody Sunday, WO2 Bob Harvey found himself transferred from Lurgan to Londonderry. The plan was that the experience he had already gained in the Province (albeit limited) would provide a sound bedrock for new operators coming in. Harvey recalls:

Londonderry was totally different from my expectations – permanent barracks, windows that did not require to be blacked out – in fact, all the comforts so dear to the British Army. It even had the luxury of being able to observe the aggro in the city from the parade ground.

The section consisted of Captain Hawkins, WO2 Beattie (who I was relieving – he left the next morning), and Sergeant Keith Adams, who introduced me into the Mess and our shared accommodation, a palatial room on the ground floor. Captain Hawkins took me out the next day and showed me the city. I got the distinct impression that the Captain was a bit 'bomb happy' – he showed a misguided bravado – deliberately exposing himself to danger when the resident troops tended to keep their heads down, especially near the Rossville flats. It seemed to me that he and Keith had psyched themselves up to believe that this was a personal war, and that the clearance of bombs was a sacred trust.

Londonderry section was quite quiet when I got there, and it was very similar to Lurgan in that there was a lot of country activity but, unlike Lurgan, it had the added attraction of Londonderry city and Strabane. However, the same system of work was used. The major difference was the vehicles. When I arrived, we handed one of the Land Rovers in and received a Humber Pig [armoured personnel carrier], which was fitted out to the satisfaction of the Captain.

The first work I did was with Keith, and I had an early introduction to the Rossville flats area. It's not until it matters personally that it becomes very apparent that the centre of the city is overlooked; there is no cover. I had my chance to shine when Keith and I were called to a suspect car on the edge of the Creggan estate. True to country practice, it got zapped in quick time. Next morning, the Captain appeared displeased that explosives had been used to clear a suspect car. He offered to show Keith and myself the 'right' way to clear a car. I declined the invitation.

The next weeks were spent learning the lie of the land, finding out how cold rides are in Scout helicopters, doing the odd job, and post-scene investigation work. Then came the start of the destruction of Londonderry. The bombers really began to hit us, and they were good at it. They used really simple devices: five pounds of ANFO [home-made explosive] in a sugar bag, a half-pound Gelamex primer, and a 30-minute burning fuse. Their timing was very good; the devices all went off at the time given. One of the devices was eventually recovered; the detonator wasn't crimped properly [not attached sufficiently tightly to the fuse]. It was taken to a lonely spot and destroyed. Imagine our consternation when it was reported in the next day's paper that terrorists had destroyed the 18th hole of a local golf course. Come to think of it, the hole did seem very conveniently shaped!

The continuance of the campaign along the High Street threw us into close contact with the Fire Brigade. As their Chief Officer, Mr Harvey, was fond of saying, 'These places are built to burn', and it was amazing that, once a device had exploded, it was only seconds before the building was truly ablaze from top to bottom. It was obvious that there had been a change of emphasis by the IRA, and that their objective was to destroy the city. All sections of the Security Forces were now being attacked, and the Fire Brigade came under mounting pressure as the fire bombs were also used as an invitation to stone the appliances and us, as we were often waiting alongside them. Mr Harvey complained to the local clergy that their flocks were getting out of hand, and it was not unusual for one of them to control the mob, always emphasising quite clearly that it was only the Fire Brigade he was minding.

The build-up carried on, and it was assumed that the IRA were setting the scene for the forthcoming NICRA marches, which had been proscribed as illegal. The march took place on what is now remembered as 'Bloody Sunday'. This was obviously a big 'do', and we were graced with the presence of the GOC, General Tuzo.

It was after Bloody Sunday that Captain Hawkins, Sergeant Adams and Private Hack were relieved by Captain Watson, Staff Sergeant Mitchell and

Private Constantine. They came just in time for the IRA backlash, which was only to be expected. The weapon that the IRA chose to use was the car bomb. The city received 21 of these in the next 28 days, and Strabane was kept on the boil as well. It was during this period that we all became aware that the IRA had identified us – the crowd now 'wished us well' by name.

Throughout January, in the build-up to Bloody Sunday, the IRA had demonstrated its growing ruthlessness and cunning in the use of explosives to cause death and destruction. A summary of the incidents for the month, issued by the Ministry of Defence, drew attention to the varied, innovative and indiscriminate nature of the attacks. On 3 January sixty-two people were injured in an explosion in Callender Street, Belfast. The street was busy at the time when 10lb of high explosive, concealed on the back of a lorry, detonated without warning. Less than a week later, on 8 January, four small explosive charges were placed on the storage tanks of a petroleum depot at Omagh. The pipes were fractured, and approximately 1,000 gallons of fuel were lost before the tanks could be drained. On the same day, an explosion at an electricity transformer at Clady was used to draw an EOD team into an ambush. As the team arrived at the scene, an IED of up to 10lb was detonated by command wire, peppering one of the Humber Pigs with shrapnel. Another 'come-on' occurred on 19 January. This time, a 5-gallon chemical drum, containing a clock and wires, and marked 'IRA bomb – do not touch', was the bait. The ATO had just set off a controlled explosion when a gunman fired sixteen shots at the team. There were no casualties. An IRA landmine, consisting of three massive charges set off by command wire, killed a soldier at Derrynoose, near Keady, in South Armagh on 21 January. Finally, on the last day of the month, the day after Bloody Sunday, an innocent shopworker was killed as a device exploded in a van outside British Home Stores, Belfast, as he tried to usher people to safety.

Luckily for the population at large, the IRA terrorists were still learning their deadly trade, and throughout February managed to kill more of their own number than innocent civilians through a series of own goals. On 4 February, two 'volunteers' were fatally injured in a premature explosion as they tried to destroy temporary council offices located in a school hall at Keady in South Armagh. Two days later, two more IRA men died instantly, again in a premature explosion, as they tried to sink several sand barges moored on Lough Neagh, near the village of Crumlin in County Antrim. In this incident, firemen had been called to the scene after a large explosion was reported. Initially, it was not realised that anyone had been killed, until a hand was seen floating in the water as the firemen pumped out a half-submerged barge. A follow-up search was then implemented, revealing two severely mutilated bodies in the Lough. On 21 February a further four IRA men died when their 20lb bomb detonated unexpectedly as they were driving with it to a target in Protestant East Belfast. Their car was completely destroyed in the blast, and hundreds of children just leaving school in the afternoon watched as the bodies were taken away. This must have been a particularly gruesome sight, since one of the bombers had been balancing the device on his knees when it went off.

But, on Saturday 4 March, the terrorists finally achieved their aim. Sometime after 4 p.m. two young women entered the Abercorn Bar, situated in Belfast city centre. It was a popular place for Saturday afternoon shoppers to rest their legs, and for young people to meet up with their friends. The two girls were both members of the IRA. When they had finished at their table and walked out of the restaurant, they appeared to have forgotten their bag. One woman at an adjacent table noticed this after they had left, but assumed that they would be back for it. The bag had not been left by mistake, nor had they any intention of coming back.

At around 4.28 p.m. an anonymous telephone call was made, claiming that a bomb would explode in Castle Lane, in the city centre, in five minutes. No exact location was given and no mention was made of the Abercorn Bar. Two minutes later, an explosion smashed the building apart. Two young Catholic women in their early twenties died instantly in the blast. They had only just sat down at the table vacated by the bombers. Rescuers racing to the scene encountered horrific sights. The front of the Abercorn had been blown out and passers-by had been hurled across the street. Around seventy people had been injured. Two sisters, Rosaleen and Jennifer McNern, received particular prominence in news reports of the time, one having lost two legs and an arm, the other losing both her legs. Most of the seriously injured were young women in their early twenties; they had all lost one or two limbs. Several victims lost eyes, and a male casualty lost both legs.

As 1972 continued, the car bomb started to assert itself as the IRA's weapon of choice. Looking at the statistics for mid-year, we see that in June alone there were fourteen car-bomb explosions, five car bombs defused and a further two found in transit. By using a car, the terrorist could deliver a massive device, rapidly, to the designated target, where it would fit in with its surroundings until it detonated without warning. Cars were therefore perfectly suited to the IRA's change of tactics, which now concentrated on striking fear into the hearts of the population at large. Women or children, young or old, even Protestant or Catholic – everyone became a potential target as the attacks became indiscriminate.

On occasions, probably when the terrorists had trouble acquiring sufficient explosives, they would make use of a car's petrol tank to achieve a destructive effect. A contemporary report describes two ways in which this could be done. One was to run a strand of detonating cord from a timer in the boot, round the outside of the car, and into the filling aperture of the petrol tank. Obviously, this could be spotted fairly readily, so evacuation could be commenced before the bomb exploded. An alternative method was to place about 1lb of explosive alongside the petrol tank inside the boot. This was far more sinister, as there was no indication that a bomb was concealed within.

The same report goes on to say that Ford cars were the most likely to be stolen for such purposes: 'No doubt there are many of the same colour and type in the Belfast area, and it is a simple operation to change the number plates.' Achieving such anonymity would be particularly important if the car was not to be used on the same day it was stolen, since its description would quickly have been circulated among the Security Forces.

The first car to be used as an ambush device appeared during January. On this occasion, some 50lb of scrap metal had been concealed in the boot of a stolen vehicle. This was intended to provide the fragmentation effect for a 30lb explosive charge placed behind it. The idea was to catch out the Security Forces when they turned up to investigate the car. The initiation mechanism relied on one of the early radio-control systems. Ever since the deaths of Constables Donaldson and Millar in August 1970, it had been standard practice for an ATO to examine any car found in suspicious circumstances, before the police would take it away, just in case it was booby-trapped. This device was perfectly configured to kill the ATO, but, by an amazing stroke of luck, it only partially detonated.

Early methods for dealing with potential car bombs had been painstakingly slow. Former WO1 G.A. Smith, who served as a No. 1 operator in the Province from May to September 1970, recalls that, rather than being classified as 'EOD tasks', suspicious vehicles were subjected to 'car searches'. This meant using a hand drill and a panel-cutter to get into them, so as to avoid the possibility of triggering a booby trap when the doors were opened. Derek Markham, a Belfast ATO captain from June to October 1971, describes opening car doors from a safe distance by means of a long cord, a screwdriver and some masking tape, 'but it relied more on artistry than science'. By December 1971, when WO2 Bob Harvey attended his pre-deployment training course, the perceived wisdom concerning the tackling of car bombs was starting to change:

> The only area which caused the course to stand in unanimous disagreement with the 'standing operating procedures' [SOPs] was the meticulous, time-consuming approach and method of entry to a suspect car. The general consensus of opinion was that time was a precious commodity that should not be frittered away, especially if a timer had been fitted. It was eventually made clear that the individual in the field would, of necessity, fit the SOPs to the circumstances as they may arise.

Faced with the growing threat of time-initiated car bombs in public places, the operators were having to develop their own novel methods for dealing with the problem. Some of these were more successful than others; all involved a huge degree of risk. Staff Sergeant B.J. Mitchell's preferred approach sounded like a stunt from a Hollywood adventure film:

> One of my brainwaves was to approach suspect cars over open ground, lying on the side of a Ferret Scout Car. After shooting out a window, I would lob a couple of sticks of plastic explosive inside with the fuse burning [with the intention of disrupting the bomb without setting it off]. Sergeant Jack Slack RWF [Royal Welch Fusiliers] was the driver. He would drive up very fast, only slowing down just before the car. I would roll off, drop the explosives onto the back seat, and leg it back to cover. The signal that I had left the Ferret, and that Jack could drive off, was to bang on the turret. This method was abandoned after Jack started to think about the consequences and, unbeknown to me, borrowed a motorcycle helmet and earplugs.
>
> After a successful deployment, we were sitting waiting for the resultant bang, when the infantry company commander asked what a car bomb would do to a close proximity Ferret. I asked him why, and he replied, 'Well, we're about to find out!' Jack was parked about ten feet from the

target, and obviously hadn't heard my tap. Frantic attempts on the radio also failed. Luckily, it was a hoax, and he barely heard the couple of sticks of plastic explosive going off.

Although our relations with the RWF were fantastic, they were a little wary of our harebrained schemes after that.

Scourfield-Evans recalls that even the more conventional approaches were not without risk:

Incendiaries were used on cars to burn them out – an attempt to burn out the 'Co-op mix' [home-made explosive] without it detonating. This often failed. Car boots were often opened with Cordtex under the lip. Prior to that, a hole was made for the Cordtex by the ATO using a .38 service revolver. There was an incident involving one ATO when the .38 bullet bounced off the boot lid. Subsequently, all ATOs were issued with [more powerful] 9mm pistols. However, the practice of shooting holes in car boots also ceased.

Former WO2 Mick Coldrick found that placing Cordtex in the near vicinity of high explosives could have a dramatic effect. One morning he was tasked to a green Ford Cortina abandoned on a garage forecourt. He was not to know it, but a 300lb IED was concealed in the boot.

On 3 March 1972, I had a very large car bomb at a garage on the A1, near the border with Southern Ireland. I tried to open the boot with detonating cord; this resulted in a monumental explosion. The Royal Scots Dragoon Guards manning the cordon were delighted with the outcome, and wanted to know when I was coming down again!

Coldrick was to be among the first to use a shotgun to blast his way into a suspect car. Subsequently awarded the George Medal for his work as an operator, part of his citation reads:

As a marksman, he led the attack on the cars by the shotgun shattering of windows. He developed the method of remotely firing at cars, and his expertise encouraged the use of this remote attack by all other bomb-disposal experts with the unit.

His cool, calm approaches to car bombs were a constant source of admiration from Security Forces at incidents. He dealt regularly with cars, which invariably required him to go up to them after suitable waiting periods and, after shooting out windows, to gain access for the placing of incendiary or explosive charges.

With car bombs appearing on a daily basis and, as yet, no remote means for dealing with them, it is hardly surprising that more operators would die. On 15 March 1972 it was to be a car bomb that would kill two Belfast operators, Staff Sergeant Chris Cracknell and Sergeant Tony Butcher. WO2 Bob Harvey attended the same pre-deployment training course as Tony Butcher, and remembers a strange incident:

The team that I was a member of consisted of Captain Simon Harvey, Sergeant Tony Butcher and myself. The course served its purpose well in bringing us together. In that respect, it was a great leveller. I had not served with Tony Butcher before, but he struck me as being a good AT, with a solid background of inspectorate work. He did not seem a fanciful man, but towards the end of the course he told a group of us fellow students that he had a premonition that if he went to Belfast he would die. We told him that was okay, as our posting was to Lurgan, so it was obvious that his premonition was wrong.

The summons came for us to go to Northern Ireland just before Christmas. The idea was to allow the homecoming teams to be back in time for Christmas. Mid-December saw us on the Liverpool-to-Belfast ferry – an uneventful trip. It seemed a stupid way to go to war – civvies and a suitcase. We disembarked feeling jaded, and were met by Tony Dedman from the Lurgan team, as well as the Belfast mob. The plot unfolded; we were to be the first team to be split up, Simon and I to Lurgan, Tony Butcher was destined for Belfast. It was all over in a flash. Before we had time to say goodbye, we were all whisked away.

On 15 March 1972, a little after 5 p.m., an Army mobile patrol in Belfast came across a car that had been abandoned in the middle of the road. It was in Willow Street, just off Grosvenor Road, one of the main thoroughfares near the city centre. The vehicle was cordoned off, and the request sent out for an ATO team to attend the scene. In Belfast at that stage, it was routine for two No. 1 operators to attend each incident. On this occasion, the two in question were Staff Sergeant Cracknell and Sergeant Butcher. Butcher was by now quite experienced. He had been in Northern Ireland for ninety-one days, having arrived on 15 December. Cracknell was still learning the ropes, with only twenty-six days as an operator under his belt.

In terms of tasks performed, between 15 December and 15 March Sergeant Butcher had attended forty-nine false alarms, of which twenty-six had involved cars with nothing suspicious found inside. Indeed, five out of his six initial jobs on arriving in the Province fell into this category. As far as his 'real' jobs were concerned, cars certainly did not feature as the greatest threat. He had been called to the scene of thirty-six explosions, of which only four had been car bombs. Of the nine live IEDs that he had actually rendered safe, only one was in a car. There is potentially a likelihood, therefore, that he had been lulled into a false sense of security where cars were concerned.

Staff Sergeant Cracknell arrived on 18 February, some two months after Sergeant Butcher. He found himself attending his first task two days later: it was a car search, which he conducted with Butcher. Nothing was found. Half of his further fourteen false alarms proved to be the same – that is, cars with nothing suspicious found inside. Out of the sixteen explosions he attended, only two were caused by car bombs. Again, the emerging car-bomb threat may not yet have been setting the alarm bells ringing. Although Staff Sergeant Cracknell had only been in theatre for twenty-six days, of the forty-six tasks that he had attended in that time, thirty had been conducted with Sergeant Butcher as his partner. They were well used to operating as a team.

One of the team's first actions was to open the boot to check the load-carrying area for a large IED. They did this by applying a controlled explosion – almost certainly a strip of Cordtex in the manner of the time. At one stage while doing this, a third operator had been present at the car with them. Luckily, he was tasked away to another incident halfway through the job. With the boot open, Cracknell and Butcher then started to walk back towards the car. But the device was not in the boot; it was on the back seat. As they came alongside the vehicle, the bomb detonated, killing both Senior NCOs instantly.

A formal investigation followed, under the Senior Ammunition Technical Officer (SATO) for Northern Ireland, Major Bernard Calladene, who had taken over from George Styles in November 1971. Calladene concluded that an important operational rule had been broken – namely, that Cracknell and Butcher had not observed the one-man-risk procedure; both had approached the car at the same time. Indeed, at one stage, three operators had been within the killing area. This was inexplicable; all three had recently attended an incident where the importance of the one-man-risk rule had been stressed by their superior officer. Furthermore, it had been precisely this same error that had allowed WO2 Taff Davies's No. 2 to be injured back in December, in the same incident in which Davies himself had been killed (see Chapter Two).

The car bombs were now coming thick and fast. At some time after 11 a.m. on 20 March a Ford Cortina was driven into Donegall Street, close to Belfast city centre, and parked up. The driver got out and walked away. Behind the Cortina, the driver of a dustbin lorry, which was slowly making its way along the road, thought that the man looked suspicious. He seemed to be hiding his face by turning it to the wall as he left the vehicle. The dustman tried to warn people nearby, but they simply ignored him. He then approached a patrolling soldier, who looked inside the car, but, seeing nothing, continued on his way.

With less than fifteen minutes to go on the 200lb time bomb that was counting down inside the car boot, a series of telephone warnings began filtering through. As would so often be the case, the warnings were imprecise and confusing. An agency in Church Street, close to Donegall Street, was called at 11.45 a.m. and told that there was a 'big bomb' in the building. Seven minutes later, the RUC was telephoned by the *Irish News* saying that it had received a warning call about a bomb in Church Street. The next call to the police came at 11.55 a.m. from the offices of the *Belfast Telegraph*. This time, the warning correctly identified Donegall Street, but again stated that the bomb was in a building. In any case, it was now too late. At 11.58 a.m. the bomb exploded.

The IRA's plan had worked. By giving the false information about Church Street, those being evacuated were channelled right into the killing area of Donegall Street. The *Belfast Telegraph* described the aftermath of the explosion:

Donegall Street looked like a battlefield. When the smoke and dust from the blast cleared, injured people were seen lying in pools of blood on the roadway. Some of the casualties lay in agony with glass splinters embedded in their wounds. A body was blown to pieces by the force of the explosion, which rocked the entire city centre. An old man was comforted on the footpath. As he lay barely conscious, he was unaware that half his leg had been blown off in the explosion.

Six people were killed in the blast and 154 injured. The total of dead eventually rose to seven when one of those wounded, a 79-year-old man, died two weeks later. Two policemen who had been trying to evacuate the area were cut down; one of them was a Roman Catholic. The Belfast EOD team was tasked to the explosion at 12.15 p.m. The 321 EOD Unit Log Book for the period shows that the two operators, Captain Stacey and Sergeant Hammond, were joined at the scene by the SATO, Major Calladene. As Officer Commanding the unit, Calladene had instructed that, following the deaths of Cracknell and Butcher, he was to be called out to any incident involving a car bomb. He was determined to find a way of dealing with the car bombs quickly, effectively and, above all, safely.

More people were to die from a no-warning car bomb on 28 March. This time the terrorists turned their attention to the western side of the Province, positioning a van loaded with explosives outside Limavady RUC Station in County Londonderry. Two men sitting in a car parked close by were killed instantly when they took the full force of the blast.

There was now a desperate need for the operators of 321 EOD Unit to find an effective solution to the car-bomb threat. The day after the Londonderry device, Belfast again became the focus of the terrorists' attention, and Bernard Calladene was eager to get to grips with the problem. Just after five o'clock on the afternoon of 29 March, a 4-ton Ford truck, bearing the registration AOI 7851, drove into position outside Belfast's Chichester Street Law Courts. On board was a 150lb time bomb. A warning was given, and WO2 P.H. Dandy and Sergeant J.S. Hammond were the operators tasked to the scene. In accordance with his previous instructions, Major Calladene was also called out. It is difficult to determine quite what degree of success the trio had. In his book *Bombs Have No Pity*, George Styles states that the Major had saved Belfast Magistrates' Court that day by dealing with a bomb in a lorry parked outside. The 321 EOD Operational Log suggests a slightly different story, recording an explosion outside the courthouse, which caused damage up to 200 yards away. The truth is likely to lie somewhere in between. The most probable explanation is that a controlled explosion brought about the partial detonation of the bomb's main charge, causing limited damage out to some distance, but preventing the total devastation that one might have expected from such a large IED.

Less than four hours later, the same trio of operators was out on the streets again. On the previous evening, an Austin 1800, with the registration 428 OTZ, had been hijacked in the Springfield Road area of West Belfast. The next day, 29 March, at sometime close to 10 p.m., it reappeared outside 10 Wellington Street, a side street close to Belfast City Hall. The police became aware of its presence via a telephone operator, who had received a call, later traced to a public house on the Falls Road, giving the location of the car bomb, and saying that it would go off in ten minutes.

P.H. Dandy was serving in Belfast as a WO2 at the time. He takes up the story:

I was on R&R when Staff Sergeant Cracknell and Sergeant Butcher died whilst dealing with a car bomb in the Grosvenor Road, Belfast. A fortnight later, at approximately 2330 hours, because of a request by Major Calladene, I asked for him to deal with a suspect car in Wellington Street, Belfast. I had already walked down to the car once before Major Calladene arrived. I briefed him, and then he set out towards it. As he walked around the right-hand side of the vehicle, it exploded. A search was instigated and he was discovered, badly injured, but still alive. He was despatched by ambulance to the Royal Victoria Hospital, but died there approximately an hour and a half later.

The bomb, sitting on the back seat and estimated to have contained only 5–10lb of explosive, had detonated at five minutes to midnight. From a distance of only 5 yards away, it had been enough to blow Major Calladene through an adjacent shop window. He was buried in York with full military honours. At the funeral, the Army chaplain said:

People will rightly wonder – even marvel – that bravery of the sort that this is before us can really be, whereby a man seems so willingly and unceremoniously to walk literally in the valley of the shadow of death, doing simply what his job and duty require of him. Instant, spontaneous acts of bravery must surely be one thing, but this conscious, calculated rendezvous with the unknown must, somehow, be another.

An operator who served under Major Calladene, WO2 Mick Coldrick, expressed his own admiration thus: 'If I could elect to pay tribute to anyone, it would be Bernard Calladene, whose selfless sacrifice was in an effort to find out what had killed Sergeant Butcher and Staff Sergeant Cracknell. He gave specific instructions that he was to be called to any suspect car in Belfast.'

All this was true. But the sad fact underlying Major Bernard Calladene's death was that, only two weeks after the two senior NCOs had died, he had defied his own instructions and approached a device before the soak time had expired. Nobody will ever know why he chose to do this. As Officer Commanding 321 EOD Unit, he would have been under tremendous pressure to prevent the bombers incrementally destroying the city. The RUC, the Fire Brigade, the Army cordon, all would have expected some sort of action – otherwise, what was the point of the bomb-disposal team? How could he stand by, just looking on? The second pressure, this one self-induced, would have been an overwhelming urge to get to the bottom of what had killed Cracknell and Butcher. He had recently 'lost' two operators; he would have been determined not to lose any more.

Unfortunately, operators do not always do the sensible thing. Following the deaths of Cracknell and Butcher, all ATOs were under strict instructions to deal with car bombs by using controlled explosions or incendiaries. Under no circumstances were they to attempt to disarm them manually – that is, by cutting wires, and removing batteries, timers and detonators. However, only eight days after the fatal explosion that had killed his two colleagues, WO2 Bob Harvey found himself doing just that:

The war carried on, and we were getting very tired. Events were beginning to kaleidoscope, and I began to understand Captain Hawkins a bit better. I can only suppose that this attitude led me to defuse the first car bomb of this present blitz. This was contrary to Top Cat's [Chief·Ammunition Technical Officer's] orders. The incident was at Shantallow, County Londonderry, on 22 March 1972. I spent nearly four hours stalking, shooting, pulling and generally trying to convince myself that it was a hoax. Eventually, I got into it. It was an alarm clock timer and one hundredweight of ANFO, with all the necessary detonators and batteries to make a bang. The non-explosive items were handed over to the police, and I returned to base. I got in at about 0200 hours, and Top Cat was on the phone soon after that. He confirmed that I was in receipt of his orders reference car bombs, and expressed his displeasure that I had contravened them. I pointed out to him that rank had nothing to do with the ability to make bombs safe, that this was my patch, and that, if he felt so concerned, why hadn't he flown over and taken command? After all, I had been on this one for almost six hours!

Such is the state of mind of the experienced, but tired, operator, who even though he knows the rules, decides for whatever reason simply to disregard them.

In the wake of the three deaths, it was clear that some means of dealing with a car remotely was urgently required. Back in England, discussions had already commenced to take forward the idea of some sort of robot, based loosely on the 'Little Willie' concept, which had been tried out at the end of 1971 (described in Chapter Two). In the meantime, though, the gap had to be covered in some other way. The method chosen was to issue the EOD teams with the 84mm Carl Gustav rocket launcher. This shoulder-fired weapon, not dissimilar to a bazooka, was intended to defeat tanks. It would normally fire a round containing a high-explosive warhead, with the charge shaped in such a way that it would readily pierce armour up to a certain thickness. The forces on firing were such that, in order to minimise the recoil, the back-blast was expelled through the rear vent in the launch tube. This meant that a danger area was imposed for about 20 metres to the rear of the weapon, which would be subjected to heat, blast and flame. It was not pleasant to fire; the noise alone was quite deafening, and the firer would ideally be supported by an assistant to prevent him from falling over when it went off.

Clearly, sending a high-explosive round into the centre of a bomb would almost certainly result in its complete detonation. But there was another alternative. In order to give the infantry plenty of opportunity to develop their accuracy with the weapon, but at minimal cost, a 'practice round' had been developed. This had all the characteristics of the high-explosive round in terms of back-blast and flight path, but it had an inert warhead – that is, there was no explosive filling. The missile could still effect considerable damage through its kinetic energy alone, and might therefore be successful in disrupting a bomb, but it was unlikely to set it off in the process.

In theory, this was a great idea. In practice, it left a lot to be desired. Staff Sergeant B.J. Mitchell was working in a patch controlled by the Royal Welch Fusiliers:

They loved the 84mm Carl Gustav practice round jobs, and could hit a car number plate from over 100 metres away. It was discontinued by us after firing up a narrow street in Magherafelt at a positive target on the brow. The round hit under the car, via the ground, bounced, and smashed a house roof 400 metres away. The back-blast took out over 100 windows on a very cold winter's morning.

Scourfield-Evans comments:

Carl Gustav was adopted as a stand-off means of disrupting car bombs, using the practice round. However, I personally never got to use it. One was actually fired in barracks during the handover/takeover of one of the EOD sections. The escorts mistook 'drill' [replica dummies] for 'practice' rounds during the demonstration.

This latter occurrence was not as unusual as it might seem. 'Drill' rounds had dark-blue markings and were simply replicas used to practise loading and unloading drills. 'Practice' rounds had light-blue markings, and were principally intended for shooting at targets on a range. They therefore contained an explosive propellant. Load a drill round and press the weapon's firing button, and all you get is a click. Load a practice round and press the firing button, and there will be an ear-splitting explosion, followed by the round disappearing off for several hundred yards, smashing through everything in its path. The effect inside the close confines of a barracks must have caused a mind-numbing sense of shock and awe.

Scourfield-Evans continues:

It became something of a fad to take out bread vans at border crossings and collect the number plates. Apparently, one ATO is reputed to have shot beer kegs one by one off a flatbed truck, until the device was revealed. A considerable number of rounds were expended in this particular exercise – not through poor marksmanship, but because there were a lot of kegs on the truck!

Former Sergeant F. Haley was a Londonderry operator who discovered that the Carl Gustav was not the easiest of weapons to use:

Ever since I had arrived in Londonderry, I had wanted to use the Carl Gustav on a job, circumstances permitting. Well, that day did arrive. A suspect Bedford van was left on the outskirts of the town. Not being trained to fire the Carl Gustav, I asked for two volunteers from the Royal Artillery, who formed the patrol at the incident.

We crawled to within about 100 yards of the Bedford, and prepared to fire a practice round into the floor of the van, and so shake up all the contents. The soldiers on the other side of the firing point, who were having a bit of aggro from the usual rioters, were warned, and the firer took aim.

The Carl Gustav round went up into the air, over the top of the target, took the top off a telegraph pole, went soaring into the distance, and came down on waste ground, which at the time was occupied by gypsies. Well, no one was hurt, so I thought, 'Let's have another go, with sights duly corrected.'

Admittedly, the second shot was better, but only just. It sailed over the top of the target and landed on the road that the rioters were doing their bit on. According to the troops who were trying to keep the rioters back, the sight of an 84mm round skidding down the road had a marked effect on the mob. Fortunately, no one was hurt.

After that second attempt, more conventional methods were used. The van turned out to have 30lb of explosives, wired to a trip mechanism, operated by opening the back doors. It was dismantled successfully.

While the operators were battling to deal with the car-bomb threat as best they could in the Province, elsewhere the back-room boys were desperately trying to come up with a remote, robotic solution. Initially, aspirations were very limited, but once the project got under way it was to develop fast.

As a result of a meeting at the Fighting Vehicles Research and Development Establishment (FVRDE) in Chertsey, Surrey, on 8 March 1972, work immediately went into devising some means of attaching a hook to a car remotely. The concept was that the car could then be dragged by a long tow rope to an area where it would cause limited collateral damage. Within eight days, the first prototype was ready, based on a three-wheeled electrically controlled wheelbarrow, which had been purchased from the Sunningdale Garden Machine Centre. Enhancements followed rapidly, and by August 1972 the new piece of equipment, now formally designated 'Wheelbarrow', could carry a range of weapons, was mounted with a CCTV camera to view a device from a distance, and had been fitted with tracks so that it could surmount steps and other obstacles. Thus appeared the first robotic bomb-disposal vehicle, the like of which is now routinely in service in hundreds of countries around the globe. The full story behind the development of the early Wheelbarrows is covered in Chapter Eight.

Wheelbarrow was a godsend. From the moment it entered service, ATO casualties dropped markedly, which was just as well, as the IRA continued to step up its campaign.

As 1972 proceeded, the IRA's tactics took a terrifying new turn – waves of devices, one after the other, deliberately targeted the population at large. On 13 April a series of coordinated bomb attacks rocked the Province. The bombers started early. At twenty minutes after midnight, a massive car bomb exploded outside flats in Ballymoney. Although a telephone warning had been given, an elderly lady was killed before she could be helped from the building by the police. Sadly, her husband had already been escorted outside, and was waiting for her. The rest of the night remained quiet, but, as morning came, the bombers started plying their deadly trade again. At 9.30 a.m. two electricity pylons were brought down in the Crossmaglen area. Just after 10.00 a.m. a security guard was shot in the leg by one of four raiders as they planted a device at the council offices in Newry. Almost simultaneously, dozens of shops in Castlederg were destroyed by a bomb, which exploded in a stolen white Mini. Two minutes after the Castlederg explosion, the temporary offices of the *Belfast Telegraph* were attacked. Two men, one armed, entered the hallway. One, who was carrying a cardboard box, lit a fuse attached to it. Staff in the offices were given two minutes to get clear, and the alarm was raised. But the bomb did not explode, and an ATO (Captain David Hourahane) dragged it from the building, using a hook and line, and defused it. Within the hour, twenty-five buses were damaged in a bomb attack on the Smithfield bus depot in Belfast city centre. Armed men had placed the device in the middle of the depot, near the canteen, and warned staff that it would go off shortly. Several houses nearby were damaged in the explosion, but, luckily, nobody was injured.

And so it went on throughout the day. At 11 a.m. a fire bomb went off in College Gardens, Belfast. Back in the Newry area, an ambush device caused a number of Army casualties thirty minutes later. Then it was Londonderry's turn, with a bomb exploding in Foyle Street at ten minutes to one. Back in

Belfast, at 2.25 p.m., Isaac Agnew's car showrooms on the Grosvenor Road were demolished. Then Sion Mills was hit by a car-bomb blast at 2.35 p.m., and, later in the afternoon, a 25lb device exploded in Corporation Street, Belfast. Throughout the evening, and right up to midnight, a further nine bombs were planted, most of which detonated. Significant among these were two explosions in Strabane, a 100lb car bomb outside the Beechlawn Hotel in Dunmurry, just south of Belfast, and the destruction of the telephone exchange at Mayobridge.

Despite the wholesale bomb attacks on 13 April, only one person died that day. The IRA was to have considerably more success on 21 July – a day to be remembered for ever more as 'Bloody Friday'. Rather than spreading their efforts Province-wide, on this occasion the target was solely Belfast. In the space of just over an hour, some 20 devices detonated, killing 9 people and injuring 130 others. The attack was planned for mid-afternoon, when the streets would be crowded with shoppers. Targets included the bus station in Oxford Street, the railway stations at Great Victoria Street and York Street, bridges, offices, garages, a hotel, a bar and shops. Pandemonium broke out as members of the public fled, seeking safety, only to be confronted with further explosions. The first bomb went off at 2.10 p.m., and the last detonated only just over an hour later at 3.15 p.m. The great majority of devices were car bombs. Some of the bodies were so badly mutilated that they had to be scraped off the roads using shovels and taken away in plastic bags.

Six of the deaths occurred at the Oxford Street bus station, where four Ulsterbus employees and two soldiers were killed, and nearly forty people injured. The other three fatalities were caused by a car bomb, which functioned outside shops along the Cavehill Road in North Belfast. This killed two women and a teenage boy. The boy, 14-year-old Stephen Parker, had been trying to warn shoppers away from the car when it exploded next to him. He was posthumously awarded the Queen's Commendation for Bravery. His father, the Revd Joseph Parker, a prominent peace campaigner, later recalled: 'I was at the mission when word came that Stephen was missing. We checked all the hospitals. We found him in the morgue. I was able to identify him by his hands, and by a box of trick matches he had in his pocket, and by the scout belt he was wearing.'

The overwhelming horror of the day was summed up by an RUC officer who, in 1997, was interviewed for the BBC television series *The Provos*. He said:

At first there was almost like a silence. Then you could hear people screaming and crying and moaning, almost as if they were winded. The first thing that caught my eye was a torso of a human being lying in the middle of the street. It was recognisable as a torso because the clothes had actually been blown off and you could actually see parts of the human anatomy. One of the victims was a soldier I knew personally. He'd had his arms and legs blown off, and some of his body had been blown through the railings. One of the most horrendous memories for me was seeing a head stuck to a wall.

A couple of days later we found vertebrae and a ribcage on the roof of a nearby building. The reason we found it was because the seagulls were diving onto it. I've tried to put it to the back of my mind for 25 years.

In the aftermath of Bloody Friday, the IRA faced a wave of public revulsion from across the entire community. The attacks had been carried out by the 'Belfast Brigade', who, in a pathetic attempt to deflect blame, issued the following statement:

We accept full responsibility for all explosions in the Belfast area today. In accepting responsibility, we point out that the following organisations were informed of bomb positions at least thirty minutes to one hour before each explosion: the Samaritans, the Public Protection Agency, the rumour service and the press.

Warnings had indeed been telephoned through, but the Security Forces had simply been overwhelmed by the sheer volume of calls. The confused situation had been further exacerbated by a large number of hoax calls. Staggeringly, various IRA leaders later suggested that the Security Forces had deliberately failed to react to warnings about the Oxford Street and Cavehill Road bombs – despite the fact that two of those killed had been soldiers who had been trying to evacuate the Oxford Street bus station.

For all its excuses and hollow words of regret, the IRA continued to favour the terror bombing of populated areas as a means of trying to bring the Government to its knees. Only ten days after Bloody Friday, the terrorists struck again. This time, rather than an urban centre, its target was the small country village of Claudy, nestling in the Sperrin Mountains, not far from Londonderry. Nine more innocent people were to die.

It was 31 July at 10.20 in the morning when the first device, a car bomb, exploded outside McElhinney's pub on Main Street without warning. Mrs McElhinney, serving petrol from a pump outside the pub, died instantly, along with a 39-year-old Catholic man and a 9-year-old Protestant girl, who had been out in the street polishing the window of her parents' grocery store. Three males, one a youth of only 15, were fatally injured in the blast. Police descended on the scene, and quickly discovered a second bomb in the back of a minivan parked outside the post office. They started to evacuate the area. As people moved away, many headed in the direction of the Beaufort Hotel, where a third device, concealed in another minivan, was lying in wait. It detonated, killing a further three people.

Yet again, the IRA tried to deny any blame. In *A Revolutionary in Ireland*, Sean MacStiofain, who had been the IRA's 'Chief of Staff' at the time, wrote:

I turned on RTE. The news was appalling. A terrible tragedy had struck the small town of Claudy in Co. Derry. Three car bombs had exploded there. Six people had been killed outright. Over 30 were injured, and some subsequently died. My heart and everything I had inside me just seemed to tighten up in a knot and sink slowly to the bottom of my stomach. 'Holy Mother of God,' I thought, 'who is responsible for this?'

The familiar tale of late warnings was heard. This time, it was claimed that the problem was down to damaged telephone exchanges. Apparently, shop assistants in Dungiven had been directed by the bombers to warn the police. However, it had proved impossible to make a telephone call from Dungiven owing to earlier bomb damage to the exchange. Eventually, one of the female shop assistants walked into Dungiven RUC Station to deliver the message personally . . . fifteen minutes after the first bomb had exploded.

The Claudy bombings, abhorrent and deadly though they were, were largely overshadowed by another significant event that occurred on the same day – Operation 'Motorman'. At four o'clock in the morning, on 31 July 1972, the biggest operation carried out by the British Army since Suez went into effect. Over the preceding months, the IRA had established so-called No-Go Areas within the hardline Catholic estates of the Creggan and Bogside in Londonderry, and within West Belfast. Here, the terrorists implemented their own version of law and order, enforced at the point of a gun. The Army and police bided their time, fearing that the use of impromptu armed force would incur hundreds of innocent casualties. But it had to stop. As the hours counted down, increasingly tight cordons of armoured reconnaissance and UDR patrols were put in place. Then, at 'H Hour', the spearhead units of the battalions assembled for this single operation moved straight to the heart of the IRA strongholds. Four battalions were assigned to Londonderry, eleven to Belfast, and a number of smaller elements to trouble spots elsewhere in the Province.

Not surprisingly, ATOs were among the vanguard of troops pouring into the former No Go Areas. One of them was Captain A. Gaiger-Booth:

During the Operation Motorman clearance of the 'No Go Areas' in the Creggan estate, the Londonderry Section deployed one ATO, including myself, to each of the four battalions. There was very little kit to split four ways! It included a Russian shotgun (ex-IRA!). I had spoken to the AVRE [Armoured Vehicle Royal Engineers] commanders – they requested that each barricade should first be cleared by ATO before they attempted to bulldoze it. I removed a 100lb device from the first one, and another operator cleared a very nasty tripwire ring-main [linked charges]. ATO reinforcements arrived in Londonderry when it was all over.

In all, total arms finds during Operation Motorman amounted to 32 weapons, 1,000 rounds of ammunition, 27 bombs and 450lb of explosives. There could be no doubt that it had been an outstanding success. The grip of the IRA on the Bogside and Creggan estates in Londonderry, and parts of Belfast, had been broken.

By the end of the first half of 1972, fifty-seven people had been killed by terrorist bombs. Bizarrely, IRA members made up the majority of casualties, with twenty being killed when IEDs they were placing exploded prematurely. Eighteen innocent civilians and two policemen had also died. Among the Army, deaths attributed to explosive devices ran at seventeen, with three of the deceased being ATOs. Given the dramatically escalating casualty rate, it is hardly surprising that more ATOs were to be killed, injured or to suffer near misses before the year was out.

The first of these was Captain John Young on 15 July. Just 22 years old, he had been in Northern Ireland since 18 May. During the subsequent two months he had had a busy time, having attended forty-three tasks. Compared to other operators, a high proportion of his jobs had been real, with only ten of them being hoaxes and four being false alarms. He had personally defused ten live devices, most of which were substantial in size. But July had been a quiet month for him. His last tasks prior to the 15th had been on 12 July, when he had attended the sites of two separate explosions. Immediately before that, there had been an uncharacteristic ten-day gap stretching back to the 2nd. Given that this was about his mid-tour point, it is possible that he took his R&R during this period. On 15 July his luck ran out. The device that killed him consisted of a milk churn with wires coming from it, which had been left at Silverbridge, near Forkhill. It contained 150–200lb of explosive. In most respects, it varied little from several other devices that Captain Young had already dealt with. It is, of course, possible that this lured him into a false sense of security. At around 11.30 a.m. he started trying to remove the lid from the milk churn using a hammer. During the process, the device, which was almost certainly booby-trapped, detonated.

The saddest aspect of Captain Young's death is that it may well have been needless. A fellow operator who had served with him in the Province in 1972 questioned the need to remove the lid at all. In his words: 'We simply blew them up.' But 'just blowing them up' does not preserve any forensic evidence for the future prosecution of a captured terrorist. It is quite possible that, in his efforts to produce the most professional outcome, Captain Young simply put his own safety last.

WO2 Alan Wright arrived in Northern Ireland as an operator in August, shortly after Captain Young's death. He had encountered the junior officer before and was deeply saddened by the event:

Captain John Young was a wonderful man, with whom I served on the Bramley 'Shadow Unit', and I still count it one of my greatest privileges to have known and served with him. We did a week's exercise with the Shadow Unit in 1971 up at Sherwood Forest, and it rained horribly for the entire visit. The Bramley lads earned a glowing report for their wonderful spirit, but it was due largely to the kindness and understanding of a fine officer and gentleman. It is through living rough in the field that you get to know and understand a person and how sincere they are. The lads of the Bramley Shadow Unit had a farewell party for him and presented him with a silver box before his departure to Lurgan – and that speaks louder than any praises that I can try and put into words!

It was to be a similar device that caused the death of WO2 William 'Nobby' Clark on 3 August 1972. A patrol from the Royal Welch Fusiliers had discovered it – a 10-gallon oil drum, tucked away alongside a metal gate, some 400 yards from the Urney Presbyterian Church, on the Sion Mills to Clady road about 5 miles from Strabane. WO2 Clark, a married man with four sons, aged between 5 and 12, was the operator called to the scene. He had been in Northern Ireland for only nine days, arriving just ten days after the loss of Captain John Young.

No doubt with the death of Captain Young still fresh in his mind, WO2 Clark stuck strictly to the rules when removing the top of the drum, using a small controlled explosion to blow it off. Unfortunately, he was then caught out when he approached the bomb for a second time. We cannot be sure precisely what happened next. There are three possible options. One is that the controlled explosion set some internal timer mechanism working, which detonated the device just as the ATO walked up to it. Alternatively, an internal booby trap might have functioned as the Warrant Officer put his hands into the now-open drum. The last option is that the booby trap was somehow connected to the outside of the drum, perhaps attached to the base, so that lifting or tilting would have set it off. Whatever the cause, WO2 Clark was buried a few days later in Middlesborough, his family receiving compensation of a mere £12,500.

Besides the deaths, near misses were being experienced on a regular basis. WO2 Alan Wright served in the Province from 10 August to 11 December 1972. He arrived at a particularly nerve-racking time. Given the small number of operators serving in Northern Ireland simultaneously – generally around ten – the casualty figures for 1972 were already horrifying. Cracknell, Butcher and Calladene had all been killed by car bombs in March, and Young and Clark by rural booby-trapped IEDs in July and August respectively. The odds in favour of survival for new arrivals were not looking good.

Wright's own brush with death came on 8 October, when he and his team were called out to an incident at Trainor's Village Supermarket and Tyre Depot, in Creggan village, near Crossmaglen. Mr Trainor had raised the alarm after making a narrow escape following a 'visit' by armed terrorists. Wright recalls:

Bombers had tied him up in his shop, and placed a milk churn containing incendiary mixture, with a second large drum on top. I tried to pull the device out of the building, using the heavy duty nylon rope threaded through the handle of the churn, but on the first pull, the bomb detonated, hurling a huge fireball across the road, and debris started to drop all around us in the field opposite. We had direct protection from the blast by the roadside wall. My driver and myself were unhurt, but a young private in 1st Battalion Staffords, guarding our rear, facing open country, was unlucky enough to catch a chunk of debris in the middle of the back. Luckily, his flak jacket protected him, and after a check-over by the Argyll and Sutherland Highlanders' Medical Officer at Bessbrook Mill, and a stiff tot of whisky, he was fine. We had a word with 1 Staffords' Orderly Room to give him a 'special mention' on his records – he was only a young lad.

Major Buchanan, of the Argylls, was in charge of the incident. He witnessed the colossal fireball shoot across the road and thought we were all 'goners'. I must confess we were a little stunned, and were gyrating like windmills for a few minutes. Thank God for the issue ear defenders! I remember saying to myself, 'Dear God, what a way to spend a Sunday afternoon!'

Not all near misses had such a happy outcome. On 28 November two youths left a time bomb at Long's supermarket on the Strand Road in Londonderry. Although they told staff that they had four minutes before the bomb would explode, it was still intact some forty-five minutes later when the team from 321 EOD Unit arrived. The operator was WO2 Kay, the Senior Ammunition Technician of the Londonderry Section. By one of those unhappy elections of fate, the team was accompanied on this occasion by 21-year-old Gunner Paul Jackson, the regimental photographer of the Royal Artillery Regiment, within whose area of operations the device had been laid. The Regiment wanted to obtain some pictures of an ATO at work. As the team drew up opposite the supermarket in their armoured Saracen, the device exploded, showering the vehicle with rubble and glass. Gunner Jackson and WO2 Kay were both attempting to peer through a hatch in the vehicle at the time. Jackson was killed instantly, as shrapnel struck him in the head, and Kay suffered serious facial injuries, losing an eye.

But the year was not yet over, and nor were the deaths. The 321 EOD Unit Log Book for 5 December 1972 bears the following entry: 'SF [Security Forces] reported that at 1810 hrs an explosion was heard and an investigation found an improvised mortar set up aimed at HQ 3 Infantry Brigade with a bomb hanging out of the mortar. Sgt Hills was called to the scene . . .'.

That evening, two home-made 'Mark 2' mortar rounds had been fired at the Army base at Kitchen Hill in Lurgan. The bombs were comparatively small, and caused little damage. No one was injured. The reaction from the troops in the base was swift, and the mortar firing point was soon found and cordoned off. It became apparent that a third bomb had failed to fire, and this live projectile, undoubtedly in a highly dangerous state, was now hanging out of the tube.

Sergeant Roy Hills from the Lurgan Section was tasked to the scene. A 28-year-old married man, Sergeant Hills had been in Northern Ireland for thirty-nine days, having arrived on 27 October. He went forward to tackle the unexploded device, which meant first removing it entirely from its tube. At some stage, he appears to have made an error – the indications are that, with fingers chilled by the cold of the winter's evening, he may simply have mishandled the bomb and dropped it. It detonated, killing him instantly.

WO2 Alan Wright knew Sergeant Hills well:

Sergeant Roy Hills was a very quiet, studious and likeable fellow, who was tragically killed while investigating a mortar attack early evening upon the Army base at Kitchen Hill, Lurgan. Roy, for interest, was an authority on the American Civil War – in fact, I think it was his whole life and time-consuming passion. I think he had in his possession almost every work of repute that had been written upon the subject. Two brothers had married two sisters, and I think they were a happy, close-knit family. Roy's sister-in-law phoned me prior to his death, seeking reassurance – and I tried earnestly to reassure her that activities had quietened considerably, and that everything would be fine. The next minute, dear Roy was gone. I felt terribly guilty and miserable for a few days, as if I had lied to his family. Life can be cruel at times. Roy Hills wouldn't have harmed a soul!

Roy Hills was the last operator to meet his death in 1972; it had been a terrible year. Indeed, over the next thirty years of the Troubles, successive annual body counts for all parties – innocent civilians, police, terrorists or

Army – were never to reach the same grim tally. As far as the operators of 321 EOD Unit were concerned, mistakes had been made, lessons had been learnt, and techniques and equipment had been developed. But, to balance the books, the unit had, without doubt, saved hundreds of lives and stymied the terrorists' goal of destroying the very fabric of society. Time after time, the operators had looked into the mouth of the dragon, and quenched its flames. Now they would join the list of most-wanted targets.

PART TWO

THE ENDURING THREAT

FOUR

SLAUGHTER OF THE INNOCENTS

From 1969, through to the end of 1971, despite the growing frequency of bombing attacks, devices remained relatively crude, simple and limited in size. Commonly, they were made up of small quantities of commercial explosive, set off by a burning fuse and a detonator. Such devices might be thrown as home-made grenades, particularly in riot situations, or used to destroy public utilities or commercial premises under cover of darkness. However, all this was to change. Several developments contributed to the change. As the casualty figures rose, attitudes hardened. This coincided with the refinement of techniques for manufacturing large quantities of home-made explosives, together with more sophisticated timer mechanisms. A series of no-warning, tit-for-tat pub bombings towards the end of 1971 led to the routine targeting of the civilian population. It soon became clear that the car bomb provided the best means of achieving a devastating effect quickly. The slaughter of the innocents had commenced.

Frequently, civilian deaths were the result of carelessness or callous indifference. Victim-operated booby traps would be placed in the hope of catching out members of the Army or RUC, but with a cavalier disregard for the safety of the population at large. On occasions, the wrong individuals died because of cases of mistaken identity. More often, innocent bystanders were blown to pieces when a terrorist's bomb detonated prematurely, whether during manufacture or in transit. Time-bomb warnings often arrived too late or lacked sufficient accuracy, making it impossible for the Security Forces to evacuate people in time. But probably the greatest number of innocent civilian deaths occurred simply because that is what terrorists do – they kill.

The first individuals to die from a booby trap intended for the Security Forces were the five BBC technicians whose Land Rover was destroyed as they drove up the Brougher Mountain to fix a damaged transmitter on 9 February 1971 (see Chapter Two). Eighteen months later, on 28 August

1972, 57-year-old farmer William Trotter was killed with his dog, when he stumbled across a booby trap on his land near Newtownbutler, not far from the border. At least, on these occasions, the IRA was able to fall back on the excuse that the booby traps had been placed in remote rural areas, which were routinely patrolled by the Army.

Less easy to explain was the death of a 9-year-old boy who died while playing Cowboys and Indians in the back garden of his own home on the Creggan estate in Londonderry, on 23 February 1973. William Gordon was one of seven children who lived in the house, and had been playing with one of his brothers when he unwittingly disturbed the 10lb device. The words of a postman who was first on the scene are deeply poignant: 'I saw a young boy crawling along the ground, covered in blood. He looked up at me and said, "Help me, Mister, I'm hurt."'

The boy was still alive when the ambulance reached Altnagelvin Hospital, but he died on the operating table, his legs having been amputated in an attempt to save him. Astonishingly, not only was a second similar device found nearby, which could have killed or maimed more children, but troops responding to the incident were stoned by a crowd of 300 youths.

Similarly beyond belief is the thought process that prompted a terrorist to rig a 10lb booby trap to the door of an Air Training Corps hut in the grounds of Cavehill Primary School in North Belfast. Sixteen-year-old Edward Wilson died instantly in the blast when he opened the door, and five other boys were injured. Who did the bomber think he was targeting? This was not some crack force of junior SAS aspirants, but a uniformed youth club for young lads interested in aircraft and flying. No doubt many of them still had Airfix plastic model aeroplanes hanging from their bedroom ceilings by lengths of thread.

Signaller G.R. Henderson, who was working as a signals operator with one of 321 EOD Unit's teams in Londonderry between November 1976 and April 1977, witnessed the outcome of a carelessly placed booby trap:

An explosion had been reported in Strabane. We left Londonderry and 'blue lighted' it all the way. At the scene of the incident, we were confronted with a trail of blood and odd bits of human flesh scattered around the area. A young boy returning from judo classes had found a rifle magazine at the base of the sangar at the end of the High Street. He had picked it up and had been messing about with it when it exploded, removing his hand from one of his arms. He had run along the street with blood gushing everywhere. A quick-thinking soldier had caught him and put a field dressing on the stump, probably saving the boy's life.

We closed off the area, and then members of the team, led by Sergeant Alan Wase, went forward to comb the area for evidence. Each item we picked up was placed in a forensic bag, and the location where it was found marked on a sketch map.

I felt quite all right until I bent down to pick up what looked like a piece of red and white jelly. It was in fact the end of a finger, minus bone, but with the fingernail intact. For the first time in the Province, I felt my stomach turn, and I was sick. We found live rounds in the street from the magazine, and it was then realised that the magazine had been left to catch an unwary soldier who would think that one of his mates had dropped it.

Mistaken identities provided many similar tragic results. Frequently, innocent civilians were mistaken for members of the Security Forces or other 'legitimate targets'. On 24 February 1979 five teenagers were walking along the road between Keady and Newtownhamilton, in South Armagh. They were heading for a Saturday night dance. To the nervous IRA man, lying hidden in the darkness, finger hovering over the firing switch as he waited for an opportunity target, they must have looked like soldiers patrolling. For some reason, he missed the fact that they were not spread out tactically but were walking close together, were not carrying guns and were not wearing uniforms. On the spur of the moment, the target must have looked good enough. The massive ambush device, concealed in a trailer by the side of the road and detonated by command wire, left a crater 5 feet deep. With the casualties writhing on the ground, the IRA death squad continued to pump high-velocity shots into the killing area, trying to finish off the wounded. Two 16-year-old boys were killed by the blast. The other three, all 15, were badly injured, one of them losing an arm, and another, partially paralysed, being confined to a wheelchair for life. An apology was issued to the families, saying: 'Tragically, the youths and their position on the road were mistaken for the movements of soldiers, and the bomb was set off.'

Sometimes it was the terrorists' faulty intelligence and planning that were behind the deaths of innocent people. When the IRA planted a victim-operated IED under the cab of a lorry at the creamery in Killen, Co. Tyrone, on 12 December 1986, their planned target was a part-time member of the

UDR. Instead, the wrong man, Desmond Caldwell, a 44-year-old father of three, died when he started the engine. Ironically, although he was not the intended victim, Caldwell had, by coincidence, been a member of the UDR – albeit sixteen years before and for just five months. As such, the terrorists would still claim him as a 'legitimate target'. The fact that innocent workers might have used the truck, or been in close proximity to it when it exploded, clearly did not feature in the bomber's considerations.

Even when the terrorists tried to execute their missions with military precision, combining forward intelligence with on-the-ground surveillance, they were still prone to careless errors. On 23 July 1988 Robert Hanna, a 45-year-old heating contractor, flew into Dublin Airport, with his wife, Maureen, and 7-year-old son, David. They had been on holiday in America. They could not have known that they would be arriving at the same time as High Court Judge Eoin Higgins and his family, or that an IRA murder squad would be waiting.

Somewhere along the line, the Judge, who was due to go to Belfast, got delayed. The Hannas, meanwhile, left the airport, heading north to their home in the Ballynahinch Road, Hillsborough, Co. Down. Unknown to them, and by complete chance, their car was following an unmarked Garda (Southern Irish Police) vehicle. This had already been identified by the IRA, and was now mistakenly assumed to be the police escort for Judge Higgins. The terrorists were obviously very certain of the Judge's likely movements that day, as they had taken the trouble to conceal a 1,000lb bomb beneath the Dublin-to-Belfast road, just across the border at Killeen near Newry in South Armagh. The fact that the Judge would be accompanied by his wife and daughter was irrelevant – they were simply 'legitimate targets'. Once the wrong description had been passed, the bomber waited until the Hannas drove over the device, then pressed the button. Death was instantaneous. In a curt statement, attempting to explain the error, the IRA said: 'The vehicle at Killeen was blown up on the understanding that it was carrying Judge Higgins and not the Hannas. There is nothing we can say in any way of comfort to the relatives of this family.'

Over the years, own goals have caused the deaths of considerable numbers of terrorists from both sides of the sectarian divide. In total, between the years 1969 and 2004, 125 terrorists died in explosions caused by their own bombs. Of these, the split is 16 Loyalists compared to 108 IRA 'volunteers'. The vast majority of deaths occurred in the early years of the campaign, with

90 IRA bombers and 15 UDA/UVF men being killed between 1969 and 1980. Unbelievably, during 1972 alone, 33 IRA men and women managed to blow themselves up. Beyond 1976, with a better understanding of the necessary safety measures, own goals became far less frequent occurrences. Of course, the worst aspect of own goals is that there is every chance that innocent bystanders will be caught in the blast. The statistics show that, over the period 1969–2000, 26 people met their deaths this way.

Some of the individual own goals caused so many deaths and injuries that they may be counted among the most significant incidents of the Troubles. On 28 May 1972 four members of the IRA's '2nd Belfast Battalion' were involved in the transit of a bomb containing a large quantity of home-made explosive in the Short Strand area of East Belfast. It seems likely that they were trying to load it into the boot of a car, which had been hijacked earlier in the Ardoyne. Something went wrong, and the device exploded. The four terrorists were killed instantly, as were four passers-by – all Catholics.

Three months later, on 22 August, nine people were killed in a premature explosion at the Newry Customs Clearing Station. The dead comprised three members of a four-man IRA bombing team, four Customs officials and two lorry-drivers, who were waiting for their papers to be cleared. Six other people were injured. From the limited information available from witnesses, it appears that the bombers entered the building at around 9.45 a.m., shouting a warning for people to get out quickly. Somebody pressed the attack alarm, but the bell rang for only about five seconds before an explosion demolished the building. All but one of those killed died instantly.

Over successive years, more premature explosions continued to take their toll of the innocent civilian population. These included one that happened on the Ballymena-to-Belfast train on 17 January 1980. The device, an incendiary being carried in a haversack, caused a massive fireball, which shot through the carriage. Three people died: the IRA man carrying the bomb, a male passenger and a schoolboy of 17. A second bomber was also caught in the blast. With 20 per cent burns to his body, he ran along the train screaming, 'I'm burning. Help me.' Despite his horrific injuries, he succeeded in getting off the train, and tried to mingle with other passengers as they were evacuated to safety. He was later arrested and sentenced to ten years in prison.

Undoubtedly, the own goal that caused the most significant political ramifications was that which blew apart Frizzell's fish and chip shop on the

Shankill Road on 23 October 1993. It was a busy Saturday afternoon, and the shoppers were out in force when two IRA men entered the shop carrying the bomb. They were both dressed in white overall coats so that they could masquerade as delivery men. The IRA later stated that it had believed that members of the Loyalist UDA's command team were meeting in a room above the shop. It had therefore been its intention to deposit the bomb on a short timer, giving just enough time for the customers and staff to flee the building, but killing those upstairs. Subsequent investigations showed that no such UDA members were among the resultant casualties.

The terrorists had barely entered the shop when the device went off, the force of the explosion ripping through the building and reducing it to rubble. One of the bombers, Thomas Begley, was killed instantly, along with nine innocent people, all Protestants. Fifty-seven people were injured. The dead included 7-year-old Michelle Baird, who was killed with her parents. They always popped into the shop to buy crabsticks as a treat for the little girl on their way back home from their regular Saturday shopping trip.

The bombing provoked outrage among the Protestant community, with Loyalist terrorists embarking on a revenge-killing spree. The sense of fury was heightened when Gerry Adams, who as the leader of Sinn Fein was supposedly pursuing the peace process, acted as a pallbearer at Begley's funeral.

Although, over the years, twenty-six innocent people have been killed in premature explosions, this statistic is tiny when compared with the numbers who have died when the terrorists simply got the warnings wrong. So frequently has this happened that, on examination, the authenticity of many such warnings seems debatable. Indeed one might readily judge that the terrorists' ensuing protests that warnings have gone unheeded, or have been acted upon too slowly, have routinely been used after the event to explain away high civilian casualty figures. On other occasions, warnings have been so vague or misleading that they seem to have been deliberately calculated to lead the greatest number of people into the killing area.

We have already looked at a number of horrific instances in the early 1970s where this happened. When a 200lb car bomb detonated in Donegall Street, Belfast, on 20 March 1972, killing 7 people and injuring 150, initial calls warned of a device placed inside a building in nearby Church Street. The correct street name was passed only three minutes before the explosion, by which time people were already heading into the danger area as a result of the initial inaccurate bomb scare. On Bloody Friday, 21 July 1972, 9 people were killed and 130 injured when the IRA let off twenty bombs in just over an hour. Afterwards they claimed that warnings had been given 'at least thirty minutes to one hour before each explosion'. Clearly with no comprehension of the difficulties involved in evacuating thousands of people from a capital city centre, in a calm, ordered manner, as twenty bombs go off at random around them, former IRA leader Sean MacStiofan made the fanciful comment:

It required only one man with a loud hailer to clear each target area in no time. The claim that the enormous British forces were overwhelmed by 22 localised explosions would not be likely to impress impartial investigators. The Republicans were convinced that the British had deliberately disregarded these two warnings for strategic policy reasons.

As described in Chapter Three, at the village of Claudy on 31 July 1972, where nine died, the problem had been that shop assistants in Dungiven had been instructed to telephone a warning to the RUC on behalf of the IRA. Nobody had checked that the telephones were working. Earlier bomb damage to the local exchange meant that they were not, with the consequence that a woman walked into the Dungiven RUC Station fifteen minutes after the first bomb had gone off. (See Chapter Three for a fuller description of the Donegall Street, Bloody Friday and Claudy bombings.)

On 21 May 1976 the IRA chose to bomb the Bangor-to-Portadown train as it passed through Belfast. Two bombs were placed on board by two IRA members, who had been informed that the target was Central Station in Belfast. They were assured that warnings would be telephoned through in time. In fact, a warning was received only after the train had already pulled out of Belfast on its way to Portadown. There was no means of contacting the train once it had left the station. Fortuitously, one device was discovered, and removed by a brave guard, who placed it on the railway line embankment. The other bomb remained hidden, finally detonating while the train was on a stretch of track between Moira and Lisburn. A 22-year-old female civil servant died in the blast.

One of the most horrifying incidents where deaths were the inevitable result of an inadequate warning was that involving a firebomb attack on the La Mon restaurant on 17 February 1978. Two functions were in progress that night: the annual dinner dance for the Irish Collie Club and a party for the Northern Ireland Junior Motorcycle Club. Over 400 people were present at the popular venue. Under cover of darkness, an IRA bombing team crept up to the outside of the building. Using a meat hook, they attached the bomb to the metal security grille that covered one of the windows. It was a blast incendiary. It consisted of several plastic containers of petrol, an explosive charge in a steel container to add to the fragmentation, and a delay timer.

When the bomb exploded, a massive fireball, around 60 feet in diameter, shot into the function room. The lights went out, fumes filled the air, and a raging inferno took hold, in which people could be seen burning alive. Twelve people were killed, and many more suffered horrendous burns. News reports of the time spoke of some of the victims having been melted into the ground by the heat. The *Newtownards Chronicle* reported:

Evidence of the intense heat and the blast became evident when the bodies were found charred beyond recognition huddled against the wall directly opposite the bomb position. It was gruesome, people with their clothes and flesh on fire trying to get out of the burning building which was a raging inferno in a few minutes.

The first warning received by the RUC at Newtownards was recorded as being at 8.57 p.m. An officer immediately rang the restaurant, only to hear pandemonium at the other end, the bomb having already gone off. A second warning came in at 9.04 p.m. – several minutes too late. The IRA trotted out the usual apology: 'There is nothing we can offer in mitigation, bar that our enquiries have established that a nine-minute warning was given to the RUC. This was totally inadequate given the disastrous consequences.'

'Do these people never learn?' is the question that must spring to mind. Well, clearly not, because this same set of circumstances was to happen time and time again throughout the years of the Troubles, culminating finally in the worst incident of all: the Omagh bombing.

On 13 August 1998 a Vauxhall Cavalier was reported stolen from Carrickmacross in Co. Monaghan, Southern Ireland. At some time over the next two days, a 500lb bomb was loaded into the boot. It almost certainly consisted of a booster charge of Semtex, with a main charge of fertiliser (ammonium nitrate) mixed with fuel oil – a home-made explosive known as ANFO.

Saturday 15 August was a warm, sunny day, and shoppers flocked into Omagh, Co. Tyrone. Probably at around 2 p.m. the car was driven into the town centre and abandoned in Market Street, where a pub, a coffee shop and clothes shops acted as magnets for the Saturday crowds. At this stage the bomb's delay timer still had over an hour to run. Just after 2.30 p.m. the first warnings started to filter in, being telephoned through to the Ulster Television newsroom and the Coleraine branch of the Samaritans. At Ulster Television the call was taken by Maggie Hall. She immediately rang the RUC's emergency switchboard, where she was recorded as saying: 'I'm only after getting a call from a man with a country accent, saying there's a bomb in Omagh main street near the Courthouse – a 500lb bomb. It's going to go off in 30 minutes.' She also passed on the codeword that had been used: 'Malta Pope'.

The calls were immediately treated as genuine, because the caller had used a recognised codeword. Indeed, it was identical to the one that had been given when the town of Banbridge had been bombed two weeks earlier. The evacuation therefore commenced without delay. Given the degree of advance warning, there was every chance that the terrorists could have avoided causing civilian casualties on this occasion – if they had only given the true location of the device. But they did not. Instead, the anonymous caller warned of a bomb at the Courthouse in the main street, at the other end of town from Market Street. The police duly began shepherding the crowds away from the Courthouse – and towards the waiting bomb.

At 3.10 p.m. the device exploded, causing instant carnage. Glass, bricks and masonry smashed into the afternoon shoppers, cutting down people of all ages, sexes and religions. The dead included a 30-year-old woman, pregnant with twins, and her 18-month-old daughter. One man of 60 had just arrived home from a holiday abroad, and gone into town with his son to do some shopping; both died. Several Spanish children were in town that day. They were on a schools exchange programme with Irish children from Buncrana, Co. Donegal. Earlier, they had visited the Ulster–American Folk Park near Omagh, and were just doing some impromptu shopping in the town before returning back across the border to Eire. One Spanish schoolboy died in the explosion, along with his 23-year-old female teacher, and three of their schoolboy hosts from Buncrana. The second youngest victim was an 18-month-old baby girl. Her mother survived, but with 60 per cent burns. She was to spend the next four months in hospital, being heavily sedated for the first six weeks. Only then was she told of the death of her daughter. The final death toll reached twenty-nine, of whom more than half were Catholics. It was reported that thirty children lost their mothers in the blast. Some 200 people suffered injuries, many of them serious, including having limbs blown off. Dorothy Boyle witnessed the immediate aftermath:

> There were limbs lying about that had been blown off people. Everyone was running round, trying to help people. There was a girl in a wheelchair screaming for help, who was in a bad way. There were people with cuts on their heads, bleeding. One young boy had half his leg completely blown off. He didn't cry or anything. He was just in a complete state of shock.

Another witness was John King, a local carpenter, who had been passing nearby. He immediately raced across to the scene to try to help:

> The first thing I noticed was what I suppose was a shop dummy lying in the middle of the street, so I knew then that there was people injured, 'cause I could see everybody come running with blood and one thing or another. After I passed the first shop dummy that I saw lying in the street, out of one of the clothes shops, the next thing I saw in the street, again, was what I thought was another shop dummy. But unfortunately that wasn't. That was either a man or a woman – I've no idea what it was – but it was just a body. And there were neither legs or arms or anything to be seen on it. It was a sight that I'll not forget anyway, that's for sure.
>
> And that was only one – there was a lot of other sights lying on that street, that really yet is still hard to describe. How anybody could do that to innocent people, I have no idea.

In response to the initial warning, a team from 321 EOD had been deployed forward from its Omagh base, only three minutes' drive away. As with the civilian population, they had been directed to what was supposed to be a safe area, where they were held awaiting further information. There had been numerous hoax calls over the preceding weeks, and there was therefore every chance that this was no different. However, the team's No. 1, Staff Sergeant Adam Modd, had taken the decision to get out on the ground, since a new No. 2 had arrived only two days previously and it was important that he should become familiar with the territory.

Within about six minutes of their arrival, the device exploded – just 75 metres away. By pure chance, the team was positioned out of line of sight and suffered no casualties. As with all explosion sites, it then became the operator's job to examine the aftermath in order to ensure that there was no likelihood of further blasts, and to gain any intelligence and forensic evidence. This was not an easy task. Absolute chaos ensued in the wake of the explosion, and it was to be at least an hour before the evacuation had been completed and a cordon put in place. During this time, team members assisted the Fire and Ambulance Services in treating the injured, evacuating the dead and searching the collapsed buildings for more casualties. They were subjected to some horrific scenes that day, perhaps made all the worse by the knowledge that, if only they had known where the car bomb was, they could have stopped it going off. Adam Modd recalls that the team members were given counselling afterwards. In his view, this 'may have helped some, but it's probably better to put it behind you and get on with life'.

In an article in the *Daily Mail* on 26 May 2004, Michael Gallagher, the father of Aidan Gallagher, who died in the explosion at the age of 21, recalled the grief of that terrible day:

It's some of the small things that make the biggest difference. I went to the hospital looking for Aidan three times that day. The first time I came back – hoping and hoping Aidan would be back at home – my daughter Cathy had lit a candle and placed it in the window.

When I finally came back the third time and all hope had gone, the candle was still there. I will always remember that candle.

He was going to buy a pair of jeans and some work boots. I told him where to park the car. I said he didn't want to be dragging his boots around town and if he parked behind the Courthouse he could get the boots nearby, drop them off at the car and then go and buy the jeans.

The Courthouse was the area everyone was evacuated from – and that's the guilt I will always feel. If I hadn't told him where to park, he might have parked somewhere else.

Once again the casualties had been made far worse by an inaccurate warning. Had the true location of the car bomb been given, the police would have had time to clear most of the shoppers from the danger area. But, whether deliberately or not, they were misled. This time, the terrorist group in question was the 'Real IRA', a dissident splinter group, which had broken away from the Provisional IRA because of the latter's perceived compliance with the ongoing peace process. It made no difference: the fundamental errors, resulting from a callous disregard for human life, were unchanged. As tradition demanded, a formal statement of apology was made, affirming that: 'It was a commercial target, part of an ongoing campaign against the Brits. We offer apologies to the civilians.'

One hopes that the injured and bereaved were suitably appeased.

While the consequences of late or inaccurate warnings have frequently been horrific, the terrorists can at least fall back on the excuse that they tried to minimise casualties – no matter how lacking in credibility that claim might often seem. There is, however, no excuse for the no-warning device when targeted against innocent civilians. Sadly, there have been many such incidents. By 2005, 180 people had been slaughtered in this way, if one counted just those killed when a time bomb exploded without warning, or when terrorists threw a fizzing blast bomb into an area where innocent deaths were likely to occur. The statistic excludes those who died despite some sort of warning being given, those killed by booby traps, or those who were collateral casualties in an attack on the military. Of the 180 fatalities, it is perhaps hardly surprising that a third of them occurred in the three-year period spanning the beginning of 1971 through to the end of 1973. This was the time of revenge pub bombings and attacks on crowded shopping areas. For some years, the most serious of these, in terms of deaths, was the attack on McGurk's Bar on 4 December 1971, in which fifteen people were killed (see Chapter Two).

A particularly harrowing aspect of the no-warning attacks is the completely random way in which people have been cut down simply because they happened to be in the wrong place at the wrong time. When Loyalist bombers attacked the Catholic clientele of Benny's Bar in North Belfast on Hallowe'en Night 1972, the only fatalities were two little girls, Paula Stronge, 6, and Claire Hughes, 4, who were playing around a bonfire in the street outside. Only six weeks later, on 14 December, 19-year-old office worker Kathleen Dolan was killed by a Loyalist car bomb in the village of Killeter, Co. Tyrone. She had been on her way to post her wedding invitations at the time. When the Osbornes family went to watch the greyhound racing at the Hannahstown track, on 9 June 1974, they little realised that a UDA bomb left outside would end the life of 13-year-old Michelle Osbornes and leave her father, brother and sister seriously injured. The seaside town of Ballycastle in Co. Antrim had suffered very few IRA attacks during the early Troubles, but when a bomb was placed at the town's Marne Hotel on 19 June 1979, it snuffed out the life of William Whitten, 65, who was on holiday there with his wife.

Almost unbelievably, when there have been fatalities from no-warning attacks, they have tended to be limited to just one or two per bomb. But there have been exceptions. At the Droppin Well pub in Ballykelly, on 7 December 1982, seventeen people died when an IRA bomb exploded during a disco, which had attracted over 150 people into the bar. Former Signaller B.M. Raine was the Royal Signals operator attached to the Londonderry EOD team that was called to the scene. He recalls: 'The longest and most horrific job that I ever did was the explosion at the Droppin Well disco in Ballykelly. The team was there from midnight until mid-afternoon the following day. That was the first and last time I'd see the carnage a small IED can do to so many people.' The bomb was indeed relatively small, consisting of just an estimated 5lb of commercial explosive. However, it was enough to blow the walls out and bring the roof crashing down on those below. As a result, most of the deaths were caused by crush asphyxia. Of the seventeen killed, eleven were soldiers from a nearby military base.

Of all the no-warning attacks, perhaps that which caused most revulsion was the Enniskillen bombing of 8 November 1987. It was Remembrance Day, and crowds of people had gathered in the town for the annual service at the War Memorial, to be followed by a parade. Not surprisingly, many of those present were elderly. Just before the service started, the device exploded. Containing 40lb of gelignite, it had been concealed in a community hall to the rear of the congregation. Masonry and bricks rained down, crushing people under the rubble. Eleven people were killed and sixty-three injured, nineteen of them seriously. All were civilians. The youngest to die was 2; the eldest was 75.

As usual, the IRA trotted out its expressions of 'deep regret'. But on this occasion, it clearly realised that it had gone too far. The desecration of a memorial service, which resulted in purely civilian casualties, was obviously not going to be an easy one to explain away. So, instead, a barely credible excuse was proffered. The story was that the terrorists had planned to initiate the bomb by radio control, but only when soldiers providing security for the service entered the target area. However, before the opportunity presented itself, they claimed, a 'scanner' deployed by the Security Forces had set it off prematurely. This was an outright lie, but it was to be another eight years before the IRA would admit as much. The fact was, the device was on a timer, and, yet again, the IRA just got it wrong.

In the early 1990s the IRA took the concept of the no-warning device, and added an evil new twist: they created so-called human bombs. A member of the public would be taken prisoner and strapped into a car containing a bomb. He would then be coerced – by direct threats either to him, or to members of his family – into driving the vehicle to a Security Force base or checkpoint. When it reached the base, the car would be detonated. We in the West have a particular form of revulsion for the suicide bomber, who will often kill innocent women and children at the expense of his own life. But at least the suicide bomber feels so strongly about his cause that he is prepared to sacrifice his own life in its pursuit. The IRA took the approach that it was probably better to sacrifice somebody else's life in the pursuit of its cause. What this approach lacked in courage, it certainly made up for in pragmatism.

The first 'human-bomb' attack happened on 24 October 1990. Patsy Gillespie was a 42-year-old, Roman Catholic, married man with three children. He was also a canteen worker at the Fort George Army base. As far as the IRA was concerned, this made him a 'legitimate target', and therefore expendable. With armed men holding his wife and children hostage, Mr Gillespie was ordered to drive a van bomb to the heavily fortified Coshquin vehicle checkpoint on the border with Donegal. As the van drove into the checkpoint, the bomb was detonated with Mr Gillespie still in the driving seat. There was a massive blast that killed three soldiers and mortally wounded a further two. Amid the carnage, gunmen poured fire into the checkpoint from the southern side of the border.

The same night, 68-year-old James McEvoy was forcibly awakened by two masked gunmen who had broken into his house. He too was ordered into a vehicle containing a bomb, which he was instructed to drive to the Killeen permanent vehicle checkpoint just outside Newry. He was told that, if he did not obey, two of his sons would be murdered. He was also led to believe that the troops would have forty minutes to evacuate the post before the device exploded. This was a lie. As soon as Mr McEvoy entered the checkpoint, he jumped out of the car and raised the alarm. Seconds later the bomb went off, injuring him and killing Ranger Cyril Smith, a 21-year-old soldier who lost his life while trying to alert his colleagues (he was subsequently awarded the Queen's Gallantry Medal posthumously).

The practice of using human bombs was savagely condemned. The Catholic Bishop of Londonderry, Dr Edward Daly, scathingly accused the IRA of 'crossing a new threshold of evil'. Even so, a further attempt to use this type of attack was made nearly a year later, on 3 September 1991, at Annaghmartin. At 8.30 p.m., six armed men took over a house occupied by a family named Quigley. Shortly afterwards, a Mr and Mrs Scott arrived at the house. They were immediately apprehended by the terrorists, and their red Nissan van hijacked. The van was then driven to a second house, belonging to a Mr Nelson, which was also taken over. With the rest of the Nelson family tied up, Mr Nelson's son and daughter were taken to a site where twenty armed men were attempting to free a bogged-in tractor with a silage trailer attached. The trailer had been inadvertently dragged into a hidden culvert as it was being towed across a field towards the Army's Annaghmartin permanent vehicle checkpoint. A second tractor had been commandeered to assist in pulling it free. Meanwhile, an illegal vehicle checkpoint was established by the terrorists in the Republic of Ireland. This was manned by armed men, who stopped five cars, which were then used to block the road. Eventually, it became clear that the tractor and trailer could not be extricated, and the operation was aborted. It seems almost certain that Mr Nelson's son would have been ordered to drive the tractor to the military checkpoint had it not bogged down.

A clearance operation, conducted by the Security Forces over the next forty-eight hours, produced eleven fertiliser bags of home-made explosive. The ATO estimated the total quantity to be in the region of 8,000lb – the largest ever IRA bomb.

In this chapter we have seen how, over the years, the Troubles in Northern Ireland produced certain events that will be forever etched in the nation's memory for their unparalleled wickedness: McGurk's, the Abercorn, Bloody Friday, Claudy, La Mon, the Shankill Road fish and chip shop bombing of 1993, Omagh and the human-bomb attacks of the early 1990s. Time and time again, innocent civilians have paid with their lives, or have been hideously maimed. Of course, the terrorists have often been quick to apologise – after all, they need popular support – but over time, their repeated excuses have come to have a hollow ring.

Throughout the 1970s the paramilitaries from both sides tried to batter each other, and the British Government, into submission. But, as the blood price paid in innocent lives rose, the tactics started to change. The Loyalists moved away from trying to deploy large explosive devices, switching instead to using guns to pursue their random assassination campaigns against the Catholics. Meanwhile, the IRA turned its attention to prosecuting an all-out war against the Security Forces, deliberately targeting soldiers and policemen on duty. In the next chapter we shall see how explosive devices were used to pursue this sustained offensive campaign.

FIVE

BOOBY TRAPS AND AMBUSHES

Constables Samuel Donaldson and Robert Millar were the first members of the Security Forces to be killed in an explosion during the contemporary Troubles. It was 12 August 1970, and the cause of their deaths was a booby trap. The IRA's 'South Armagh Brigade' had decided that it wanted to kill policemen, and, in order to do this, it needed to draw its targets into the chosen killing area. The easiest method was to entice the police to respond to a crime. A stolen car provided the perfect scenario. It could be left abandoned, in the knowledge that, sooner or later, it would be reported. Once reported, it could hardly be left where it was; at some stage the police would have to take it away. In order to move it, it would have to be opened, and a car interior presented many options for the concealment of explosives. The RUC had never faced anything like this before. Despite the nightly rioting in Belfast, the focus of the police was still on fighting everyday crime; they were not yet fighting a war on terror. Approaching a supposedly stolen vehicle with this mindset, Donaldson and Millar did not stand a chance. A bomb was hidden in the car, with its detonator wired in to the internal courtesy light circuit. As soon as any door was opened, the circuit would be completed and the device would explode. Like all good booby traps, it was simple, effective and quite deadly.

Initially, the IRA was slow to use booby traps. There were some obvious reasons for this. In 1969 the Troubles had ignited surprisingly quickly out of the sectarian hatred that had, for years, smouldered just below the surface. At that stage, the IRA had been long dormant, and was in no state to start prosecuting a cohesive terrorist campaign against the Security Forces. Its members therefore tended to concentrate on the 'protection' of the Catholic enclaves in the major cities of Belfast and Londonderry, using whatever weapons came to hand – principally guns and simple blast bombs. Throughout 1970, and into 1971, the organisation continued to grow and regroup, its numbers boosted by such events as the introduction of internment in August 1971, and Bloody Sunday in January 1972. As it grew in size and confidence, it began to diversify in terms of tactics and weaponry.

When Captain David Stewardson, the first ATO to be killed, died on 9 September 1971, he was only the third member of the Security Forces to be killed by a booby trap. Thirteen months had already passed since the deaths of Donaldson and Millar. Stewardson had been caught out by the notorious Castlerobin, with its micro-switch anti-disturbance mechanism. No doubt inspired by such early successes, the IRA learnt quickly. By the start of 1972 it was engaged in an all-out war against the Security Forces, and the booby traps started to come thick and fast. In that year alone, seven soldiers, one policeman and two civilians were cut down by booby traps – the two civilians both being innocent victims of devices that had been left in place for patrolling troops.

Booby traps do not need to be technically complex or sophisticated. In many respects, the simpler they are the better. For that reason, the basic designs and types have remained very much the same throughout the history of the campaign. Invariably, the terrorist will set up an explosive device, reliant on an electrical circuit to initiate it, leaving just one element to complete the loop. The aim is then to lure the victim into unwittingly completing that circuit while they are still in the bomb's killing area.

There are many ways of doing this. We have already seen how a clothes peg might be incorporated into a bomb's electrical circuit, with wires leading to drawing-pin contacts, one in each jaw. An insulator – probably just a slip of plastic – can be inserted between the pins to prevent them touching. However, once the insulator is snatched away, perhaps when someone stumbles across a fishing-line tripwire, the pins make contact, the circuit is completed and the device explodes. It was just such a device that killed the five BBC technicians on Brougher Mountain in February 1971. This might lead one to think that, once a tripwire has been discovered, then merely cutting it will render the booby trap safe. Well, it will, so long as the device has been set up to operate on a 'pull' mechanism. In the case of a 'release' mechanism, the cutting of a tripwire might have the opposite effect and be quite deadly. For example, that would be the case if the jaws of the peg were actually held open under tension, perhaps with one jaw nailed to a door frame, and the other pulled open by a tripwire. As soon as the operator cut the wire, the jaws would snap shut, thereby completing the circuit. Game over!

Another favourite is the mercury tilt switch, which is used to provide an 'anti-disturbance' mechanism. These are readily available commercially, although they are also very easy to make. The principle is that a drop of mercury is placed inside a small glass phial, the open end of which is then plugged. Two metal pins are inserted through the plug, so that the ends protrude inside the phial – parallel, but not touching. Each pin is then wired in to the bomb's electrical circuit. So long as the mercury comes nowhere near the ends of the pins, the circuit remains open. However, as soon as the phial is disturbed, through tilting or rocking, the mercury globule will slide down the tube. Being metal, as soon as it touches both pins, it will immediately close the circuit; the current will flow and the bomb will explode. Mercury tilt switches are the most common means of initiating under-car booby traps.

One common booby trap is the 'pressure pad'. As its name implies, this requires the victim to stand or sit on it in order to set off the device. In its simplest form, it might consist of no more than two sheets of aluminium foil, each wired in to the bomb's circuit, but held apart by a thin layer of insulating material, such as rubber or foam. The insulating material would have holes cut into it, so that any significant downward pressure would allow the foil sheets to touch, thereby initiating the device. Pressure pads can be adapted for either urban or rural environments with equally devastating effect. In the town, one might typically be hidden under the stair carpet of a derelict house, waiting for the first footfall. In the country, the terrorist might conceal a pressure pad under a lightweight turf, adjacent to a more readily visible hoax device, hoping to catch out an unwary ATO.

Most booby traps operate on these simple principles – that is, something must be pulled, disturbed or released, or pressure must be applied, in order to make the bomb function. The trick is not in the complexity of the device, but in the ingenuity with which it is placed. The terrorists will either aim to catch out their victims in the routine performance of their everyday actions, or will entice them into performing a specific action. The most common type of booby trap, which falls into the first category, is the 'under vehicle (UV) IED'. All the terrorist has to do is watch and wait. Once he has identified the intended target's car and established his or her pattern of behaviour, he simply inserts the device and allows the victim to do the rest. Of course, one might assume that people who suspect that they might be a terrorist target would check their vehicle thoroughly before entering it. Not so. Time after time, members of the Security Forces in Northern Ireland have been caught out. The reasons are understandable: 'It won't happen to me'; 'I didn't have time'; 'It would give my cover away if somebody saw me checking'. Such excuses led to the deaths of forty-eight members of the Security Forces and thirty-one civilians in incidents involving booby-trapped vehicles between 1969 and 2000.

Frequently, the innocent casualties have been the result of the wrong person getting into the car. A typical case occurred on 8 November 1981, when 17-year-old Trevor Foster, who was only just learning to drive, offered to put his father's car away in the garage. Unfortunately, as a part-time member of the UDR, his father had come to the attention of the IRA, who had placed an 8lb IED under the vehicle. As the car nudged forward, it exploded, killing the teenager instantly in the driveway of the family home at Ballymoran just outside Armagh city.

On other occasions the civilians have been wives or children accompanying the terrorists' real target – but then, as we have seen, innocent collateral casualties are irrelevant when it comes to spreading terror. A typical example was the death of James Sefton and his wife, Ellen, on 6 June 1990. As a retired officer in the RUC Reserve, he would always remain on the IRA hit list – despite the fact that he had reached 65 years of age. The device placed under their car exploded as they drove past a primary school near their home in North Belfast. Both were killed.

But some civilian casualties are quite deliberate. No matter how much terrorists might like to claim that they are fighting a legitimate war, and dress themselves up with all the trappings of a real army, their true colours will always show through when it comes to their casual disregard of the Laws of Armed Conflict. The death of Mrs Rosemary Nelson on 15 March 1999 is a good example. As a leading human-rights lawyer, she had seriously upset the Loyalist terror group, the Red Hand Commandos. Her 'crime' was to bring complaints against the RUC for their treatment of Catholics, particularly those living in the Portadown area. When terrorists commit a crime against the state in a democratic country, they are generally locked up. However, when somebody crosses a terrorist organisation, the only sentence available is death. And that was the punishment meted out to Rosemary Nelson. As she drove away from her home in Lurgan, an under-car booby trap functioned, inflicting fatal wounds. Despite her terrible injuries, she survived the journey to hospital, but sadly died within a few hours.

The statistics show that almost half of all the booby traps that have killed people, whether civilian or military, during the Troubles have been placed in or under cars. However, these require little imagination on the part of the bomber. It is when the terrorist tries to kill somebody away from a car that he must use maximum cunning and ingenuity. The rash of Castlerobins in late 1971 was deliberately aimed at killing an ATO (see Chapter Two). The IRA had observed operators moving devices as they cut into them, and decided to take advantage of this weakness in procedure. After the death of Captain Stewardson, ATOs approached unexploded IEDs with far more caution.

An early tactic for catching out the Security Forces was to set up booby traps in unoccupied or derelict houses. These would often attract Army patrols because of the suspicion that weapons had been stashed inside. With experience, the Army learnt that all derelicts should be treated with extreme caution, and that any search of such buildings should be mapped out well in advance and conducted as a 'planned operation'. But the lesson came hard.

The first soldiers to die in these circumstances were Sergeant Major Arthur McMillan, Sergeant Ian Mutch and Lance-Corporal Colin Leslie, all of the 1st Battalion, the Gordon Highlanders. They were killed and four other soldiers injured on 18 June 1972, when they went to search a house at Bleary, near Lurgan. Later in the year, on 15 October, Colour Sergeant John Morrell of the Staffordshire Regiment was fatally injured in similar circumstances, dying in hospital ten days later. Realising the potential of this form of attack, the IRA repeated the tactic in late November. By this time, the Army should have known better and, indeed, lives would have been saved if only the correct procedures had been followed.

On 18 November 1972 an anonymous telephone call was made to the RUC Station at Newtownhamilton. The caller stated that he had observed suspicious activity in the vicinity of a derelict farmhouse near the village of Cullyhannah in Co. Armagh. The alarm bells should have started to ring immediately. Who was this caller? What was his motivation in telephoning the police? Were the Security Forces deliberately being lured into a place of the terrorists' choosing?

The following day, an Army patrol from the Argyll and Sutherland Highlanders descended on the house. With the help of arms and explosives search dogs, they discovered some rounds of ammunition and a rifle butt. The circumstances were now starting to look distinctly risky, so the patrol commander decided to back off from the house and put in a request for an

ATO. The request was passed through to the Lurgan Section of 321 EOD Unit, but, by that time, the afternoon was drawing on and the light was starting to fail. Not surprisingly, the Lurgan ATO decided that the sensible course of action would be to stake out the house for a further night, rather than trying to play 'find the booby trap' by torchlight. The patrol therefore went firm, and prepared for a long, cold night in the field.

By eight o'clock the next morning there was still no sign of the ATO, and the troops on the ground were starting to get impatient. A discussion ensued between the two senior soldiers present, Captain William Watson, 28, and Sergeant James Strothers, 31. Shortly after eight o'clock, with the ATO still en route, the two entered the house, with a view to lifting any arms and ammunition concealed inside. Within seconds of stepping inside, they were dead. A massive explosion destroyed the farmhouse, killing the two soldiers instantly.

Amazingly, these were not to be the last deaths to be caused by booby traps planted within vacant or derelict houses. On 8 March 1973 Corporal Joseph Leaghy of the Royal Hampshires died after being fatally injured in an explosion while searching a derelict building near Forkhill in South Armagh. Three months later, Corporal David Smith, Royal Welch Fusiliers, was blown up during the search of an unoccupied house in Strabane, which had already been 'cleared' by a 'sniffer' dog. Several more deaths were to follow. Only with time, and through painful experience, did the Army start to adapt to this particular threat.

Once it became apparent that the Security Forces were approaching the likely sites of weapon hides more cautiously, the IRA moved to booby-trapping the actual weapons themselves. In concept, this was only one step beyond the well-tried practice of concealing an anti-handling mechanism within an apparently straightforward IED, such as those that had killed ATO Captains David Stewardson and John Young. As with all terrorist techniques, the bombers were to score a number of successes before Army and police tactics changed in response.

The first successful use of this technique was seen on 21 November 1975. The lure, or 'come-on', on this occasion was a burning car spotted at a road junction just a mile outside Forkhill – well inside the IRA's so-called bandit country. A patrol from the 3rd Battalion, The Royal Regiment of Fusiliers, under the command of a lieutenant, approached the vehicle cautiously. Initial impressions were that an ambush had taken place, but the troops were

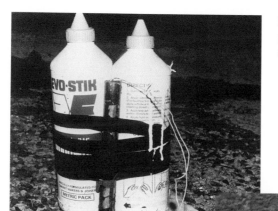

Blast incendiary. The plastic bottles contain petrol, and a pipe bomb is taped to the outside. *(N.D. Rees)*

Typical IRA timing and power unit recovered from a blast incendiary. *(DLSA Archives)*

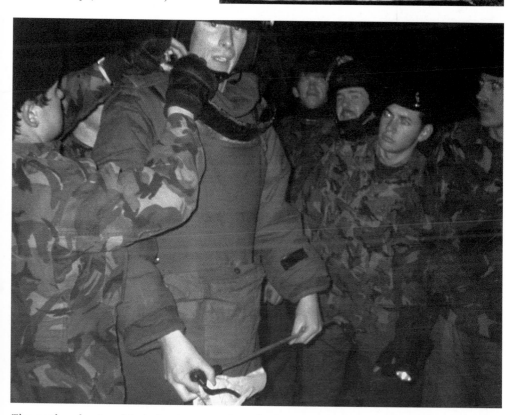

The author having his helmet strapped on by his No. 2 before taking the 'long walk'. *(S.P. Smith)*

Castlerobin Orange Hall – the site of Captain David Stewardson's death, 9 September 1971 (see Chapter Two). *(G.J. Lawrence)*

Two soldiers were killed when they entered this house near Cullyhanna, Co. Armagh, to investigate a rifle butt seen with wires leading to a fireplace, 20 November 1972 (see Chapter Five). *(G.J. Lawrence)*

Sergeant Roy Hills, seen here checking a find of home-made explosives near Newry. He was later killed while attempting to render safe a misfired IRA Mark 2 mortar bomb in Lurgan, 5 December 1972. *(G.J. Lawrence)*

Top: An operator places a small explosive charge into a suspect car to clear it of potential booby traps.
Below: Controlled explosion! No booby traps found.
Near Carrickmore, 22 August 1972.
(G.J. Lawrence)

Aftermath of the explosion at Trainor's Village Supermarket and Tyre Depot in Creggan village, which almost killed WO2 Alan Wright, 8 October 1972 (see Chapter Three). *(A.J. Wright)*

The effects of a 1,000lb horse-box bomb at Kinawley, 18 March 1979. (*P. Forshaw*)

Aftermath of the bomb explosion at the Droppin Well discothèque below the Shoppin Well Centre, Ballykelly, which killed seventeen people, 7 December 1982 (see Chapter Four). (*S.J. Clarkson*)

A controlled explosion being used on a suspect car, Londonderry, 5 July 1984. (*A.J. Hinton*)

The human cost of the terrorists' actions. *(D.S. McAdam)*

This barn was believed to contain weapons. A booby trap exploded when a suspect device was pulled by hook and line (the line is on the right of the picture). Lowe's Barn, Coalisland, 25 March 1972. *(J.M. Coldrick)*

An operator checks an arms find in Portadown, 23 November 1972. *(A.J. Wright)*

One soldier was killed and another injured in this command-wire attack near Lisnaskea, 11 April 1974. *(D.S. McAdam)*

Top: Clearance of a radio-controlled milk-churn bomb. Shortly afterwards a secondary device exploded under the churn's original location beside the road. No casualties resulted.

Below: Crater caused by the booby trap linked to the radio-controlled milk-churn bomb. Near Silverbridge, 19 October 1984 (see Chapter Five). *(F.W.R. Smith)*

Controlled explosion of a pressure-pad booby-trap device during a clearance operation near Silverbridge, 16–23 October 1984 (see Chapter Five). *(F.W.R. Smith)*

Top: An Army Saracen blown over a hedge and into a field by a 400–500lb bomb. Three soldiers were killed.
Below: The crater caused by the bomb that destroyed the Army Saracen. The Mini driver was unable to stop in time. Near Dungannon, 10 September 1972 (see Chapter Five). *(G.J. Lawrence)*

A 200lb radio-controlled device. The photograph was taken during the operator's first manual approach, while the bomb was still 'live'. Flurrybridge, 4 November 1972 (see Chapter Five). *(G.J. Lawrence)*

Two radio-controlled bombs killed eighteen soldiers at Warrenpoint, 27 August 1979 (see Chapter Five). *Top:* Shortly after the second explosion *(A.A. Burns). Below:* The aftermath of the two bombs *(P. Forshaw).*

Top: IRA Mark 10 mortars mounted
on a lorry. Used in an attack on
Rosslea RUC Station, 9 May 1981.
Inset: Close-up of IRA Mark 10
mortar tubes (see Chapter Six).
(C.M.G. Hendy)

Centre: IRA improvised projected
grenade and two launchers
(see Chapter Six). *(C.A. Storey)*

Below: IRA improvised hand grenade
(Mark 13A). *(A.J. Hinton)*

Lt-Col Derrick Patrick (right) and an operator sprint from a building that is about to explode, 1976. *(DLSA Archives)*

An operator under training dismantles a culvert bomb. *(AS of A Archives)*

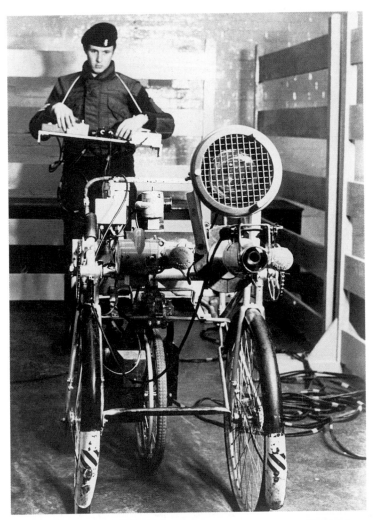

'Little Willie', the forerunner of Wheelbarrow, based around an electric wheelchair and developed by Queen's University, Belfast, December 1971 (see Chapter Two). *(R. McDermott)*

Mark 1 Wheelbarrow. *(AS of A Archives)*

Mark 2 Wheelbarrow. *(AS of A Archives)*

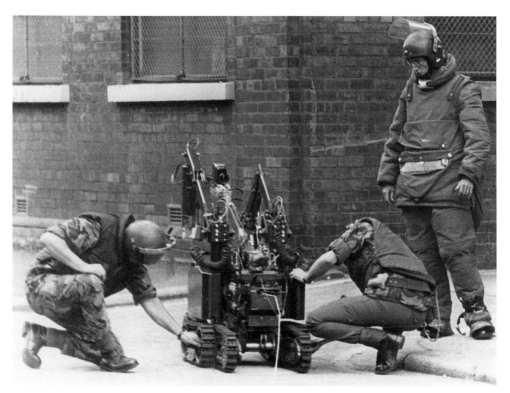

A team prepares Marauder for action on the streets of Belfast, 1977 (see Chapter Eight). *(R. Noutch)*

A car bomb explodes while Wheelbarrow is alongside. The robot was destroyed. *(P. Forshaw)*

Mark 7A
Wheelbarrow.
(P. Forshaw)

Foaming pig in
action in Belfast
city centre, 1974
(see Chapter Eight).
(N.N. Wylde)

The Mark 1 EOD
suit, 1974.
(J.M. Gaff)

The Belfast teams with a selection of their equipment, mid-1980s. *(R. Noutch)*

The Omagh team carries out a controlled explosion, 1974. *(D.S. McAdam)*

Remains of the van used to fire a Mark 15 mortar into the Crossmaglen base, 10 January 1994. The EOD operator was seriously injured by a concealed booby trap (see Chapter Ten). *(PATO Archives)*

Staff Sergeant Ron Beckett (centre) pictured shortly before his death at Tullyhommon, 30 August 1973 (see Chapter Ten). *(D.S. McAdam)*

Remains of the booby-trapped car that killed WO2 Mick O'Neill near Newry, 31 May 1981 (see Chapter Ten). *(PATO Archives)*

attuned to the possibility of being set up themselves. Some loose ammunition could be seen lying in the road. Sergeant Simon Francis picked up one of the bullets, pocketing it, before noticing a rifle discarded nearby. His last words were, 'Ah, it's a Garrand', describing the make of weapon as he stooped to lift it. The ensuing explosion killed him instantly.

As always with the IRA, once it had developed a successful method of attack, it would continue to exploit it until the Security Forces found an effective counter. Within two months, on 22 January 1973, it managed to catch two more victims, this time policemen, with a similar trick. On this occasion, yet another anonymous telephone call alerted the police to 'suspicious activity' at the back of a derelict house just off the Donegall Road in Belfast. An RUC patrol attended the scene, and discovered a shotgun, wrapped in a quilt, concealed in an outhouse. The weapon was transported to the nearby Donegall Pass RUC Station, where several policemen gathered round to watch while it was dismantled. An explosive charge of only 4oz does not sound very much, but within the close confines of the police station it was enough to kill two policemen and wound four others when the booby trap hidden in the shotgun detonated.

Lieutenant-Colonel Peter Istead (later Major-General Peter Istead OBE GM) was the Chief Ammunition Technical Officer in Northern Ireland from August 1977 to August 1978. On the subject of booby traps, he observes:

I never ceased to be amazed at the way the forces on the ground constantly fell for the same sort of trap – particularly the 'come-on'. It was a fairly regular occurrence in South Armagh and Fermanagh for a comparatively simple incident to draw in Security Forces to an ambush situation. I do not recall a body being booby trapped, but a booby trap in the vicinity, particularly at a likely incident control point, was a high probability. Just before my arrival, there had also been a shooting incident, after which the firing point had empty cases lying around. One of these cases was attached by a piece of fishing line to 15lb of explosive just under the turf. Luckily, the device failed. There were also the more obvious baited traps, such as the girlie magazine in the hedgerow, or a tricolour on a telegraph pole – in each case connected up to a device.

Just how easy it was for the terrorist to get soldiers to fall for a simple trick is brought out by the following extract from 321 EOD Unit's Log Book for

26 May 1972. It covers an incident at Lifford Bridge near Strabane, where an ATO rendered safe a booby trap IED. In the 'Remarks' column we read: 'Army torch which had been found by soldiers 4 days ago – would not work! Inside were pink gelignite, No. 6 elec [detonator] and PP3 battery. Battery was flat.' Clearly, the soldiers had retained the torch for several days, and only discovered the concealed booby trap when investigating why it would not work.

The setting of booby traps in the vicinity of dead bodies has been one of the IRA's more repugnant tricks. The first instance of this happening was in connection with the death of Corporal James Elliott, a 36-year-old member of the UDR. Having just driven his firm's lorry over the border from Eire, he was stopped by the IRA and ordered from the cab. Over the next day and a half, he was interrogated, before being executed with a shot through the back of the head. The body was then dumped in a ditch about a mile and a half from Newtownhamilton, and close to the tiny village of Altnamacken, in South Armagh.

David Barzilay was, at the time, a reporter with the *Belfast Telegraph*. News of the discovery reached the newspaper's offices 40 miles away in Belfast, and he was ordered to get down to the scene quickly to see if it was true. In his book *The British Army in Ulster, Volume 1*, he recounts what he found on the ground:

At the border I forked left and started to drive along the desolate road. It was a crisp morning and the sun was shining. I turned a sharp corner, went down a slight hill and then up an incline, round another corner and saw what I thought was a sack lying beside the road.

But it wasn't. As I drew nearer I could see the shoulders of a man sticking out of the top of the sack. His head seemed to be buried in his hands and there was a lot of blood. I drove slowly by, completely shaken. The area was absolutely quiet except for the lowing of cattle in a nearby field.

I couldn't understand why nobody was around and then I thought perhaps it was an ambush. This frightened me even more, as I thought of gunmen concealed in the undergrowth a short distance away across the border. And as I looked towards a coppice on the other side of the river, I thought I saw somebody move. I didn't once think that the body might be booby-trapped. I accelerated and drove away fast until I came to the entrance to a farm a few hundred yards off. Here I stopped and tried to collect my thoughts. Should I ring the office first? Should I go back and try to identify the body?

After a few seconds' thought, I decided to go back and have another look. I drove as fast as the winding lane allowed and passed the body at high speed. Eventually, I found a gateway, turned the car and drove back again to the body.

By this time I was feeling extremely sick and I make no excuse. I drove up to the body and stopped. But something told me not to get out and touch it. I watched for several seconds and there were no signs of life

Again I looked across the border. This time I could see no movement. But I had the uncanny feeling that I was being watched. I put it down to general nervousness. I started the car and set off back to the farm to ask if I could use the telephone.

WO2 P.H. Dandy, who at that stage was an operator with the Lurgan Section of 321 EOD Unit, was tasked to the scene. As a result of his subsequent actions, he was awarded the George Medal. The following extract from his citation describes the tense situation that he had to deal with:

On 19 April 1972, WO2 Dandy was sent to the border area of Altnamacken, County Armagh, where the body of a man had been found very close to the Eire/Northern Ireland border. WO2 Dandy well knew that this was a dangerous stretch of the Border, on which shooting and mining incidents directed at the Security Forces had occurred before. He also had good reason to believe that the body itself might be booby-trapped.

Escorted and covered by infantry soldiers, WO2 Dandy approached the body, at one time wading along a stream, which at that point was the border line. In the stream, he discovered wires leading from the Eire side of the Border. He cut the wires and followed them towards the body. The wires led first to a culvert, which, on inspection, was found to be packed with six containers of explosive and two Claymore-type anti-personnel mines. All these devices were some 70 yards from the body.

Working completely alone, in order to provide only one-man risk, WO2 Dandy defused each of these devices, which were later proved to contain a total of about 550lb of explosive. This was the biggest multiple explosive device found in Northern Ireland up to that date.

Still working entirely alone, though covered by the infantry, WO2 Dandy examined the area around the body, and the body itself, and satisfied himself that they were clear of explosives. Only when all possible safety precautions had been taken did he allow the other soldiers to approach and remove the body (which proved to be that of Corporal Elliott of the Ulster Defence Regiment).

Several days later, on 27 April, the *Belfast Telegraph* reported the incident thus:

Feeling ran high in Rathfriland last night after news of the finding of the UDR man's body, shot through the head and back and surrounded by a minefield of six Claymore devices and a huge 500lb bomb only feet from the body. Youths smashed windows in Roman Catholic premises in the town before they were dispersed by security forces. Trip-wires ran from the body to explosives and across the border to a farm building. The booby-trap was set so that the bomb would go off if the body was moved.

Sometimes, the recovery of booby-trapped dead bodies presented ATOs with some unexpected problems. The following incident describes the recovery of a body close to the Eire border in the 1980s. During the operation, a number of devices were discovered in the immediate area, including a radio-controlled IED, set to catch out the Security Forces. The events are recalled by the Team No. 2, then a corporal. The reader should note that, although the No. 2 refers to sticking a hook 'into the body', the practice was actually to insert it into the corpse's clothing in order to move the body and disturb any booby traps. Occasionally, the operator's actions might cause unavoidable damage, but every effort would be taken to minimise this, both out of respect and in order to preserve forensic evidence. Clearly, if a body had been exposed to the elements for a period of time, it would become more fragile as it started to degenerate.

Because our Incident Control Point was on the downward slope . . . and the body was on the opposite slope, towards the border (i.e. we were working over the brow of a hill), we sent Wheelbarrows over, only to find that they either broke down or that we could not stick the hook into the body. Eventually the Officer Commanding the resident unit accused us of breeding Wheelbarrows down by the body.

After four attempts with the Wheelbarrows, which included the new, remote, radio-controlled model, we decided to get the remote Eager Beaver [a radio-controlled fork-lift truck] in. But, lo and behold, its camera stopped working once alongside the body.

Eventually, it was decided to coax the Eager Beaver to stick the hook in whilst using the last remaining camera on the radio-controlled Wheelbarrow. This was successful. However, whilst we were all pulling the body over the hill using the car towrope, the hook slipped and pulled his trousers down to his ankles.

This was not the end of the incident. As we dragged the body over the hill, level with the radio-controlled IED, the head fell off. Once we'd dragged the torso back to the Incident Control Point, WO2 —— [the No. 1 operator] and I put the corpse into a body bag and had it flown out. What a bloody day!

The next day:

We arrived early on the scene (approximately 0600 hours), with Captain ——, who had come over from sleepy Lurgan. He was giving advice and expressing a wish to deal with the radio-controlled IED. My boss readily agreed, but first insisted on recovering [the victim's] head. This he does successfully, then bags it up and asks me to look after it!

On arriving back at Bessbrook with the job complete, I offered the head back to my boss, who told me to give it to the Operations Officer, or the RUC Liaison Officer, or anyone who would take it. But nobody would, as it was so late. So I put it under the bed for safe keeping while I went for something to eat.

The next morning, I tried to get rid of the head again, but to no avail. So I ambled off down to the RUC Station, and asked them to pass it on to the relevant authorities, as it had two bullets in it, which were forensic evidence (not true!). Of course, this story got blown out of all proportion, and I became known as 'Mark the Head' for the short time I had left of my tour.

The same day, Captain —— defuses the radio-controlled IED, linked to two milk churns of explosive, and grabs all the glory.

While the above description might sound insensitive, it should be taken in the context of a situation in which the IRA had deliberately set out to kill members of the EOD team as they recovered the body. Typical 'squaddie humour' often tends towards grim cynicism; under desperate circumstances it is a useful coping mechanism. During that operation, four devices were made safe in the vicinity of the deceased.

Once an ATO is out on the ground, anything might be there to catch him out: an ambush device en route, a sniper attack, a booby trap in his Incident Control Point, a pressure pad hidden under the turf as he approaches the known suspicious object – the possibilities are endless, and he must plan to counter each one. One typically tense encounter is described in the George Medal citation for Lieutenant-Colonel John Gaff, who was CATO Northern Ireland from 13 February to 1 November 1974:

One incident, which deserves special mention, took place on 21st March 1974. Lt Col Gaff was summoned to the Railway Signal House at Dunloy Halt, where three armed men had placed a bomb in the building and a second bomb on the railway track. Lt Col Gaff himself quickly defused the bomb on the railway track. However, the bomb in the Railway House proved to be more difficult to neutralise, as its exact position was not known, and it was suspected that it was booby-trapped because the terrorists had spent such a considerable amount of time in the building.

For nearly eight hours Lt Col Gaff investigated every inch of the Signal Box, despite the extreme danger involved in this activity. Finally, he noticed a small bump at the bottom of a stairwell, under a piece of linoleum, and this turned out to be the pressure switch of the booby trap. It was clearly a sensitive device, and Lt Col Gaff had to place the disruption equipment alongside the pressure switch, knowing that the slightest pressure in the wrong place would trigger the device, resulting in him being killed or badly injured.

His action proved successful, and the booby trap circuit was defused. He then searched for the main explosive charge, which he found under the stairs. It consisted of 70lb of explosives. This whole operation took nearly 15 hours, during which time Lt Col Gaff was under extreme personal danger. This successful neutralisation avoided any damage caused to the Signal Box and its equipment, and enabled an important railway line to be kept open.

Another incident at which several secondary devices had been planted with the specific aim of killing the operator, is described by former WO1 F.W.R. Smith:

On 15 October 1984, a Shell tanker full of petrol was hijacked near Silverbridge and was dumped approximately 150 metres north west of border crossing point H29(c), on the Concession Road. A phone call to the Samaritans stated that there was a bomb on the tanker.

A planned operation was initiated to clear the tanker. A reconnaissance flight was flown on 16 October and 42 Commando, Royal Marines, inserted a cordon on 17 October. The clearance started at 0730 hours on 19 October. The Royal Engineers Search Team, whilst clearing a route, eventually located a device – a radio-control pack linked to a buried milk churn beside the Concession Road. The radio-control pack was cleared and the milk churn pulled out of the ground (1728 hours). As weather was closing in and helicopter extraction was due, the churn was cleared and forensic evidence collected. Whilst clearing up, a secondary device under the original location of the milk churn exploded. The signals operator, a signals warrant officer, two infantry escorts and myself were approximately 30 metres from the device – there were no casualties.

On 20 October, we cleared the site of the explosion. The Search Team started to clear another route and found a plastic lunchbox and command wire beside the road. The lunch box, containing a timing and power unit, was cleared, and all agencies extracted.

On 21 October, the Search Team followed the command wire and located a pressure mat. I cleared the pressure mat and located explosives. It was decided to destroy in situ after taking samples. An estimated 100–200kg of home-made explosive were in the device. The agencies were then extracted again.

On 22 October, we eventually started the clearance of the tanker, which was declared clear at 1040 hours, 23 October 1984. Nothing was found on the tanker. It had been placed there to lure Security Forces into the area where booby traps had been laid.

Sadly, not all such incidents go according to plan, one former CATO recalls:

Just to show that we were not always as clever as we might have been, I will mention an incident at Forkhill. The Mark 9 mortar bomb had been used on various occasions, but we had never seen the mortar itself. The police post at Forkhill was eventually mortared, and a truck left in the village, on which the mortar tubes were mounted. Incidentally, the residents of the houses behind which the mortars were fired had 'gone shopping for the day'. There was considerable excitement at the discovery of the mortars and, by the time I arrived, the police had managed to persuade the AT concerned to let them swarm all over the vehicle, and they were preparing to take it away to Armagh. I went to the target end to look for fragments of the bomb. I then heard a loud explosion from the village.

When the police had started up the truck, a bomb was initiated which was in the wash bottle under the dashboard. To my knowledge, this was the only occasion on which the IRA had initiated a device using the electrical system of the vehicle. It is perhaps not surprising, therefore, that the AT missed it. Both the policemen survived, albeit with fairly serious injuries. The incident led to questions, including from the Cabinet Office in Whitehall. When the Chief of the General Staff visited, he questioned me about it. He asked me how the device came to have been missed. I told him, 'It was well hidden.' My respect for him was considerable when he replied, 'Oh, as simple as that.' The terrorists did, of course, catch us out about once every 18 months – nobody is perfect.

While booby traps have claimed numerous casualties, both military and civilian, over the duration of the Troubles, it is the ambush device that has been the IRA's most successful weapon against the Security Forces. In the first thirty years of the ongoing violence, 172 serving members of the Security Forces were killed by ambush bombs, compared with 98 being lost to booby traps.

The principle of the ambush device is that an explosive charge is hidden in an area that is likely to be visited by the Security Forces. The terrorist lies in wait, and detonates the device remotely when his target appears. The simplest way of doing this is by means of a command-wire IED. The command-wire IED has three main parts: the power source, the command wire (simply a length of electrical flex) and the bomb itself. Most frequently, the power source will be a 'battery pack'. This comprises several batteries linked together to provide sufficient power to send an electrical current down several hundred metres of cable and set off the explosive charge at the far end.

The first deadly use of the command-wire IED was on the Camlough Road at Derryberg, near Newry, on 6 September 1971. By later standards, it was a relatively small device – just 10–15lb – but it was still enough to blow

Trooper John Warnock of the 16th/5th Lancers off the tailboard of a passing Land Rover. He was evacuated to Daisy Hill Hospital, Newry, but died some four hours later. Two other soldiers were also seriously injured in the blast. More command-wire attacks followed thick and fast, and, within twelve months, twenty-three soldiers had been killed in this way. Although some attacks were made on soldiers on foot and in urban areas, the majority were against vehicles patrolling in the countryside. Throughout the twelve-month period, most of the deaths came in ones and twos, as individual Land Rovers, Saracen armoured cars and Ferret scout cars were attacked. The biggest toll was on 24 June 1972, when a massive double-landmine, containing 120lb of explosive, packed into milk churns, destroyed a Land Rover escorting a damaged Sioux helicopter from Ballykelly to RAF Aldergrove. Three soldiers died and three more were injured.

As the IRA grew bolder in its use of the ambush bomb, the devices started to increase in size. On 10 September 1972 a massive 400–500lb bomb was used to take out an Army Saracen armoured car near Dungannon. At that stage, it qualified as the biggest device of its type yet encountered. The Saracen was blown into the air, landing almost on its roof. Three soldiers inside died as a result of the violent concussive effects of being thrown around. The blast left a crater measuring 30 feet in diameter and 25 feet deep. Unable to stop in time, a civilian motorist following behind drove his Mini straight into the gaping hole in the road. Soldiers who witnessed the incident later recounted having seen several cars approach the scene, only to turn around and drive off without offering any assistance.

Even the EOD teams were to pay the price of being lured into the killing area of a command-wire IED. WO2 Gus Garside and his No. 2, Corporal Calvert Brown, were among a party of four soldiers involved in a rural clearance operation near Forkhill on 17 July 1975. As they crossed a gap in a hedge, a terrorist, hiding 400 yards away, pressed the button on a 70lb bomb. All four were killed.

Four years later, on 2 August 1979, two members of the Armagh Section died when their vehicle was caught by a 400lb command-wire ambush bomb hidden in a culvert. Signaller Paul Reece was the team's signals operator, and Gunner Richard Furminger was the escort. Both were only 19, and both had been in the Province for only nine days. At the time, they were part of a three-vehicle convoy that was returning from checking out a car for booby traps, in which an RUC officer had been shot dead.

The most devastating command-wire attack on the Army occurred on 20 August 1988. The 1st Battalion, The Light Infantry, was at that time based in Omagh, where it was undertaking a two-year 'resident' tour, of which it had completed eighteen months. A regular bus run had been established to pick up soldiers returning from leave at Belfast International Airport and Belfast Harbour Airport. In order to avoid being targeted, the bus drivers were under strict instructions to take routes that did not simply follow the major roads. However, this meant that the journey would take considerably longer. On this occasion, the driver had planned a route through the rural villages of Clogher and Fintona, but, for some reason, at a roundabout he diverted onto the main A5 Omagh road, which had been placed out of bounds. There is the possibility that the IRA deliberately brought about the diversion by erecting false signs, but this remains unproven. For whatever reason, the bus was now heading straight into the killing area of a command-wire IED, which had been dug in alongside the road, near Ballygawley.

From a firing point some 330 yards away, the IRA man pressed the trigger that detonated between 25 and 35lb of Semtex high explosive. The blast wave smashed into the side of the passing vehicle, demolishing the superstructure and causing it to slew across the road. Nine soldiers died, eight of them instantly. One managed to crawl several hundred yards before succumbing to his terrible wounds in a cow shed. All the dead were between 18 and 21 years old. A further nineteen were injured.

The command-wire IED has proved to be a simple and effective weapon, which remains popular with terrorist groups worldwide. Nevertheless, it does have its drawbacks. Unless well dug in or concealed, it can be spotted by the Security Forces. It takes time to lay, so the operation has to be planned well in advance, and the command wire must be put down either in a remote area where there is little danger of discovery, or under cover of darkness. Hence, it cannot be deployed quickly to take advantage of opportunity targets. Furthermore, the terrorist must remain in relatively close proximity to the device; he must therefore have a quick and well-planned escape route.

In order to overcome these difficulties, very early in the campaign, the IRA began to experiment with radio-controlled IEDs – that is, those that require no physical link, such as a command wire. Instead, the command signal to initiate the device is sent over a frequency band in the electromagnetic spectrum, using radio, microwave or light frequencies. Since a remote detonation system is no more than a form of communication link, the essential elements are a transmitter and matching receiver.

From simple beginnings, advances in technology have meant that a rapidly expanding range of options has become available to the terrorist. Early IRA radio-controlled devices exploited the sort of equipment that would normally be used to send radio signals to model cars, boats or aeroplanes. These operated on a fixed frequency basis, lacked range and were susceptible to false triggering. The terrorists have since moved through a variety of increasingly sophisticated options, including radio pagers, keyless garage-door opening devices, mobile telephones and police radar guns.

The IRA triggered its first radio-controlled IED attack on a border post at Aughnacloy on 19 January 1972. As chance would have it, the intended target was an EOD team responding to a hoax bomb call. The initial incident involved of two terrorists placing a supposed bomb at the Aughnacloy Customs Post. The hoax device consisted of an engine-oil can, filled with sawdust, sealed with plastic adhesive tape and fitted with black and yellow plastic-covered wiring. The plan was to take out the EOD team at the point when it would be dealing with the hoax. Accordingly, a stolen Mini was pre-positioned nearby. Inside was a Claymore-type mine, containing approximately 30lb of plaster gelatine and some 50lb of scrap metal to provide fragmentation. The radio-control receiver was linked to the Mini's radio aerial, and was intended to fire a commercial detonator, which was connected to the main charge by detonating cord. Luckily, the device failed to function as intended, and there were no casualties.

The initial British Army response to the new threat was typically Heath Robinson, as former Captain S.H. Scourfield-Evans recalls:

The first radio-controlled device was discovered in my area by Staff Sergeant Dedman, who was permanently detached at Enniskillen. He was called to a device that had a model aircraft radio receiver and a wound rubber band actuator! This discovery, and others like it, led to EOD sections trying to jam possible radio-controlled devices using service radios mounted in Pigs.

While the Army was doing its best, in its inimitable amateurish style, the back-room boffins were working on some form of kit that would detect the latest menace. By autumn 1972 the first version was already being deployed into the field. For security reasons, within this book I shall refer to it as 'Scanner', although that is not its real name. Hugh Heap was an ATO captain in Londonderry from September to November 1972. He remembers using an early Scanner on a task on 19 October 1972:

Based on an intelligence tip-off, Commander 8 Infantry Brigade became convinced that the IRA were to attempt to float a bomb down the Foyle in order to attack the Craigavon Bridge. As radio-controlled devices were appearing around the Province, it was considered just possible that the threat was real. So, from my limited resources, I had to deploy a team, with a [Scanner], to the bridge for 24 hours a day. On the second night, when I happened to be doing my shift, the equipment detected a signal, and we saw a tea chest, complete with wire trailing from the lid, floating towards us on the current. My orders from Brigade were that the device must not be allowed to reach the bridge, so I had previously decided that small arms fire was the best render-safe procedure.

My marksman, a Royal Horse Artillery Battery Sergeant Major, fired 15 rounds, during which the lid and aerial came off, and the trace disappeared. The tea chest floated under the bridge and, although we failed to grapple it in, I did see it was filled with bags of apparent home-made explosive. An early morning search by me in a boat, and later by Royal Navy frogmen, failed to produce any evidence, but this is recorded as a radio-controlled IED incident. I believe it was also the first success of the equipment in detecting an RCIED.

Just over two weeks later, Sergeant John Lawrence, operating out of Lurgan, was to have a face-to-face encounter with a live radio-controlled IED just north of the border with Southern Ireland, at Flurrybridge. The incident had been sparked by a report to the Garda that a large bomb, contained in two barrels, had been dug in next to a road. The informants had claimed that there was a strong smell of almonds coming from the barrels; this would indicate the presence of home-made explosives.

As soon as Sergeant Lawrence's team arrived on the ground, the Royal Signals operator set about trying to detect the presence of a radio-controlled device using Scanner. As the machine went through its paces, he would have been staring attentively at an oscilloscope, looking for one key indicator – a clear spike rising above a uniform wave pattern. On this occasion, the result was immediate and dramatic. The pattern displayed on the screen was so clear that it could have been a textbook example taken from the training manual.

As they were out in the countryside, the first solution that sprang to mind was to 'fire the device'. Early radio-controlled receivers generally incorporated a 'servomechanism'. This consisted of an arm mounted on a spindle. When a radio signal was transmitted, the spindle would rotate, causing the arm to move. In this way, it could be used for such purposes as steering a radio-controlled car. In a bomb, the arm would rotate onto a microswitch, applying sufficient pressure to close it, thereby completing the circuit and activating the device. Servomechanisms can be so sensitive, however, that, if a transmitter on the same frequency comes within range it can cause the arm to judder, potentially causing the device to detonate prematurely. This knowledge had prompted the Army to use its vehicle-mounted radio sets to try to trigger concealed devices in rural areas. With this in mind, a first attempt was made to set the bomb off. It failed. Sergeant Lawrence allowed a soak period, just in case there was a delayed response, then directed his signals operator to try again. Once more, there was no result. After four or five attempts, the signaller, a very junior soldier, was starting to lose confidence and beginning to doubt the existence of the bomb.

'It's a carrier wave, Sergeant,' he said.

'What's that?' asked Sergeant Lawrence.

'It's a wave that carries another wave,' came the helpful reply.

Sergeant Lawrence then recalls being subjected to 'some more signals mumbo jumbo', before allowing himself to become convinced that this was indeed a spurious signal, and that they were dealing with a hoax. Some considerable time had now passed since they had arrived, so the only thing left was to walk down and have a look. Taking his camera and a hook and line, Sergeant Lawrence set off towards the area of the suspect device. With the target area overlooked by sloping ground to the south of the border, Lawrence could see a small group of people in civilian clothes observing his movements. On reaching the spot, he looked down from the road to see that the earth had been dug away. Two barrels, standing upright, side by side, stared back at him. Clearly visible on top was a Cordtex link, along with what appeared to be a radio-control mechanism. The spot reeked of almonds.

Several actions might have been open to him at this point. The one that most operators might have taken would have been to bolt back to the Incident Control Point like a frightened rabbit. John Lawrence did something that, to this day he cannot explain: standing over a massive device that could have been detonated at any time . . . he took a photograph. After that, he immediately rendered the device safe by hand. The main charge consisted of 200lb of 'Co-op' home-made explosive.

In presenting the photograph to the unit's chain of command, he resorted to a small white lie. Rather than admit that he had acted like a tourist in the face of such overwhelming danger, he explained that he had taken the device apart, then, once it was safe, he had reassembled parts of it for the benefit of the camera. In his words: 'If I hadn't done that, I would have got the most almighty bollocking.'

Despite the Army's newly developed ability to detect radio-controlled IEDs, the IRA continued to have occasional successes with the technique throughout the 1970s. However, the unreliability of the modeller's radio-control kits meant that the simple but reliable command-wire IED remained the preferred ambush weapon for most of the decade. With improving technology, use of the radio-controlled IEDs started to creep up again from the late-1970s onwards. The most notable success ever scored by the IRA using this form of attack came on 27 August 1979. The place was Narrow Water, on the edge of Carlingford Lough. In the history of the Troubles, it is more infamously known as Warrenpoint.

During the lead-up to the Warrenpoint attack, the summer of 1979 was already proving to be a hot one for the Security Forces in terms of radio-controlled devices. On 3 June two policemen were killed when a 200lb IRA bomb exploded at Clonalig, near Silverbridge, in South Armagh. The device, contained in a milk churn, detonated at 9.05 p.m., after a day-long planned operation in the area. One month later, 19-year-old Private John McMillan of the 1st Battalion, The Queen's Own Highlanders, was fatally injured when a device went off behind the door of a house in the village square at Crossmaglen.

On 27 August 1979 a small military convoy was making its way from one Army barracks at Ballykinler to another at Newry. The convoy consisted of two 4-ton trucks, led by a Land Rover. The troops on board came from A Company of the 2nd Battalion, The Parachute Regiment. The journey was obviously one that had become predictable, because, on this occasion, an IRA hit team was lying in wait. At Narrow Water, the convoy was just accelerating into a stretch of dual carriageway, with Carlingford Lough and the border with the Irish Republic on its left. As the trucks drew level with the ancient edifice of Narrow Water Castle, the terrorists on the far side of the Lough transmitted the attack signal. The receiver was wired in to an 800lb bomb, hidden in a trailer by the side of the road, and concealed under bales of straw. The rear vehicle in the convoy was passing the trailer as the device detonated.

The vehicle was instantly ripped apart by the explosion, with what remained of the chassis careering across the road. It is believed that six paratroopers were killed in this initial blast, and several more were seriously injured. From across the southern side of the border, IRA gunmen immediately opened up, and the paratroopers responded, during which a civilian holidaymaker was killed in the crossfire. A patrol from the Royal Marines in the near vicinity heard the sounds of gunfire and radioed in for assistance. As fire was exchanged, the Quick Reaction Force from the nearest Army battalion, the Queen's Own Highlanders, was crashed out to race to the scene. The Commanding Officer of the Battalion, Lieutenant-Colonel David Blair, took the decision to deploy personally onto the ground by light 'Gazelle' helicopter.

Over the next half-hour, two helicopters, the Gazelle and a troop-carrying Wessex, and several Land Rovers, arrived at the scene. The paratroopers had by now taken up defensive positions alongside the gates and wall of Narrow Water Castle. Lieutenant-Colonel Blair moved to join them there, along with his radio operator, Lance-Corporal Victor McLeod, in order to link up with the Officer Commanding A Company, Major Peter Fursman. Well versed in the Army's tactics, the IRA had already predicted the likely response. Hidden beside the castle's gates was a second radio-controlled device – it was another 800-pounder.

The Wessex helicopter had been loaded with the casualties from the first explosion, and was just taking off, when the terrorists transmitted the second attack signal. The resulting explosion caused immediate devastation. Twelve more soldiers died in the blast, including Lieutenant-Colonel Blair, who was so close to the device that he was effectively vaporised.

Eighteen soldiers died that day, and several more were very seriously injured – one lost his left eye and others suffered amputations. More British soldiers were killed in this one incident than in any other during the history of the Troubles. It served to prove the efficacy of the radio-controlled bomb as an ideal ambush weapon, and the 1980s and 1990s were to see the technique used increasingly as more sophisticated hardware became available.

Before leaving this chapter, we should look at one last type of ambush weapon, which, after a only couple of appearances, passed into obscurity. That said, its novelty value alone makes it worthy of mention. It is the 'projectile command IED'.

At about 5.30 p.m. on 26 April 1983 two masked and armed men burst into a family home in West Belfast. They demanded the keys to the red Renault van parked outside. Two of the men then stayed with the family while the third man drove the van away.

Some twenty minutes later, this same van, along with another one, a blue Ford, was stopped by police manning a vehicle checkpoint on the Falls Road. They had both been heading in the direction of the city centre. On seeing the checkpoint, the drivers abandoned their vehicles and ran off. After a quick look at the vans, the police requested the assistance of an ATO.

The operator who attended the scene was Captain Gary O'Sullivan. He spent the next couple of hours going over the suspect vehicles with a fine-tooth comb. In the Renault, the only suspicious item was a hand-held radio. The Ford yielded a much greater prize. Stashed in the back was a 45-gallon oil drum, containing a main charge of approximately 500lb of home-made explosive, and two black plastic bags, which together held a 5lb 'booster' charge. Along with the usual other bomb components, such as the timing and power unit, detonators and detonating cord, there were some most unusual items.

Captain O'Sullivan extracted two plywood boards, each about a metre square, which had been bolted together to form a sandwich. The inside face of each board was covered with a copper sheet, and one of those sheets was itself covered with a layer of tracing paper. Three wooden battens at the centre of the sandwich kept the metal plates from touching. A length of electrical wire had been soldered to each copper plate. The intention was obvious. The boards would be wired up to the rest of the device and placed in the back of the van, positioned along one of its internal walls. The timing and power unit would give the terrorist the opportunity to get clear before the bomb became 'armed'. On the outside of the van, a marker of some sort, such as a large trade sticker, would mark the position of the boards in the back. From some distance away, a sniper, armed with a high-velocity rifle, would take up position overlooking the van. As the first Army patrol walked past the vehicle, the sniper would squeeze off his shot. The round would smash through the side of the van and into the boards. As it ripped through the two copper sheets, it would distort them, causing them to touch, thereby completing the circuit and allowing the device to initiate.

It seemed like the perfect ambush weapon. With no physical link between the terrorist and the device, it would be impossible to detect. The firer could be several hundred yards away and therefore well sited to make his getaway. The size of the boards meant that he did not even need to be a particularly good shot in order to guarantee a hit. Whatever the target was on this occasion, the device was well put together, and it would almost certainly have functioned as intended.

The same could not be said of a similar device which turned up in a 'find' several weeks later. In the second instance, it almost seemed as if the individual who had put it together had been working off a set of instructions passed badly over the telephone. Whoever it was clearly did not have the faintest idea about electricity, because, rather than separating the copper plates with the wooden battens, the plates were actually touching, with the battens stuck on the outside. Had the terrorist connected the device up, the circuit would have been completed immediately, and the bomb would have functioned there and then. For whatever reason, that was the last appearance of the projectile command IED, and it was never used in anger thereafter.

As the seventies wore on and the terrorist campaign continued into the eighties, the IRA gradually reduced its no-warning attacks on the innocent civilian population, and began to concentrate on its all-out war with the Security Forces. For this, as well the booby traps and ambush bombs described in this chapter, it required a whole range of 'prestige' weapons, both factory built and home-made, which had the potential to wreak death and destruction on a massive scale. These would also demand the attention of the operators of 321 EOD Unit.

SIX

DO-IT-YOURSELF PROJECTS

The greatest loss of police lives in a single incident over the period 1969–2000 was caused by an IRA improvised weapon. The IRA's Mark 10 mortar bomb looked like an ugly black torpedo. Over a metre long and 16cm in diameter, it was fabricated from an oxyacetylene gas cylinder, containing some 45lb of explosive. The propellant was black powder – a mix of potassium nitrate and sulphur – packed around a flash bulb. When an electric current from a firing box caused the bulb to flash, it ignited the propellant. The resultant high-velocity gases were sufficient to hurl the missile with its deadly payload over a range of around 200 metres. It was designed to explode on impact. The launch tubes, frequently mounted in multiples in order to send a wave of bombs crashing down around the target, would be fixed within a frame made of box tubing or angle iron, and bolted or welded to a solid steel 'base plate'. This would then be positioned aboard some type of vehicle.

At around 1 p.m. on 28 February 1985 a red Ford flatbed truck was hijacked by two gunmen in Drumackavall, near Crossmaglen. Throughout the afternoon, IRA engineers worked on the stolen vehicle. By the early evening, it was fitted out ready for action, with nine Mark 10 mortar tubes bolted to the back, concealed beneath a plastic tarpaulin and surrounded by wooden pallets. Shortly after 6 p.m., the truck reappeared in Newry, where it burst through locked gates barring access to waste ground off Monaghan Street. The driver, his identity concealed by a Ronald Reagan mask, lined the mortars up to fire at the town's Corry Road RUC Station nearly 200 metres away. A tall radio mast within the base, surmounted by a red light, served as his aiming point. Once he was happy with the launching position, he quickly and quietly made his escape.

At 6.37 p.m. the tubes began to fire in quick succession, launching the bombs in a ripple over the rooftops of neighbouring houses. Eight bombs overshot the target, with two of them failing to detonate. The only bomb to land within the perimeter came crashing down through the roof of the flimsy Portakabin canteen building, where it exploded on impact. Those inside had no time to take cover. Nine police officers, two of them women, died, and several others were injured. One of the dead was Chief Inspector Alex Donaldson, the brother of Constable Sam Donaldson, who had been killed by a booby-trapped car near Crossmaglen in August 1970 – one of the first policemen to die in the present Troubles. Twenty-five civilians were also injured in the attack. For some thirteen years the IRA had worked to develop a weapon that could project a lethal blow from a distance. With the Newry attack, their patience had finally paid off.

Most terrorist organisations rely on sympathetic foreign governments to provide their weaponry. This was most obviously the case during the Cold War years, when the United States, the Soviet Union and China vied for influence with various international insurgent groups. The Provisional IRA has always been different in this respect. Although it is true that thousands of weapons have been procured from external sources, ranging from Libya to the United States, the organisation has continually sought to develop and refine its own manufacturing capability. From simple petrol bombs, the armoury of improvised weapons grew to include home-made mortars, anti-armour projectiles and improvised hand grenades. Indeed, the Provisionals' expertise in this area has never been equalled, either by the Protestant paramilitaries or by other breakaway Republican groups.

The 'Engineering Department', which developed as part of the IRA's General Headquarters element, became responsible for the design and production of home-made weapons. From the outset, it operated mainly within the Republic of Ireland and border areas, where it could count on greater security and freedom of movement. Although a loosely defined structure could be identified, it would be more accurate to think of it as a series of small, close-knit, groups of individuals, brought together through contacts in academic institutions, local IRA cells and prison. Many of those who became involved in the Engineering Department would never play a direct part in actual terrorist attacks. Often, they would not even be known to the Active Service Units they supported. In some cases, their identities were further protected by not taking up formal IRA membership. By distancing themselves from overt terrorism in this way, they could disguise their activities as being for legitimate commercial or domestic purposes, and thus avoid coming to the attention of the Security Forces.

Two subdisciplines arose within the Engineering Department: 'Heavy Engineering' and 'Electronics' (although the groupings were so loose that these definitions were assigned by the Security Forces in an attempt to clarify the organisational structure, rather than by the IRA itself). The 'Heavy Engineering Group' became responsible for the design and manufacture of actual weapons, such as mortars, anti-armour projectiles and grenades. As far as possible, the engineers would try to use simple components that were conducive to mass production, employing the standard tools and machinery available to garages or light industrial units. Whenever more complex components were required, they would be obtained commercially, using some artificial but plausible pretext. The 'Electronics Group' became responsible for the production of the initiation systems used to set off explosive devices, such as timer mechanisms and radio-control components.

In development terms, the road to Newry had been a long one. As early as 1972, the IRA had shown enthusiasm for manufacturing some form of stand-off weapon that could deliver a lethal blow into a designated killing area from a concealed or protected position. Such a weapon would allow rapid strikes to be made against static Army and RUC bases, with a good chance of making a clean getaway. The obvious choice was to create a home-made mortar. A mortar is basically a smoothbore launch tube, which lobs a bomb in a high trajectory towards its target, usually over comparatively short ranges. Accuracy is generally imprecise, although it is good enough for hitting an area target.

The first IRA mortar was fired in anger in May 1972. The bomb was constructed from a simple copper pipe, 50mm in diameter, which could carry 10oz of plastic explosive. Plugged into the tail section was a cartridge from a .303 inch rifle. With the launch tube braced against the ground by hand, a trigger was pulled, firing the cartridge, and sending the bomb flying over several hundred metres towards its target. On impact, a pointed steel striker, housed in the bomb's nose, was driven into a second, smaller, rifle cartridge – this time a .22 inch, the size used for indoor target shooting. This in turn set off a detonator, which initiated the main explosive charge.

A new improvised design, the Mark 2, made its appearance a few months later, on 5 December 1972, when a wave of attacks took place across the Province. Just after 6 p.m., an explosion rocked the front sangar of the Bligh's Lane Army post in Londonderry. Following the attack, an ATO was tasked to recover a further eight bombs, which had failed to explode. At around the same time, the Green Jackets came under attack, with mortars firing from three positions at their base in Killrea. Two bombs landed short and a third landed in the television room without inflicting any casualties. At ten past six, there was an attack on the home of Headquarters 3 Infantry Brigade at Kitchen Hill in Lurgan. A single mortar tube was aimed at the base and two bombs launched, but a third projectile misfired and was left hanging out of the barrel. Sadly, within two hours, this same bomb was to kill Sergeant Roy Hills, the AT tasked to defuse it (see Chapter Three).

The Mark 2 used the cartridge from a 12-bore shotgun as its means of propulsion. It was notable for having a built-in five-second delay between impact and detonation, so that the bomb could penetrate the roof of a target before exploding in the room below. As a result of the sudden appearance of this very real threat in such well-coordinated attacks, the Londonderry Section ATO, Captain J.J. Gordon, was tasked to advise on defensive countermeasures. The favoured solution was to construct some protective screens to catch the incoming bombs. Bizarrely, the trials involved Gordon being strapped to the outside of a helicopter and, in his words, 'dropping weighted "mortars" onto various materials from 100 to 200 feet'.

Despite early technical hitches and a failure to inflict the hoped-for devastating casualties, the IRA continued with the concept of improvised mortars. As with so many of the organisation's weapon developments, it is hardly surprising that such experiments resulted in an early 'own goal'. The Mark 3 design was an inherently volatile and unstable weapon, which used home-made explosives to provide both the propellant and the 5lb main charge. In 1973 it had already been used without mishap to attack the bases at Creggan Camp, Londonderry, and Lisanelly Barracks, Omagh. However, a later attack on Pomeroy RUC Station in Co. Tyrone, on 16 August that year, went badly wrong. A lorry stacked with hay bales had been used to drive the launcher into position. Once it was lined up with the target, IRA men Patrick Quinn, 16, and Daniel McAnallen, 27, began dropping mortar bombs into the launch tube on the back of the truck. Two had already been fired successfully when the third detonated in the barrel, ripping the tube apart. Five pounds of explosive going off in close proximity to the human body is sufficient to cause death through the overpressure alone. With steel fragments from the shattered launch tube scything through the air at the same time, the two did not stand a chance. Despite damage to the vehicle, it could still be driven, so the surviving members of the team headed off towards the border. Along the route, they abandoned the bodies by the side of the Dungannon-to-Ballygawley road, covering them with a sheet. At three o'clock in the morning, a Dungannon priest was awoken by an anonymous telephone caller, telling him the location of the corpses, which were later discovered by some labourers on their way to work. The truck was abandoned at a quarry at Ballynahaye, some 3 miles from where the bodies had been left. Its windows had been blown out in the blast, and the hay on the back was soaked in blood. Tellingly, a further twenty-five improvised mortar bombs, along with a revolver and various types of small-arms ammunition, were found with the lorry.

By February 1974 the IRA's engineers had corrected the design faults that had led to the own goal at Pomeroy. The result was the Mark 4 mortar, which could attain a maximum range of around 400 metres, bettering its predecessor by more than 100 metres. The only documented occasion on which it was used was in an attack on a base at Strabane on 22 February 1974. In May, a raid on an IRA arms factory at Cushendall, Co. Antrim, led to the discovery of a completely new mortar, the Mark 5, although this version was never used operationally.

It was with the emergence of the Mark 6 that the IRA finally found what it was looking for: a military-style mortar that was safe to use, reliable, and that could be deployed quickly and recovered after use. The design appears to have been based on the standard 60mm mortar then in service with the US Army. The warhead of the Mark 6 projectile consisted of a length of steel pipe, 65mm in diameter and some 160mm long. It was therefore about the size of an aerosol can, and contained just over half a pound of home-made explosive. In later versions, this would be replaced by Semtex. It was designed to explode on impact. Extending from the warhead was a tail unit – a much narrower steel pipe, with four stabilising fins welded onto the bottom. This contained the propellant charge of black powder – a mix of potassium nitrate and sulphur – and a .22-inch blank firing cartridge to set it off. The system was operated in typical military fashion, with the bomb being dropped, tail first, into the muzzle of the launcher by hand. As the bomb hit the bottom of the tube, the rifle cartridge housed in the tail unit would impact on a fixed firing pin (essentially just a spike). The resultant flash would set off the propellant charge, which would launch the bomb up to 1,000 metres.

The first use of the Mark 6 mortar was on 28 September 1974, when the IRA used a number of single-tube launchers to fire thirty rounds over some

300 metres at an Army observation post at Drumackavall, near Crossmaglen. Twenty-three rounds exploded, including one direct hit on the roof of the observation post. While the single-tube launchers were designed to be portable, and therefore capable of being removed after the attack, later models incorporated several tubes mounted side-by-side on the same base plate. Rather than being hand fed, these would be driven into position, already loaded, on the back of a truck or trailer, and then initiated electrically, by timer, command wire or radio control. The advantage of this tactic was that the firer could distance himself from the weapon before it fired, thereby getting a head start on making his escape. It also positioned him well clear of any possible premature explosion, such as that experienced in the Pomeroy incident that had caused two IRA deaths.

In 1972 Major George Styles had been awarded the George Cross for leading the fight against the Castlerobin booby-trap devices. Seventeen years later, the second George Cross to be won by a member of 321 EOD went to WO1 Barry Johnson for his tremendous courage in tackling six live Mark 6 bombs. It was not to be without significant personal cost.

On 7 October 1989 a van containing six IRA Mark 6 mortar tubes had been abandoned in the middle of the Waterside housing estate in Londonderry, very close to a hospital. The intended target was a Security Force base, but, for some reason, the weapon failed to fire. WO1 Johnson was therefore left with the task of trying to make safe the six live bombs that were still lying dormant in their launch tubes. Most IRA mortars are fired in rural or semi-rural locations. This was different. Any carelessness on the part of WO1 Johnson could send one or more of the bombs hurtling towards the target. As the Mark 6 system possessed only rudimentary accuracy, this would also endanger any civilians still in the danger area, particularly those in the hospital. Assessing that Wheelbarrow would lack the precision to guarantee completely safe neutralisation, WO1 Johnson set about removing the bombs so that he could dismantle them by hand. While doing this, he would have been fully aware that the firing tubes might yet be wired into a concealed timer, and that they could fire at any time. He would also have known that the IRA had a history of booby trapping its mortar-firing platforms.

Assisted by his No. 2, WO1 Johnson very carefully shifted the firing tubes from the back of the van and placed them on the ground, facing well away from the hospital. Having ordered his No. 2 to return to cover, he then began the physically arduous, yet precarious, task of removing the bombs from their tubes one by one and dismantling them. By this time, it was dark, and an icy cold, finger-numbing drizzle had commenced.

With five mortar bombs lying dismantled on the ground, WO1 Johnson turned his attention to the sixth. As he worked on it, it suddenly exploded. The force of the blast blew him across the road, and several high-velocity fragments hit him in the face, blinding him. Despite the size of the explosion, he was still alive, albeit in great pain. Although the six bombs were no longer a threat, WO1 Johnson knew that the task was far from complete – there still remained the very real threat of a secondary device somewhere aboard the van or connected to the mortar tubes. It was obvious that another ATO would have to be tasked to the scene to take over from him. WO1 Johnson therefore insisted on briefing his No. 2 on the precise state of play before allowing himself to be evacuated.

Although WO1 Johnson suffered serious injuries to his face and legs, and lost the sight in one eye, he was not completely blinded. After months in hospital, during which he underwent numerous operations, he was able to return to Army duty.

As the IRA continued to perfect the improvised mortar, it became necessary for the Security Forces to enhance their base defences. This, in turn, drove the terrorists to seek a design that could drop a much greater explosive charge onto the target. Throughout the late 1970s, the IRA produced ever larger models of mortar. The Mark 7 and Mark 8 were effectively just longer versions of the Mark 6 bomb, but proved so unstable in flight that many failed to detonate on impact. The Mark 9 deviated significantly from this standard design, the bomb being built around a cut-down gas cylinder in a radical attempt to increase the explosive payload. During its first appearance, on 23 October 1976, ten bombs were fired from an array of launchers against the Army base in Crossmaglen. All the bombs exploded, with seven penetrating the target area. Even so, nobody was killed. The fact therefore remained that, over the period 1973–8, the IRA had made seventy-one mortar attacks against the Security Forces, and the only death had been that of Sergeant Roy Hills as he was trying to defuse a misfired bomb.

This changed with the advent of the Mark 10, which could hurl an evil-looking, metre-long projectile over 200 metres to deliver a devastating punch with its 45lb payload. It was to be this weapon that would cause the nine police deaths at Newry in 1985, described at the beginning of this chapter.

The Mark 10 mortar was first seen in an attack on RUC Newtownhamilton on 19 March 1979. Nine bombs were fired at one-second intervals, using an electronic timer, which activated just ninety seconds after the terrorists had leapt from the mortar truck. A tenth bomb was set to explode on the lorry thirty minutes later, with the aim of catching out any troops involved in the follow-up. It would also destroy potentially incriminating forensic evidence. Private Leslie Woolmore of The Queen's Regiment, who was 21, was killed in the attack, with four other soldiers, two policemen and two female civilians being injured. Launched from a truck parked approximately 100 metres from the base, the bombs caused considerable damage to nearby houses, a hotel, shops and a bookmaker's. The hotel suffered a direct hit, and rescuers had to use their bare hands to dig out the owner's 82-year-old mother.

The IRA experimented with a wide range of vehicles for mounting the Mark 10 mortar – from a twin tube in an estate car, to eighteen tubes on a flatbed lorry. In rural areas they were often mounted on hay wagons and tractor trailers. However, the most common options were Transit or HiAce vans, or small box lorries, with the mortars firing through a hole cut in the roof, camouflaged by spray-painted cardboard and adhesive tape. Once the launch tubes and frames were complete, and the bombs installed, the whole assembly could be fitted to the vehicle, wired up and prepared for deployment within an hour.

Martin Medcalf was a captain running one of the Belfast teams in 1982 when he was tasked to the scene of a Mark 10 mortar attack:

Late one evening in early 82 I had just returned to Girdwood Park Barracks from a task in Belfast city centre when I heard a series of explosions. A few minutes later we were tasked to a 'single explosion', which was actually a multiple mortar attack on Woodburn Camp, a joint Army and RUC base. Following a very quick series of questions, and having ensured that the area had been evacuated, we moved to the scene and established an Incident Control Point. Mortar attacks in the city were very rare at this time, and some effort had to be expended in securing a large area before work could commence.

The base plate, a tipper lorry with ten Mark 10 mortar tubes, was parked in a small wooded car park. It was easy to find as the cab was burning fiercely from a charge to destroy the firing pack. This had the added advantage of lighting the area nicely for observation, from which it could be seen that all of the tubes had fired. Unfortunately, the fire burnt itself out after a short period, so the vehicle still had to be cleared for booby traps.

During the reconnaissance with Wheelbarrow, it could be seen that the truck was full of rubbish and plastic barrels. I was able to remove some remotely, but eventually, the rear of the vehicle had to be opened to clear the remainder. It took three attempts to get the back open – this truck was made to last! I cleared the remainder of the rubbish, which consisted of large amounts of home-made explosive in barrels. I also confirmed that all of the tubes were empty.

I moved to the impact area and accounted for all of the bombs, less one. Fortunately, much of the camp had been abandoned some time before, and this is where most of the bombs landed. All had exploded, but what was particularly upsetting (and slightly scary) was that my old bedroom, from when I had been based in Woodburn, had been completely destroyed.

I next cleared the flight path, which was approximately 200 yards over open ground. It was in clear view of a Republican area, so I was keen to finish the task during darkness. In all this distance, there was only one obstacle – a small stream, approximately eight feet wide – and right in the centre was the mortar bomb that fell short. After some choice words, I waded in up to my waist, removed the bomb to the bank, and made it safe. The whole task took eight hours, finishing at something like seven o'clock in the morning. Tired and soaking wet, I was immediately tasked on to another incident!

Following the devastating Mark 10 mortar attack on Newry RUC Station, which had claimed nine lives, the Security Forces commenced the massive task of hardening their bases. In an enormously expensive programme, virtually every barracks and police station had to be 'mortar-proofed'. The IRA response was to strike back with bigger and better bombs. Using gas cylinders to provide the basic container, and trying to combine maximum payload with maximum range, several versions were trialled with limited success, before coming up with the optimum solution – the Mark 15, or 'Barrackbuster'. Making its first appearance in an attack on Ballygawley RUC Station on 5 December 1992, this was a truly terrifying weapon. Domestic 'Kosangas' cylinders were adapted to house around 150lb of home-made explosive, which could be hurled on an elevated trajectory over ranges between 75 and 275 metres.

The Mark 15 was used regularly throughout 1993, and into 1994 (up until a seventeen-month IRA ceasefire was agreed on 31 August), following a pattern of one or two attacks per month. Although only one death was attributed to the Mark 15, many were wounded, and the bombs inflicted extensive damage. The fatal casualty was a civilian building worker, Nigel McCollum, who was killed on 8 March 1993. He had been driving a crane to unload a portable cabin from a lorry inside the Security Force base at Keady in South Armagh when three Mark 15s were fired over the perimeter fence. He was at the centre of one of the explosions and died instantly.

Given the massive destructive payload of the Mark 15 bombs, the Security Forces were extraordinarily lucky not to suffer heavier casualties. On 9 October 1993 the IRA launched an attack against the Kilkeel base in Co. Down. Ten bombs were fired from multiple launch tubes, but only three functioned. Nevertheless, considerable damage was done to the base. Amazingly, there were no casualties, probably due to the alertness of soldiers who saw the base-plate vehicle being moved into position and sounded the alarm.

At twenty-one minutes past five on Monday, 10 January 1994, a single Mark 15 struck and destroyed the generator building inside the Crossmaglen base. It had been fired from inside a Toyota HiAce van parked up inconspicuously a short distance from the perimeter fence. The duty operator based at Bessbrook was tasked to the scene. Bad weather prevented an immediate response by helicopter, so it was not until late evening, sometime after 10 p.m., that the clearance commenced. For the next two hours, the AT worked in difficult conditions to clear the site of the explosion and the launch vehicle. By midnight, he had confirmed to his own satisfaction that the van was free from booby traps, and started to drive it into the base for subsequent forensic examination by the police. As he pulled into a predetermined parking space inside a hangar and applied the brakes, an undetected victim-operated device functioned under the bonnet. The damage to the vehicle appeared catastrophic, but, miraculously, the operator survived, although both he and a nearby soldier were seriously injured (see Chapter Ten).

Another close call with death came on 19 March 1994, when terrorists opened fire on a Lynx helicopter, which was hovering at 100 feet over the base at Crossmaglen, having just dropped off an underslung load. The projectile hit the tail of the aircraft, causing it to crash land inside the base, where it caught fire. An RUC officer on board was hit in the chest and stomach by shrapnel. Unable to get himself out of the burning wreckage, the constable was dragged clear by Corporal Wayne Cuckson, who, at the time of the attack, had been marshalling the helicopter from the ground. Cuckson was later awarded the Queen's Gallantry Medal. Eight military personnel were treated for minor injuries and smoke inhalation. Four months later, another helicopter, this time a Puma, was almost destroyed when it was hit in the tail by a Mark 15 bomb as it hovered over the base at Newtownhamilton.

The Mark 15, and variations of it, continued to be used right up to and into the new millennium. On 13 September 2000 a single bomb was fired at the RUC station in Newry Road, Armagh, from the back of a Ford transit van. On 23 January 2001, at about a quarter past midnight, another single-tube attack was launched, a single bomb being fired from the back of a blue Isuzu van into Ebrington Barracks, Londonderry. The projectile bounced off the wall of the Officers' Mess, some 40 metres away, but luckily failed to detonate. In April of the same year, a freelance journalist received a telephone call stating that a device had been abandoned in the Altmore Forest in Co. Tyrone. He drove to the forest and made a video recording of a red Toyota HiAce van, containing a single Mark 15 launch tube. He then informed the police, and a clearance operation was mounted, which resulted in the recovery of a bomb containing some 180lb of home-made explosive. As the mortar was already wired up and ready for use, the obvious deduction was that a planned attack had been abandoned at a late stage. What these attacks since 2000 show is that, whatever the Provisional IRA's public stance on decommissioning its weapons as part of the peace process, the technology has already migrated to those breakaway factions, such as the 'Real IRA', that are still prepared to wage an armed campaign.

While the mortar proved to be an immensely successful weapon for the IRA from a publicity and propaganda point of view, it had one irredeemable drawback – it was only intended to be fired against static targets. Given the extent to which the Army and RUC relied on armoured vehicles to protect their patrols, it became apparent that anti-armour weapons would be required to strike at the Security Forces on the move. Early on in the Troubles, attacks on armoured vehicles had invariably been made by using massive, command-detonated, roadside bombs – often referred to as 'landmines'. This approach had a number of disadvantages. Such large devices could not be deployed quickly to ambush an opportunity target; it would take time to put them into position, and hence the risk of being intercepted by a patrol was great. After the attack, significant quantities of forensic evidence, such as command wires and battery packs, would inevitably be left at the scene, thereby raising the likelihood of a subsequent prosecution. Furthermore, devices of the size that would be required to destroy an armoured vehicle would be too likely to cause massive, indiscriminate collateral damage and civilian casualties if deployed in an urban, rather than a rural, environment. What was needed was a shoulder-launched weapon, similar to a bazooka, that could be deployed rapidly to an ambush position, then spirited away in the confusion following the attack. The RPG-7, used by most of the world's communist-aligned armies and terrorist groups, provided the ideal answer, but such weapons could not be guaranteed in sufficient numbers. Hence, from the mid-1980s onwards, the Engineering Department began to experiment with a range of shoulder-launched missiles and off-road anti-armour projectiles.

The first shoulder-launched anti-armour weapon to emerge was the improvised projected grenade, or IPG. The grenade was very similar in general appearance to a military rifle grenade, but was fired from a rudimentary tubular launcher. The warhead contained just over a quarter of a pound of Semtex, which was set off on impact. The grenade would be loaded tail first into the launcher. A cut-down shotgun cartridge in the tail section provided the propellant to fire it. In the early models, the recoil was so violent that the firer would suffer a huge bruise on the shoulder and might even be knocked over. In order to counter this, the size of the propellant charge was reduced, but this also reduced the range of the weapon, so that most attacks were made from under 20 metres.

The IPG first came to the Security Forces' attention in February 1985. From undercover sources, it became apparent that an IRA Active Service Unit operating out of Strabane had been assigned the mission of attacking an RUC mobile patrol. It was known that improvised anti-armour weapons had been developed specifically for the task, and that small-arms fire would be used to finish off any survivors as they emerged from the vehicles. With this knowledge, various routes were placed out of bounds to mobile patrols while the SAS and elements of the RUC attempted to interdict the ambush party. This cat and mouse activity was played out over several days, eventually coming to a head on the night of 22/23 February 1985. In the early hours of 23 February, after several fruitless hours lying in ambush, five Active Service Unit members decided to abandon that night's attempt. Two began to make their way home, while the other three took the weapons and headed off to return them to their hiding place. Unknown to them, the SAS were lying in wait. As the IRA men passed within metres of the SAS observation post, still wearing their balaclavas, and carrying automatic weapons, they were engaged with 117 rounds of small-arms fire. All three were killed before they could return any shots; it was later found that two of the weapons still had their safety catches applied. In the follow-up, the first IPGs were recovered from a holdall.

The IPG did not prove to be a great success. At 10 p.m. on 6 August 1985 IRA man Charles 'Chuck' English died when one exploded as he tried to fire it at a police Land Rover in Londonderry. A second man with him, Eddie McSheffrey, was badly injured. The two were discovered later that night by the RUC when McSheffrey drove into Altnagelvin Hospital seeking treatment for himself, with English's corpse in the car beside him. Overall, the short-range, slow, unstable flight and poorly designed launcher made it unpopular with IRA operators, and it was never used in an attack after 1987.

The IPG was eventually succeeded by the Projected Recoilless Improvised Grenade, or PRIG. The PRIG was an attempt by the IRA to produce a home-made version of the military light anti-tank weapon, of which the RPG 7 is typical. The requirement was for an effective, recoilless, anti-armour weapon, which could be fired from a tubular launcher and discarded after an attack.

The warhead element of the grenade was formed from a 1lb food tin, filled with just over a pound of Semtex. Inside, the explosive was shaped in the form of a hollow cone, with the base of the cone facing the target, to produce the 'shaped charge effect'. On impact, an initiation mechanism situated in the tail of the grenade would set off the Semtex, and the cone would invert, being forged into a highly directional jet of explosive energy, capable of penetrating armour. The launcher was an open-ended length of steel tube with a trigger mounted on the outside. The propellant was housed in a small chamber situated in the centre of the tube, and was ignited electrically when the weapon was fired. The grenade was loaded into the front end of the launcher.

Part of the reason for the earlier IPG's unpopularity had been the violent recoil imparted on firing. In order to minimise the recoil effect from the PRIG, a novel but effective solution was devised. As the high-velocity gases from the burning propellant projected the missile out of the front end of the tube, a counterweight, weighing the same as the grenade, was ejected from the rear. Given that the two masses were equal, and travelling at the same speed in opposite directions, the forces would cancel each other out, and no recoil would be transmitted to the firer. The choice of counterweight could hardly be described as 'high-tech'. It consisted of two packets of digestive biscuits, wrapped in 'J-Cloths', which would break up into harmless crumbs as they were expelled.

The PRIG made its first appearance in an attack on an RUC Hotspur Land Rover in Belfast on 20 May 1991 and continued to be used sporadically throughout the 1990s and even into the twenty-first century (on 26 May 2001 a PRIG was used to attack RUC Strabane). Although very few casualties were caused by PRIG attacks, one did result in the death of Constable Johnston Beacom when his Land Rover was ambushed in the Markets area of Belfast on 17 February 1994. Two other policemen were injured in the same attack. A man delivering leaflets for the nearby St Malachy's Church was one of the first on the scene following the explosion. He described to the BBC how he entered the Land Rover and cradled PC Beacom's head while praying to Jesus, but the policeman died before an ambulance could arrive.

The year 1989 saw the emergence of a new type of anti-armour weapon. Employing the technology used in the IRA's improvised mortars, it was dubbed the 'Mark 12 mortar'. Despite its title, the Mark 12 barely qualifies for the title of 'mortar' at all. Rather than lobbing its projectile in a high arc towards the target, the weapon would be placed at the side of a road and fired horizontally into the side of a passing Army or RUC vehicle.

On 28 May 1988 the Gardai in the Republic of Ireland recovered two projectiles and a launch tube in a rural area near Multyfarnham, Co. Westmeath. A subsequent find at Coolock, Co. Dublin, on 30 June 1989, indicated that mass production of the components for the Mark 12 system had started. On 26 October 1989 the IRA mounted its first attack on a Security Force base, at Crossmaglen, injuring three soldiers.

The Mark 12 projectile was similar in general appearance to a military mortar round. It was made of welded steel sheet, being approximately 60cm long by 13cm in diameter at its widest point. The warhead contained a charge of around 5lb of Semtex, and was designed to explode on impact. It was fired from a launch tube consisting of a 1-metre length of steel tubing, and was almost certainly issued to an Active Service Unit as a complete assembly, rather than being manufactured locally. It would have come ready for firing, and could be deployed by one man. The weapon was normally used in the horizontal mode at ranges up to 20 metres, primarily against vehicles.

While the Mark 12 did cause a number of deaths, it was often unreliable, frequently failing to detonate when it hit the target. Typically, on 16 May 1990, a single tube was mounted on a mound of soil at the side of the Clogher Road, Crossowen, Co. Tyrone. It was fired by command wire at a moving RUC car, which was passing just 10 metres away. It hit the car but failed to explode. Again, on 11 July 1990, a single Mark 12 mortar was fired by command wire, from a house, at an RUC saloon car passing just 15 metres away. The launcher flew back through the house with the recoil after firing, but the warhead failed to go off despite scoring a direct hit.

However, on 1 March 1991, the terrorists got lucky. On this occasion, the first Land Rover of a two-vehicle UDR patrol was attacked as it pulled away from temporary traffic lights at roadworks on the Killyleagh Road, near the Mullaghcreevie housing estate, just outside Armagh City. The launch tube had been positioned on a mound of earth in a garden adjacent to the traffic lights, with a command wire running back through the garden. The missile slammed into the vehicle at close range, demolishing the back and blowing the roof off. One soldier, 24-year-old Private Paul Sutcliffe, died instantly, and another, Private Roger Love, died later in hospital. Two other occupants of the vehicle were injured. Later in the same year, on 2 August, three Mark 12 mortar bombs were fired simultaneously from a triple-tube base plate at a Puma helicopter unloading troops at the Newtownhamilton base helipad. Luckily, the projectiles overshot the target, two exploding 100 metres beyond the helipad. The third broke up on impact without detonating.

The Mark 12 proved to be a particularly versatile weapon, and the IRA became adept at concealing it in carefully selected ambush positions. A typically imaginative ambush occurred on 27 March 1992, in Newry. On this occasion, a Toyota Corolla was parked up, with its nose facing the kerb, on a route commonly used by RUC patrols. In its boot was a single Mark 12 mortar. Just short of midnight, a two-vehicle mobile patrol was travelling along Merchants' Quay in the town when the device was set off, hitting the second vehicle from a distance of 2 metres. The projectile was launched through a hole cut in the boot lid, which had been camouflaged by spray-painted cardboard. It was fired from the opposite side of the Newry Canal using a photographer's 'photoslave' flash initiation system (adapted so that a flashgun could set off the device from a distance). Constable Colleen McMurray died several hours after the attack in Daisy Hill Hospital, Newry, and PC Paul McShane lost both legs.

By March 1993 the Mark 12 had been superseded by an improved version, designated the Mark 16, which required only half the quantity of Semtex to achieve virtually the same target effect.

Besides the relatively sophisticated projected weapons that have been described above, right from the outset of the Troubles the IRA employed both military and home-made grenades to mount attacks on Army and RUC patrols. Although inherently short-range weapons, grenades could be lobbed unseen from behind walls or from buildings, giving the thrower the chance to make his escape. Young IRA recruits were often ordered to undertake grenade attacks as a means of proving their courage and determination.

Over the years, the IRA managed to procure some military hand grenades, of both NATO and former Warsaw Pact manufacture; however, it also developed its own improvised grenades. The simplest early form of grenade was the nail bomb – essentially a lump of commercial explosive with nails positioned around it to provide fragmentation, and set off by a length of burning 'safety fuse' and a detonator.

Simple though it was, the nail bomb could be quite deadly. The first fatality that can be attributed to it during the Troubles happened at Mackie's factory on Springfield Road on 9 August 1971. Despite the factory being situated in a Catholic area, Mackie's workforce was largely Protestant. That evening, amid scenes of violent disorder on the streets outside, some of the factory's windows were broken and a security grille wrenched off. A nail bomb came flying through one window into a room where 40-year-old William Atwell was standing. The device exploded, showering the confined space with its lethal spiked fragments. One nail penetrated Mr Atwell's head, entering his brain and killing him on the spot. The fact that somebody had died did not deter the rioters, who, as the evening wore on, made several attempts to set the factory ablaze.

Nail bombs were superseded by a range of improvised metal grenade bodies, filled with commercial or home-made explosive. The means of initiation was modelled on that used in military grenades – a safety pin would be pulled, releasing a fly-off lever, and allowing an internal, spring-loaded, striker to slam into a cartridge. The spark from the cartridge would set a fuse burning down, over several seconds, to a detonator, which would initiate the explosive filling. Variations on this theme were trialled, using an electrical means of initiation to set the fuse burning.

In 1985–6, the arrival of large quantities of Semtex from Libya enabled the IRA to develop relatively advanced models of grenade. The first of these was the Mark 14. Using the standard fly-off lever and safety-fuse method of initiation, the Mark 14 consisted of a length of steel pipe, 8.5cm long by 5cm wide, containing nineteen grooved metal fragmentation rings and about 120g of Semtex. On exploding, the grenade would throw out a considerable quantity of metal fragments from both the body and the rings over a radius of about 20 metres.

The Mark 14 grenade was used several times before an IRA man was killed in an own goal in Belfast on 2 May 1987. Finbarr 'Finn' McKenna (33) had been in the act of throwing the grenade at Springfield Road RUC Station when it exploded prematurely. A long-time IRA member, he had joined the Republican movement at the age of 15, being arrested and interned in October 1971, on his eighteenth birthday. He had been arrested a number of times since, and it was alleged that on one occasion he had been beaten by members of the Security Forces while being detained in Palace Barracks. As a result of McKenna's death, widespread deployment of the Mark 14 ceased, its last use being in an attack at Coalisland in 1989.

With access to large quantities of Semtex, the IRA also began to experiment with hand-thrown grenades designed specifically for attacks on armour. The first of these, known as the Improvised Anti-Armour Grenade (IAAG), appeared in an attack in Belfast on 17 July 1987. Luckily, it failed to function, and was recovered intact. Like the PRIG, the IAAG employed the 'shaped-charge' principle to enhance its penetrative effect. This entailed packing the explosive around a cone-shaped cavity, with the base of the cone facing towards the target. The warhead was made from a food can containing approximately 500g of Semtex, and a tail unit, which contained the initiation mechanism. To gain maximum advantage from the shaped-charge principle, it was vital that the grenade should hit the target nose first. In order to achieve this, a small drogue parachute would deploy from the tail on throwing, providing sufficient drag to ensure that the nose impacted first. The alternative was simply to drop the grenade vertically onto a passing vehicle from an overlooking building or bridge.

On 25 January 1988 an IAAG was used to attack an RUC Land Rover that was patrolling along the Falls Road, being dropped onto the vehicle from the upstairs room of a derelict house opposite the Royal Belfast Hospital for Sick Children. On detonating, the explosive jet from the grenade punched its way through the Land Rover's armour, killing 27-year-old Constable Colin Gilmore. One year later, on the evening of 29 January 1989, Constable Stephen Montgomery was killed in a similar attack at Sion Mills in Co. Tyrone. He had been sitting in a police vehicle parked outside a discothèque when the grenade was lobbed from a nearby rooftop. Another officer received serious injuries. As troops and police responded to the scene, a mob from the disco bombarded them with bottles and stones.

Despite these successes, the IAAG enjoyed only a limited period of popularity in the late 1980s to early 1990s. Confidence in the weapon must certainly have been in doubt. For example, after the Mark 2 version was deployed in May 1990, the grenade failed to function in fourteen out of twenty-two subsequent attacks. Another reason for the IAAG falling out of favour may have been that the action of throwing it could be sufficient to cause the internal striker to travel forward and hit the detonator, thus causing the grenade to explode close to the thrower. Not good for instilling user confidence!

The next development was the Mark 15 grenade, which emerged in May 1991. This was a complete departure from any previous design. Colloquially known as the 'coffee jar grenade', it comprised a glass jar containing a quantity of Semtex and an electrical circuit incorporating batteries, an electric detonator and a pressure release switch. On hitting a solid object, the jar would shatter. Without the jar to restrain it, the switch would no longer be held under pressure, so it would close, completing the circuit and initiating the device.

During the early 1990s, the Mark 15 coffee-jar grenade became the IRA's frequent weapon of choice for ambushing patrols and hitting static locations in urban areas. Between its first use in May 1991 and the ceasefire on 31 August 1994, nearly 200 were thrown Province-wide, although this caused only one Security Force fatality. This particular incident occurred at around 5.30 p.m. on 25 May 1991 at the North Howard Street Mill in Belfast. It was a sunny Sunday afternoon, and Corporal Terence O'Neill (Royal Regiment of Fusiliers), an Army dog handler, had paused in the open yard within the base to chat to another soldier. He had just come from feeding his Labrador dog at the kennels. The yard was overlooked by the adjacent Conway Street Mill, another crumbling factory building similar to that which housed the base. The throw would have been an easy lob over the wall. The grenade landed at the feet of the two soldiers, detonating on impact. Corporal

O'Neill was killed instantly, but his colleague suffered horrendous injuries to his legs. Still conscious, he began screaming at fellow soldiers to shoot him on the spot. He survived, but both his legs had to be amputated.

From 1972 onwards, the array of improvised weaponry produced by the Provisional IRA has been truly formidable. The other terrorist organisations within the Province have tried to follow suit, but with nowhere near the same degree of success. Sometimes, such weapons have cost IRA lives, generally through premature explosions resulting from failed safety mechanisms. On other occasions, the effect on the Security Forces has been devastating – such as the Mark 10 mortar attack on Newry RUC Station that claimed nine lives. But, on balance, it is apparent that the tremendous effort put in has been out of all proportion to the effect in terms of actual casualties – witness the one Army fatality resulting from over 200 Mark 15 grenade attacks. That being the case, why has the IRA persisted down this technically demanding and high-risk path? Two answers spring to mind. First is the effect on the Security Forces' morale. The fact that comparatively few fatalities have resulted from a very high number of mortar attacks may not be as important as the thought that the terrorists could reach inside a base and cause death and destruction whenever they wished. The response by the Security Forces was to spend millions of pounds on base protection measures. Secondly, real armies employ a range of weapons in aggressive attacks on their enemies. They do not just blow up civilians in shopping centres using time bombs, or wait until the enemy stumbles across one of their hidden bombs. Real armies take the war to the enemy. The ability of the IRA to demonstrate that it could utilise mortars, anti-armour weapons and grenades in offensive operations was therefore vital to its image. In short, such weapons have been as important to IRA propaganda as they have been to its offensive capability.

PART THREE

COUNTERING THE THREAT

SEVEN

SELECTION AND TRAINING

The disposal of improvised explosive devices in Northern Ireland is just one aspect of the wider trade practised by the Army's Ammunition Technical Officers and Ammunition Technicians. Indeed, it is the understanding and experience that they gain in routinely handling munitions and explosives that underpins their expertise in tackling terrorist bombs. Prior to 5 April 1993, these individuals were found within the Royal Army Ordnance Corps (RAOC), but, since the amalgamation of several corps on that date, they now wear the cap badge of the Royal Logistic Corps (RLC).

The involvement of the RAOC with ammunition stemmed from its role as the supplier to the rest of the Army. The Corps had been formed in 1896 in an attempt to improve supply processes, particularly on deployed operations. Initially, the non-commissioned ranks were enlisted into the Army Ordnance Corps (AOC), and the officers into the Army Ordnance Department (AOD). Despite the different titles, the two organisations effectively operated as a single corps.

The first real test of the new corps came with the Boer War in 1899, when over 1,000 of its men were deployed to South Africa to operate depots, containing food and ammunition, along the Army's lines of communication. With the end of the war, Ordnance personnel found themselves disposing of enormous quantities of ammunition that had deteriorated in the field and could no longer be considered safe to use. An article in the *Army Ordnance Corps Gazette* of November 1908 describes how, in 1900, shells ranging from 4.07 inch up to 9.45 inch were arranged in a demolition pit for mass destruction by guncotton charges. The pit, which was 3 miles from the town of Bloemfontein, measured 20 feet square by 20 feet deep. When detonation occurred, the resultant smoke column rose 500 feet in the air, with fragments from the explosion falling 2,000 yards away. The task described in the article was apparently by no means unusual, and the entire demolition programme extended beyond two years. At this time, the AOC employed a very limited number of 'laboratory foremen', who were the nearest thing the Army had to 'experts' in inspecting, repairing and disposing of ammunition.

During the First World War, the Army was faced with handling massive stockpiles of high-explosive ammunition, frequently in harsh conditions. Not surprisingly, serious accidents were inevitable. In March 1916, during the build-up for the Somme offensive, there was an explosion at the depot at Quevily, partially wrecking it and claiming three lives. In July of the same year, a single accurate bomb from an enemy aircraft destroyed 9,000 tons of ammunition at Audruicq, causing an oblong crater 60 feet deep. Live shells thrown clear by the explosion were found up to 2 miles away. A number of similar incidents pointed to the need for more men with appropriate training to look after such a valuable commodity. Accordingly, in 1917, ammunition schools were set up in France at Zeneghem and Blargies.

The schools in France set the pattern for the way ahead, and, in 1922, a permanent Army School of Ammunition was established alongside the Central Ammunition Depot at Bramley in Hampshire. Although initially intended to produce civilian ammunition examiners, within its first year the school switched to training the military. Both officers and soldiers attended the school, with the former originally qualifying as 'Inspecting Officers Munitions' and the latter as 'Ammunition Examiners' (the original title of 'Laboratory Foreman' having been dropped in 1923). Although the detail of the respective courses has altered over the years, the underlying theme has stayed pretty much the same. Some preliminary scientific education in explosive chemistry would be followed by instruction in the recognition, composition, construction, safe handling, inspection, repair, storage, modification and disposal of all types of UK land-service ammunition.

In 1960 the title of 'Ammunition Examiner' was dropped in favour of 'Ammunition Technician'. Meanwhile, the officers, who, since just before the Second World War, had been known as 'Inspecting Officers Ordnance', had their title changed to 'Ammunition Technical Officer'. Those who have qualified as either ATOs or ATs can be identified by a small red, black and gold flaming grenade badge worn on the right arm. The badge for soldiers is slightly larger than that for officers and is distinguished by a gold letter 'A' in its centre.

Those who apply to become ATs are among the brightest new recruits to the Army. The stipulated minimum entry standard requires civilian educational qualifications in mathematics, the sciences and English, although exceptions may be made for good-quality serving soldiers who wish to transfer into the trade. There is also a stiff selection board, designed to assess intellectual ability, motivation, mechanical reasoning and technical aptitude.

Officers who wish to become ATOs must initially pass through the Royal Military Academy Sandhurst and then be commissioned into the Royal Logistic Corps (or formerly the RAOC). They will then serve for at least two years as lieutenants in 'generalist' units within the RLC, becoming familiar with operational logistics, before being selected to attend the ATO course. As with soldier entrants to the trade, they will be expected to have educational qualifications in mathematics and the sciences, and many will have degrees in related subjects.

Once selected, both officers and soldiers will follow basic trade training along similar lines, although the officers will receive more detailed instruction in certain areas. This is principally with regard to the underpinning scientific knowledge in disciplines such as explosive chemistry, electronics, metallurgy, plastics, mathematics and ballistics. In broad terms, though, the syllabus for both will cover all aspects of ammunition: its make-up, how it works, and how to inspect, repair, store, move and dispose of it. Potential ATOs and ATs will spend considerable time out on the demolition ground, learning about the safe handling of explosives, and will also be taught how to conduct investigations into performance failures, accidents and defects.

It is only once the potential ATO or AT has gained this level of technical knowledge that he or she is ready to progress along the road to becoming a skilled counterterrorist bomb-disposal operator. As all officers emerge from the ATO course as captains, they are trained from the outset as No. 1 operators – that is, as team leaders, who will be responsible for all aspects of rendering a terrorist device safe (including undertaking 'the long walk' down to the bomb). By contrast, soldiers are trained as No. 1s only once they have attained the rank of sergeant. Therefore, while still lance-corporals or corporals, they will initially qualify only as No. 2s – learning to prepare EOD weapons for firing and driving and maintaining the Wheelbarrow robotic vehicle.

Even after an ATO or AT has gained his initial qualification as a No. 1 operator, he is still not ready to deploy to Northern Ireland. Although the earliest operators in 1969/70 had received no special training to prepare them for service in the Province, it quickly became apparent that the British

Army was facing a terrorist threat of unparalleled menace. Consequently, a 'Special to Theatre' course was put in place to train the operators in the most effective manner possible.

Not surprisingly, the early attempts were somewhat 'hit and miss'. The RAOC had to adapt its wealth of experience gained from such theatres as Cyprus, Aden and Hong Kong to face the emerging threat. This was fine in theory, but the existing procedures were geared towards combating comparatively simple devices, using the most basic EOD tools – a cumbersome portable X-ray machine, the hook and line set, wire-cutters, a Stanley knife and a limited range of demolition explosives. One operator even recalls deploying to the Province with a toolbox containing such useful items as a 'depth of cavity gauge and a stencil brush' – tools that are indispensable in an ammunition-processing laboratory, but that would prove of limited value on the streets of Belfast. Overall, there was very much a feel of learning as they went along, and trying to draw on the knowledge of those who had done it before. Former WO2 Bob Harvey comments:

> The course passed without much incident, considering the course personnel not only covered a cross-section of all ranks of the ammunition world, but at least 50 per cent had been involved in EOD/IEDD in one form or another during their long service. Thus the confrontations were dealt with as part of the debating society that the course inevitably became. Information was freely exchanged and all things new discussed, dissected and weighed for usefulness.

John Lawrence deployed to Lurgan as a sergeant No. 1 in July 1972. He describes much of the early training as being classroom based, with little attention being paid to replicating realistic situations. Students would be told to make up dummy bombs for their colleagues to take apart. The aim of the game was to build in complex traps to defeat the operator, involving 'pull', 'release', 'anti-tilt' and 'anti-intrusion' mechanisms. Students would crouch over the mock devices, using their limited tools to dismantle the 'bombs' with infinite care.

Such nerve-racking exercises are almost certainly what the general public expects most bomb-disposal training to consist of – one man hunched over a dummy bomb, snipping away with pliers as the sweat gathers on his brow. In fact, this type of training covers only a tiny element of the wide range of essential skills. During the course of an incident, an operator will have to take control of the immediate situation, question witnesses, assess the likely threats, discuss options with the Security Forces and emergency services, formulate a plan, render the device safe, then assist with the gathering of forensic evidence. The best analogy is that it is like learning to drive a car. Being able to execute a perfect gear change is a necessary skill, but in itself will not get a learner driver through the test unless it can be combined with the appropriate use of mirrors, timely signals and precise manœuvres. Also, both the car driver and the bomb-disposal operator must constantly guard against unexpected hazards. Only when the full range of skills are practised in a realistic environment will they become second nature.

The combination of skills required to make a successful EOD operator is summed up extremely well by an anonymous ATO captain in Max Arthur's book *Northern Ireland: Soldiers Talking*:

They may have a great deal of manual dexterity, or the right technological background, or they may be very good in the field as commanders, but it takes an odd, difficult-to-define mixture of qualities to find someone who's going to make a really good operator.

An ATO has got to be able to command the situation. He's going into a situation where people are already rather tense; they've found what they think is a bomb, and certainly, thinking in Northern Ireland terms, they know what that means, and they know what to expect. So when an ATO comes on the scene they think they're getting an expert. Of course, it could be the guy's first job. He's done a lot of training, but suddenly everybody is looking at him to take the lead, and say what to do next, and there are usually a lot of very experienced people on the street: RUC men who've seen it all before, firemen, and troops on the ground who've maybe had several tours there before. Therefore it does take somebody who can naturally take command of that situation and give everybody confidence in him, and the kind of decisions he's taking. Secondly, perhaps, the ability to think logically through a situation which may be constantly developing because you're getting new information all the time. You arrive at the scene of the incident absolutely cold, and you've got to find out what's going on from asking questions of people. You've got to be able to draw conclusions very coolly, and decide what to do next. You've got to be able to make decisions whilst you're talking and look confident, while actually you may have absolutely no idea! So there's a little bit of the actor required in some respects, not too much, because you naturally want somebody who does know what he's doing, and can draw logical conclusions, and then take the right course of action.

In order to stitch all of these skills together, realistic assessed tasks were soon being devised for a 'Test Week' at the end of the course. Apart from some minor variations over the years, the basic principles have remained sound and have come to be regarded as the standard for all UK-based, counterterrorist bomb-disposal courses, including that which still prepares operators for Northern Ireland. For Test Week, the operators are tested against the full range of scenarios that they are likely to face in Northern Ireland. In the early years, such exercises were conducted in disused industrial complexes and Army barracks, but in 1994 a purpose-built complex was completed. This is effectively a small town, with all the facilities to test operators in both urban and rural environments. These include various houses, shops, a bank, farm, garage and even a railway station, complete with its own train.

Once on the training area, the operators are formed into small teams, each with its own vehicle, Wheelbarrow robot and full array of EOD tools and weapons. From a central holding area, the teams are scrambled to respond to a task out on the area, with the students taking it in turns to be tested as the team No. 1. Junior NCOs (corporals and lance-corporals) attend the same course to qualify as No. 2s for Northern Ireland, as do members of the Royal Signals who have been appointed to join the bomb-disposal unit as signals operators. Both are integrated into teams alongside the No. 1s. Each candidate will be assessed over four tasks, of which he must pass at least three.

An underlying premiss is that each task must be as realistic as possible, reflecting a situation that has actually occurred in Northern Ireland. Were this not the case, then the instructors might be tempted to build in a series of increasingly complex situations over which few students could hope to triumph. Even so, the overall average pass rate rarely exceeds 50 per cent, and it is common for students to have to attempt the course more than once before they get through. Just as with the driving test, students will fail for a whole variety of reasons – inadequate questioning of witnesses, poor threat assessment, failure to anticipate secondary hazards (such as gas mains or fuel tanks), poor command and control of the incident, errors of safety, pure clumsiness, or, ultimately, getting themselves 'killed'.

In fact, in the same way that it is rare for a learner driver under test to crash the car, so it is rare for a trainee operator to commit an error of such magnitude that he loses his 'life'. But, every now and then, this inevitably happens. Small explosive simulators that produce a sharp 'crack' are used to feign devices detonating. They are wired in to the circuit in exactly the same way as a detonator would be in a real bomb. If the operator is standing alongside one when it goes off, he knows that in reality he would be dead.

A typical scenario that would catch students out with alarming regularity in the mid-1980s was the 'case of the extra shotgun cartridge'. At that time, Wheelbarrow carried a shotgun as part of its armoury of weapons. This was principally used for gaining access to a device – for example, by shooting in car windows. *In extremis*, it could also be fired into an obvious timer or battery pack in order to achieve a crude but effective means of disruption. The shotgun would always be loaded with its maximum capacity of five cartridges. After each shot, the empty cartridge case, similar in size and shape to a lipstick holder, would be ejected out of the side of the weapon and fall onto the ground.

Over a period of time, the IRA watched the ATOs establish a pattern when using the shotgun. They noticed that it was common for more than one cartridge to be fired during a single task, and, frequently, all five would be discharged. The Army had learnt through hard experience that items of military equipment should never be allowed to fall into terrorist hands in Northern Ireland, as they would often turn up again as the bait for a booby trap. Hence, at the end of each job, the operator would ensure that all the shotgun cartridges were picked up.

Using this knowledge to their advantage, the terrorists created an incident in which an obvious device was planted, partially dug in, under the surface of a recreation ground. The operator was expected to react in a standard manner and pump a couple of shotgun rounds into the area of the suspected bomb. However, this was just a lure. The terrorists had also left an empty shotgun cartridge, of the type used by the Army, nearby. Leading from it was an almost invisible fishing line, the other end of which was attached to a massive booby-trap bomb buried beneath the surface. The intention was to catch out an unwary operator who would start collecting his cartridges at the end of the task, not realising that an extra one was present. When the IRA tried this for real, the operator was too alert to be caught out by the trap. But, in the more forgiving environment of the school, the task frequently climaxed with a red-faced student standing sheepishly holding the spare cartridge case while smoke rose from the simulator that had just gone off nearby.

Often, a student's fatal error may be the result of just a moment's lapse of concentration. Up until that point, the task may have proceeded perfectly well, but then, for some inexplicable reason, the guard slips. For example, students fully understand that dealing with a bomb is like trying to feed a vicious tiger – if you do it by hand, you risk getting bitten. Nevertheless, they will frequently move suspicious objects by hand without thinking twice, when they know that they have tools to do this for them, remotely, from a safe distance.

SAS selection is extraordinarily difficult to pass because of the exceptionally high levels of fitness and general soldiering skills required. The course for EOD operators selected to go to Northern Ireland is difficult to pass because many students are unable to bring all the requisite skills together simultaneously when faced with a mock task. Irrespective of the different reasons for failure, both organisations ultimately face the same challenge. That is, they must continue to fill the operational requirement with fresh troops, while not allowing their very high standards to slip. In both cases, any drop in standards would almost certainly result in deaths.

Over the years, substantial effort has been put into ensuring the best possible pass rate on the Northern Ireland course, while in no way compromising quality. The most detailed study was carried out in 1997, when a department of the MOD specialising in the behavioural sciences was tasked to investigate and make recommendations. The study proved to be a major and complex piece of work, collecting and analysing an enormous amount of data. Numerous questionnaires were sent out to both former students and instructors. The questions ranged over such areas as the benefits of pre-course experience, the number of previous attempts a student had made, the impact of self-induced pressure, and environmental influences, such as the weather or the time of day when assessed tasks were undertaken. The relationship between No. 1s and No. 2s was also examined, to see whether a poor No. 2 would drag down a reasonable No. 1. Furthermore, students were quizzed as to whether they thought their performance was unfavourably assessed simply because they did not get on with their instructors – the 'face doesn't fit' syndrome.

The end result was a detailed and comprehensive report, but one that perhaps simply served to highlight what the practitioners had known all along – counterterrorist bomb disposal is a terribly demanding skill, and individuals will fail for a whole host of reasons. Some students will always arrive on the course rusty or inadequately prepared. Others might be inherently clumsy or careless. Some will have a comprehensive knowledge of the training manuals, but will panic so much under pressure that they simply cannot bring it all together. The No. 2 might well let down his No. 1 on a task, causing both to fail. And, ultimately, the student might simply be the victim of bad luck – darkness, tiredness, bad weather and malfunctioning equipment will all play their part. Nevertheless, the report was extremely useful in defining the precise factors that might lead to a successful result, enabling significant improvements to be put in place subsequently.

This is not the only area in which experts in the behavioural sciences have been involved with the selection of improvised explosive device disposal (IEDD) operators bound for Northern Ireland. With the casualty rate among No. 1s seeming to rise inexorably throughout 1972, it became apparent that an operator's state of mind might play a significant part in his chances of survival. Although good training and procedures might reduce the level of risk, operators would still be exposed to a high degree of stress over a sustained period. Some might simply not be able to cope with this, and should be weeded out immediately; others might react in unpredictable ways.

The stresses are easy to picture. The ATO or AT operator must undertake a tour of several months, with a single break of just a few days halfway through. He will be on call for most of that time, dealing with many and varied, life-threatening tasks. As well as being technically competent, he must be able to exert authority and command respect at the scene of an incident. He will inevitably face numerous pressures from a variety of agencies – the cordon commander will want to get his exposed troops off the ground at the earliest opportunity, while the police will want to see the traffic flowing again. He will work very much in the limelight, and may be exposed to hostile crowds, snipers or secondary devices. He will be aware that his environment is extremely hazardous, yet when taking the 'long walk' he cannot disperse the tension through vigorous physical activity. His accommodation will generally be poor, with limited recreational facilities, and no opportunity for going 'off base', except when deploying on a task. He will have subordinates to look after, and will have to do his best to instil high morale and a good team spirit. If he can, he will have to stop his mind straying to 'what if?'

Former WO2 Alan Wright describes a typical sleepless night, during which the operator battled with his own personal 'what ifs?':

Messages and reports were sometimes garbled and misleading, causing much hot air and excitement, but little action. Typical example: I was tasked to investigate the scene of an explosion on the Dungannon to Moy road, where a patrol reported wires running in all directions from a GPO manhole cover, and [therefore] a possibility of several linked devices.

As it was dark at the time, it was decided that we should rise at first light and go and see what all the fuss was about. It was readily apparent at the location that a milk churn type device had exploded, bringing down overhead telephone wires. These had been blown to the winds in several directions, and some looked as if they were coming from the GPO manhole cover. Imagination always runs riot in the hours of darkness. I must confess to a lot of anxiety and loss of sleep, which could have been prevented by a little extra care being taken by the patrol.

Sometimes, the operator has just enough information in advance of a task to let him know that he is in for something unpleasant. This will inevitably cause the level of stress to rise – even if only unconsciously – on the way to the scene. Such an occasion is described by W.B. Squires, who, as a captain, was ATO Londonderry from June to October 1973:

A bloated body was found during a helicopter reconnaissance. It was suspected of being booby-trapped. Therefore, I was tasked. I made a manual approach with my imagination running riot – thoughts of the stench and maggots crawling out of eye sockets. Great relief when I found that the 'body' was a scarecrow!

In *Northern Ireland: Soldiers Talking* by Max Arthur, an unnamed ATO major is quoted thus:

Physical manifestations of fear are very difficult to disguise. You may be a good actor, but fear grips you, and it brings out certain physical reactions which you can't hide. Shortness of breath, when it becomes difficult to actually get through a sentence of more than three words because your adrenalin is pumping so much, and you're sweating, and your hands are shaking. I've seen that in others, working as their number two, very experienced people too.

Clearly, even after passing through the rigorous training regime, not every individual possesses the ability to cope with such pressure consistently for the duration of a tour. In his book *Fetch Felix*, Lieutenant-Colonel Derrick Patrick recounts an incident that occurred shortly after the death of an operator in Omagh in 1976. In the immediate aftermath, a sergeant, already serving with 321 EOD Unit in the Province, was switched to take over the leaderless team. In due course, a permanent replacement, a staff sergeant, was flown out from England. As was usual, his first two days were spent on 'induction' at the unit's headquarters in Lisburn. Recognising the inevitable tension that would be involved in taking over from a deceased operator, during the induction phase the new staff sergeant was given every assurance that all would be well so long as he stuck to the rules. In order to boost his confidence, he was soon despatched to conduct a planned clearance operation of a suspect device that had been located in the Omagh area. With the task successfully under his belt, he was formally assigned to take command of the Omagh team. That very evening he made a phone call to the Officer Commanding 321 EOD Unit.

The conversation must have been one of the most painful to which an officer in charge of a unit can be subjected. The man on the other end of the phone broke down and confessed that he was frightened – so frightened that he could not do the job. Coming from a senior rank that was a very serious admission. But it was serious also for the troops serving in the area and for the public, too, for that matter. For the second time in a matter of days the EOD team was leaderless and the area was exposed. The OC of 321 EOD Unit had no option but to order another NCO [non-commissioned officer] to take over (the sergeant who had done such a good interim job) and to send home the staff sergeant who had cracked. In less sympathetic days, the staff sergeant might have been dealt with severely – the kindest comment from operators in Northern Ireland at the time was that he should have been court-martialled for 'cowardice in the face of the enemy'.

Someone suggested he should have been sent to a psychiatrist but we didn't have one in the Province at the time. In any case, when he saw one later, he was found to be perfectly normal, and I am pleased to say that later he returned to Northern Ireland and completed a four-month tour satisfactorily.

Very early in the Troubles, it became obvious that the pressures of conducting an EOD tour in Northern Ireland did not simply manifest themselves in the standard, recognisable symptoms of fear. The situation also seemed to breed a degree of overconfidence in some, or, certainly, a willingness to take unnecessary risks. Over 1971 and 1972, the rising death rate among operators was proving to be far higher than expected. Not only this, but the subsequent investigations into the deaths of five operators over a six-month period concluded that unaccountable human error and the disregard of basic safety procedures had played a significant part. Such errors included breaking minimum safe waiting times before walking down to a device and exposing more than one operator to a device simultaneously. Over the same period, in addition to the five deaths, a further two operators had to be released from their duties because of temporary inability to face the dangers involved.

Clearly, something had to be done. A working party was therefore set up in late 1972 to study all the factors involved in the selection, training and employment of ATOs and ATs. Stemming from the working party's recommendations, in December 1972 a series of psychometric tests was administered to operators prior to their tours. The aim was to identify those individual personality traits that might affect their performance on hazardous EOD duties. At first, only doubtful operators were referred to a psychiatrist, but, as the selection process developed, all candidates were interviewed in order to complement their test results.

During 1973 the tests were refined, and all operators were being tested before deployment as a matter of course. Potential ATOs were screened shortly before the selection process for the course began, while ATs were tested immediately before attending their training for Northern Ireland. Three tests were introduced: the Clinical Analysis Questionnaire (CAQ), the 16 Personality Factor Questionnaire (16 PF) and the Dynamic Personality Inventory (DPI). Between them, they were designed to measure ten psychological characteristics.

The CAQ consisted of questions relating to an individual's approach to life – for example, his sleeping habits, behaviour at school, attitudes to home and mistakes he had made in his life. It covered 144 statements, such as: 'I am happiest away from people', 'I feel worn out and I can't get enough rest', and 'I worry and think a lot about things that may go wrong'. The subject would be required to mark the appropriate boxes to show agreement, disagreement, or, as infrequently as possible, an indeterminate response. Also measured within the CAQ was something known as 'suicidal disgust'; clearly anyone with the faintest, even unconscious, inclination towards suicide would be ruled out immediately. The 16 PF, which was more comprehensive, dealt with intelligence and the subject's personality make-up, opinions and attitudes. Finally, the DPI was intended to measure qualities such as willingness to pay attention to detail and any unusual fascination with fire, winds and storms – the latter traits not being seen as ideal for bomb-disposal work.

From these tests it proved possible to build up, in a structured way, a good impression of the operator and his personality. That said, all such written tests are prone to two possible problems. First, the individual may be motivated to fake his responses, particularly if he feels that failure may be detrimental to his career. Secondly, the individual's self-perceptions may differ widely from those of an unbiased observer – if he deliberately tries to portray socially desirable traits, then the test results will be distorted. Therefore, in order to provide a balanced overview, on completion of the three tests, the operator would be interviewed by a psychiatrist.

The following extract, taken from a conference address given by the then Director of Army Psychiatry, Brigadier D.C.V. Stewart, in March 1977, explains in some detail what the interviewer is looking for:

Involvement in pioneering activities, such as parachuting, pot-holing, mountaineering, and so on, may reveal a man's attitude to risk taking and his ability to cope with crises or anxiety. Reaction in critical sporting or danger situations may also suggest how a man may perform in Northern Ireland. One tries to find out if the subject is patient, imaginative, whether he can take decisions (sometimes without all the information ideally required), but yet be flexible enough to change them if new information comes to hand. We look for someone who can get a grasp of the total situation, and not get over-involved with one aspect, which may lead to human error of the unawareness type. Self-confidence is important, but should not be unjustified and prevent the operator seeking advice from his superiors or listening to his colleagues. We try to discover whether the subject feels anxious, and in what sorts of situations, and whether this affects his concentration or performance. In particular, we try to find areas of vulnerability, which might show themselves when the man is tired, hungry, cold or short of sleep – or even just frightened and uncertain.

Although some questions are direct, much of the time the subject is asked to talk and think about his own personality, weaknesses and attitudes – an interview approach which is unfamiliar to them and which many find difficult. Indeed, it often leads to revelations which the subject will admit he had not intended to disclose. We look for the man who will think clearly, logically and critically at all times and under all pressures. Inspirational thinkers may prove suitable, so long as they invariably check the logic of their inspiration before acting. The interview is also concerned with medical history, any background of psychiatric illness or excessive drinking, and with certain minor conditions, such as hay fever, in which the soldier may take antihistamine tablets during the summer months, since, as you know, these drugs, and others found in proprietary cold remedies, may affect concentration and vigilance.

Although the format has been amended slightly over the years, psychometric testing of Northern Ireland IEDD operators has remained in place into the twenty-first century. The obvious question must be whether all this investment in psychometric testing really pays off. Certainly, the death rate among operators fell significantly from 1972 onwards, when testing was first instituted. Of the seventeen operator deaths in Northern Ireland during the first thirty-five years of the Troubles, eight (amounting to 47 per cent) occurred over the period 1971–2, before the tests were applied. However, this statistic should be treated with some caution, since it was towards the end of 1972 that Wheelbarrow was refined to become a highly manœuvrable and multi-capable EOD asset that could kill a bomb at a distance using a variety of weapons. From that point on, its impact in saving operator lives cannot be overstated. It might therefore be fairly argued that this development is likely to have had a far greater effect in reducing deaths than the introduction of psychometric testing.

In an effort to test the correlation between a good psychometric test result and an exceptional performance as a Northern Ireland operator, a study was carried out by R.S. Hallam, BA Ph.D., and S.J. Rachman, MA Ph.D., on behalf of the Psychology Department of the Institute of Psychiatry. Their report, *Courageous Acts or Courageous Actors?*, was published in 1980. The researchers chose to concentrate on one particular personality factor, which they deemed to be of particular significance. That was, the operator's awareness of his bodily sensations under stress, and how, if perceived, he was able to control them. In order to test this, three groups of soldiers were selected and subjected to a mild stress situation, with their reactions being closely monitored. The groups being tested consisted of former Northern Ireland operators who had won gallantry decorations, former operators who were undecorated, and a third group of less experienced soldiers.

The stress test required the subject to move a lever in the correct manner to avoid an unpleasant, but quite tolerable, electric shock. The direction in which the lever had to be moved would depend on the subject's ability to differentiate between 'high' or 'low' audio tones. The basis of the tone discrimination would become progressively more difficult, so errors would inevitably be incurred. In order to increase the level of stress, on occasions, whether the subject got the answer right or wrong, an electric shock would be unavoidable.

The major finding of the study was that the decorated operators were able to maintain a lower cardiac rate while making difficult decisions under threat of shock. The undecorated operators, in turn, maintained a lower cardiac rate than the less experienced soldiers during the difficult phases of the stress test. As a further part of the study, the CAQ test results of the three groups were compared. The main result was that the decorated operators, and George Medallists in particular (the highest gallantry award considered), were deemed to be a particularly well-adjusted and stable group. These findings were consistent with research conducted elsewhere on people who perform exceptionally well under stress. Indeed, more detailed analysis of the George Medal winners' results showed them to be happy, clear thinking, not concerned with bodily functions or health, calm in an emergency, confident, not tense or easily upset, relaxed, considerate, and involved with other people.

Certainly, these are the results that one would expect to see. However, some areas remain open to question. For example, did the George Medal holders perform particularly well because their self-esteem had been boosted immeasurably by receipt of the medal? Did they now feel that they had to live up to the perception of being 'brave'?

In the view of one former lieutenant-colonel (Hugh Heap, who had himself served twice as an operator in Northern Ireland as a captain in 1972 and 1973), confidence in the training and equipment dispels a large element of fear in the bomb-disposal operator, and this confidence increases greatly with operational experience:

I do not consider that the behaviour of an EOD operator under stress is any different from that of any other soldier on active operations. One of my own personal experiences of this is reflected in an incident in Londonderry, after midnight, when in order to get to the suspected device it was necessary to insert me into a foot patrol of the Scots Guards for movement some 300 yards through deserted back streets. My feelings were extremely fearful, as I expected an attack from one of the overlooking rooftops or windows. My fears were not relieved until I got to the scene to concentrate on the suspect device. When discussing this later with the patrol commander, a corporal, it was clear that he had no fears on the patrol but was scared stiff by the thought of dealing with a device. Four men of the Scots Guards had been killed by snipers during the preceding few weeks. The motto 'Knowledge Dispels Fear' clearly applied to both of us in our missions.

This is true of parachuting and other apparently hazardous pursuits, and it is true of IEDD operators to a certain extent. Confidence in his training and equipment and the skills he has acquired dispels a large element of fear in the IEDD operator, and this confidence increases greatly with operational experience. He will remain fearful, however, of the unknown dangers that are beyond his control in any situation, and this is supported by the fear of sniper fire by otherwise very confident operators.

Not surprisingly, there is no cut and dried answer. Psychometric testing will certainly help to weed out those who are most unsuited to counterterrorist bomb-disposal operations in a high-threat environment, but some will always slip through the net, perhaps by faking their responses. The bottom line is that, while psychometric testing will generally screen out those operators most likely to put themselves at unnecessary risk through basic errors, success, and eventual survival, will hinge on many other crucial factors. These will include the level of terrorist incidents, the actions of other troops on the ground, the ingenuity of the terrorist, the reliability of one's equipment at a critical time and, sometimes, just downright luck. Knowledge certainly does dispel fear, and, while it might be a commonly held view that bomb disposal is 'the most dangerous job in the world', that is probably not a view shared by many ATOs or ATs. A comprehensive, progressive and demanding training regime, combined with the best equipment in the field, means that few operators nowadays embark on a tour thinking that it might be a one-way ticket.

EIGHT

BRING IN THE BACK-ROOM BOYS

The first operators to find themselves dealing with terrorist bombs in Northern Ireland had to make do with the tried and trusted tools that had served ATOs for decades: the Stanley knife, a length of cord with a hook on the end and a pair of pliers. They were provided with some protective clothing, but it was rudimentary. This was all very well when trying to deal with the simple devices of the early days. The majority of bombs were reliant on a length of safety fuse burning down to a detonator. The principle was simple: if it was still burning, it was likely to go off at any minute; if not, then it had probably failed and the operator could approach it with a reasonable degree of safety. When a terrorist uses safety fuse, he is not looking for a long delay. Hence, by the time an operator has been tasked and arrived on the scene, the outcome will already have been determined.

An analysis of the statistics in the month before the death of the first ATO shows the nature of the campaign at that time. As an example, taken at random, over the forty-eight-hour period covering 10 and 11 August 1971, the operators were tasked on sixty-one occasions. Of those tasks, over half turned out to be hoaxes or false alarms. A further twenty were in response to explosions that had already happened. The remaining tasks resulted in ten bombs being rendered safe. Only one of these involved an electrical circuit (clothes peg initiated), one was a petrol bomb, and eight were blast bombs relying on a burning length of fuse to set them off. Although Constables Donaldson and Millar had been killed when opening a booby-trapped car one year earlier, booby traps were still rarely encountered. Even so, as a result of that particular incident, cars were treated with great suspicion, and it had become standard procedure for ATOs to clear them. Hence, during 10 and 11 August 1971, three cars were cleared in this way, but no booby traps were found. Given these circumstances, the operators no doubt felt reasonably confident in walking up to a suspect device with little more than a sharp knife.

However, the pattern of attacks was already changing. Following Captain David Stewardson's death on 29 September 1971, the ATOs were confronted with increasing numbers of electrically initiated devices. For example, on 2 October alone, four Castlerobin devices, with electrical circuits deliberately wired to catch out an ATO, were encountered. Battery-powered bombs opened up a whole new range of possibilities with regard to booby traps and ambush devices, and gave the terrorist much greater flexibility in terms of the degree of delay he could build in. A longer delay gave the bomber more time to get clear, which meant that he could increase the size of his devices considerably. From that point on, the car bomb was only one short step away.

The car bomb could be driven into position quickly and abandoned with its clock ticking. It would then explode, usually within the next hour, causing massive devastation. The operators needed to adapt to the new threat quickly. They had been accustomed to dealing with cars as suspicious objects that might harbour booby traps. In a potential booby-trap situation, only the carelessness of the operator will set it off. He can afford to take his time, and the early training was therefore geared towards conducting slow, methodical and extremely careful clearances. Such luxury could not be countenanced when confronted with a large, ticking time bomb, with no way of knowing how much time was left on the clock.

Back in England, staff officers working in the ATOs' parent headquarters, and the back-room boys employed within one of the MOD's experimental establishments, turned their attention to providing some sort of robotic solution to counter the new threat. One individual's interest in gardening was to provide the breakthrough.

On 8 March 1972 a meeting was held at the Fighting Vehicles Research and Development Establishment (FVRDE) at Chertsey, in Surrey, to discuss the provision of some kind of equipment for moving suspected car bombs. George Styles, the former Officer Commanding 321 EOD Unit, attended. Styles had now been promoted from major to lieutenant-colonel, and posted from Northern Ireland back to England, where he had taken up an EOD staff appointment. As a result of the meeting, Mr Dennis White, a senior engineer in FVRDE's Logistic Vehicles Branch, was given the task of coming up with a solution. Mr White's proposal involved inserting air bags on a frame under the car by remote control. The bags would then be inflated, and the car gently lifted off the road. A long tow rope would then be used to tow it to an area where the bomb would cause minimal collateral damage.

Later that same day, Lieutenant-Colonel Styles was taken aside by the Deputy Director of the Trials Wing and introduced to Peter Miller, a retired lieutenant-colonel, who was employed at the establishment as a weapons and explosives trials officer. Peter Miller was, by that time, very experienced in weapon trials. He had previously commanded the Investigation Section at the Army's Gunnery School at Lulworth, as well as the FVRDE Armament Wing at Kirkcudbright. Styles and Miller began to examine weapon-oriented solutions to the problem of lodging some form of tow hook under a car by remote control. Before he left, Styles emphasised in the strongest possible terms the urgency of the requirement.

Peter Miller went to work immediately. His first thought was that a hook should somehow be fired at the car in such a way that it would latch on. Three possible options sprang to mind: a Royal Marines cliff assault grapnel, a Royal Navy line thrower and an RNLI rocket used for launching flares. To each of these, he attached an 80-metre length of 2-inch rope, with a breaking strain of 11,000lb. He had determined that this length was adequate to protect the operator from a blast caused by 200lb of plastic explosive. On 16 March he was ready to undertake the first practical trials. They were unsuccessful.

Peter Miller had not been present at the main meeting on 8 March, so was still completely unaware that Dennis White of the Logistic Vehicles Branch had already been directed to provide a solution to the car-bomb problem. In the meantime, he launched himself at the project with immense enthusiasm, spurred on by the fact that his own father had served in the RAOC, the parent Corps of the ATOs. Despite the failure of the initial trials, he continued to worry away at the problem. Then a novel idea struck him. As a keen gardener, he had invented a labour-saving technique by modifying his Suffolk Punch lawnmower so that it could be operated by remote control.

With this in mind as the possible solution, Miller immediately took himself off to the local garden machine centre with the intention of buying a gutted lawnmower. He discussed his requirements with the sales manager, who suggested that the chassis of an electrically powered, three-wheeled wheelbarrow might be more suitable. Without hesitation, he bought one on the spot, assuming that FVRDE would pick up the bill in due course. He recalls:

At this time, the urgency was such that I did not consider following the procedure that protocol demanded and going through orthodox channels when initiating a project. I decided to depend on my initiative, without reference to anyone in authority. I expected to get retrospective assent from my superior officer, the Superintendent, Weapons Trials; he gave it unstintingly.

I designed a spring-loaded hook, capable of going under a car, and used the same sort of controls I had on my lawnmower. In fact, the mechanical performance of the wheelbarrow chassis was much the same as that of my lawnmower. I tried the equipment on a car and, after some practice, I found that a car could be hooked up by remote control and towed away at the end of a very long towrope. Although it was a crude solution, I had met Lieutenant-Colonel Styles's requirement.

The first model did indeed look like a crude solution. The short, stubby, three-wheeled vehicle, with a Heath Robinson-style hook protruding from the front, would be pointed in the direction of the car and set in motion. Thereafter, the primitive steering was by means of two long ropes attached to a tiller. The principle was the same as reins on a horse: pull one and the vehicle veered to the left; pull the other and it veered to the right.

Peter Miller invited two ATOs, a major and a captain, to view his new invention. They came on the afternoon of Maundy Thursday, 30 March 1972, after the establishment had closed for the Easter break. The previous day, Major Bernard Calladene, and a fortnight earlier, Staff Sergeant Cracknell and Sergeant Butcher, had been killed in Northern Ireland by car bombs. Both ATOs knew the deceased, and rightly considered the situation to be desperate. In their opinion, any way of beating the car bomb would be acceptable. Miller recounts:

I demonstrated my equipment, which became known as 'Wheelbarrow Mark 1'. Within the known limitations of its three-wheel configuration, it operated satisfactorily. So the ATOs who witnessed the demonstration recommended that it be sent to Northern Ireland as soon as possible. In fact, I was able to send it the same evening. That a viable equipment could be devised and developed to a state acceptable to the user in 22 days must surely constitute a record.

Within a few days of the arrival of the prototype Wheelbarrow Mark 1 in Northern Ireland, the Chief Ammunition Technical Officer (CATO),

Lieutenant-Colonel Crosby, asked for reinforcements. So I bought six wheelbarrow chassis from the Garden Machine Centre, Sunningdale. By the end of April, I had sent five more Wheelbarrows to Northern Ireland.

It was not until about mid-April that Peter Miller became aware that Dennis White was still working on a solution under the authority of a 'General Staff Operational Requirement'. Similarly, White had no idea that Miller was simultaneously involved in developing a wheeled solution. 'Had he known, he informs me, his branch would have objected in the strongest terms. After all, it was not the duty of a member of a weapons trials wing to compete with the Logistic Vehicles Branch in vehicle design!'

With the six Mark 1 Wheelbarrows already in use in Northern Ireland, Miller set about improving the design. By this stage, he had learnt about the alternative project, and had even witnessed a demonstration of the airbag equipment during its development trials. It was during those trials that he identified that the electrical controls being used on the airbag system would be ideal for the Mark 2 version of his own machine. One of the problems with the Mark 1 was that, once the hook had been embedded in the car, there was no way of detaching it remotely. Therefore, if the car blew up, the Wheelbarrow was immolated. The new electrical controls provided both a means of collapsing the hook on command, and a more reliable method of steering to replace the two long lengths of rope.

In May 1972 Mr White's airbag system and the Mark 2 Wheelbarrow were assessed by a panel of ATOs at the Army School of Ammunition at Bramley. Amazingly, neither equipment was greeted with much enthusiasm. However, it was soon realised that the Wheelbarrow could easily be adapted to perform wider tasks than just the removal of cars. On one of Miller's frequent visits to the Province, the Chief ATO told him that he wanted a means of inserting incendiary devices remotely into suspect cars. These were already being used to burn out car bombs without setting them off, but required the operator to place them by hand. Miller therefore designed a jib for Wheelbarrow. Originally, it could be adjusted to suit the estimated height of the car window only by hand in the Incident Control Point. Later designs incorporated actuators, which meant that the configuration could be adjusted remotely when the Wheelbarrow was actually at the target. In order to break the car windows to gain access, Miller produced a window-breaking gun. This was copied from a device he had made when working in Combined Operations during the Second World War to fix a limpet mine onto a wooden Rhine barge. Once inside the car, an electrical release would allow the incendiary to drop. Wheelbarrow would then withdraw and the charge would be fired.

Within weeks, the Mark 2 was sent to the section in Lurgan, where, despite its limitations, it performed well. At that point, work on the airbag solution ceased. Thereafter, Peter Miller was formally assigned to continuing his work on Wheelbarrow, in addition to his normal weapons trials commitments.

In order to give Wheelbarrow greater manœuvrability, in August 1972, a four-wheeled version was designed, and designated the Mark 3. This model had the added enhancements of a closed-circuit television camera to view a suspect device from a safe distance, and a clamp that would allow the Pigstick disrupter to be carried. An order was sent out to the Sunningdale Garden Machine Centre to build nineteen of the latest model. Former Staff Sergeant R. Noutch (No. 1, Ballykinler, July 1973–July 1974) remembers the Mark 3:

When I arrived in Ballykinler, the bombing campaign in our area of operations had only just begun. Our equipment consisted of a Land Rover and a half-ton trailer, in which we carried a four-wheeled version of Wheelbarrow. This machine was very unsophisticated, with a single upright arm upon which an actuator was bolted. The other end of the actuator was then bolted to a horizontal arm. Different angles of attack were possible by a colour coding system on the holes of the vertical and horizontal arms. The machine worked well, but would often fall over if it came into contact with the edge of the pavement. Things improved as the number of IED incidents increased.

With each successive design, the user's expectations grew. Now the operators wanted something that could surmount obstacles, and Wheelbarrow Mark 3 could not even climb small steps. Undeterred, Miller simply used heavy-duty fan belts to create tracks for three of his Mark 3s. These were then labelled 'Mark 4s'. They proved to be a huge success, but all three were soon destroyed by terrorist bombs (potentially saving the lives of three operators in the process!). Additional modifications to the track geometry quickly resulted in the Mark 5. This was greeted with huge enthusiasm, and set the pattern for Wheelbarrows for years to come.

Peter Miller remained responsible for the Wheelbarrow up until March 1973. Throughout this time he went to great lengths to ensure that suggestions from the user in the field were incorporated into the machine. On one occasion, he learnt from an incident report that a Wheelbarrow had been driven into a shop to deal with a bomb, but became trapped by its control cable when the spring-loaded door slammed shut behind it. In trying to manœuvre within the shop, Pigstick was knocked out of alignment, and was therefore unable to engage the device. The bomb eventually detonated, destroying the Wheelbarrow.

This incident gave rise to three new ancillary devices: radio control to overcome the problem of a trapped cable, a new Pigstick clamp, based on an 81mm mortar bipod clamp, and a gun designed to fire a masonry nail into the ground or floor to act as a doorstop. This gun was copied from one designed to fire a blob of paint from a Nimrod aircraft to mark the position of touchdown.

In this way, over time, Wheelbarrow was equipped with a portfolio of weapons and tools, which either came off the shelf or were devised or designed specifically to meet the latest requirement. Wheelbarrow was a godsend. From the moment it entered service, ATO casualties dropped markedly.

Although Peter Miller played an enormous part in the development of the early Wheelbarrows, there was another civilian employee at the Research Establishment whose name was to become inextricably linked with the machine. Such was his involvement that he is still virtually revered by ATOs of a certain generation. That man was 'Lofty' Pattinson.

Lofty threw himself heart and soul into the Wheelbarrow project, and for years it was to dominate his life. When not conducting trials at the Military Vehicles Experimental Establishment (MVEE) – which title had replaced the Fighting Vehicles Research and Development Establishment (FVRDE) – he would be out on the streets of Northern Ireland watching his 'baby' do its stuff. Such was his immersion in the whole EOD world that he was to become the only civilian to qualify for the award of a 'Felix tie'. In 1971 'Felix' was assigned as the radio nickname for all EOD operators in Northern Ireland. As such, a logo based on the cartoon cat became the insignia for 321 EOD Unit. Over a few beers, four of the early operators had designed a tie using the logo as its basis. The tie had a green background and was embroidered with small Felix faces, interspersed with red hands of Ulster. The tradition arose that an operator would receive his tie once he had tackled his first live bomb in Northern Ireland. Gaining a Felix tie was therefore no mean achievement.

Sadly, Lofty died in 2002. His funeral was attended by a huge number of serving and former operators from the EOD community, including one who had travelled from Australia. As his coffin was lowered into the ground, a rocket flare was fired overhead. He was buried wearing his Felix tie.

Derek Pickford served as a staff sergeant operator in Belfast from July to December 1974. He recalls Lofty's early involvement:

Certainly of most significance, in my view, at the end of November [1974] Lofty Pattinson brought a Mark 6 Wheelbarrow to the Province. He took it to Lisburn for evaluation by the Headquarters. On his way back to the mainland, he called in at Albert Street Mill to await his ferry. Having time to kill, he gave us an impromptu 'look and learn' on his latest toy. He was so impressed by the comments and feedback he was getting from the users that he decided there and then to take the Wheelbarrow to each section's location for more user evaluation.

Some years later, I met Lofty again, and reminded him of this incident. I remarked how impressed I was by the spontaneity of his decision, and how I, and the other operators, had appreciated his action. In reply, he told me that he had got a slight rocket for taking the decision, but in fact it had paid off, because he went back with much useful criticism and some very good ideas which could be incorporated into the production model.

I believe many people would agree with me when I say he deserves a vote of thanks from us all.

It was during Lofty's time that trials commenced to develop a technologically superior version of Wheelbarrow. In May 1977 a prototype of the new equipment, named 'Marauder', was sent out to Northern Ireland for an eight-week trial. It was allocated to one of the Belfast teams so that it could be assessed under real conditions on the streets.

Although it shared many of Wheelbarrow's basic features, there were some significant differences. The most obvious of these was its track geometry. Whereas Wheelbarrow had just one track on each side, rather like a miniature tank, on Marauder each track was broken up into three sections. The theory was that, by changing the track configuration, the machine would be better able to climb stairs – it could virtually walk up them. Instead of a single boom for mounting weapons, Marauder had two separately controlled arms. One could be used for carrying the shotgun and disrupters, while the other was equipped with an advanced gripper hand that would, for example, facilitate the opening of car doors.

During the trial, Marauder was used on 113 bomb-disposal tasks. It was good, but it was also complex, heavy and expensive. For the price of a single Marauder, one could buy four Wheelbarrows, and rarely could it successfully conduct a task that would defeat Wheelbarrow. The control box was not popular with the No. 2s, being unwieldy and complicated to use. Former WO1 R.N. Blakely was an operator during the trials. He remembers Lofty Pattinson's enthusiasm for Marauder:

> During the Marauder trial, a certain Mr 'Lofty' Pattinson was present as one of the experts/evaluators. One bright morning we were called to a suspect car on the Lisburn Road, which appeared to have a tilt device attached to the underside. 'Just the job for Marauder,' cries Lofty.
>
> I then became the token ATO while Lofty demonstrated the amazing machine. Unfortunately, Lofty's driving was a little haphazard, and he rammed the side of the car (a new Mercedes estate). The car was written off by the resulting explosion, and the Marauder retired to the REME workshops for repairs for the next 24 hours.

With the demise of Marauder, more effort was put into perfecting Wheelbarrow. Over the next few years, the operators saw the arrival of the Marks 6, 7, 8 and 8B, each being a significant improvement over its predecessor. One of the major steps forward was the addition of a radio-control facility as an alternative to cable. Either control mechanism could be employed, depending on the circumstances. For example, if the area in which a team was operating proved particularly difficult for the radio signal, it would revert to cable. Sometimes, the wrong choice was made, as recounted here by former Corporal S.R. Futcher, who served as a No. 2 in Armagh and Londonderry from April to August 1984:

> Sergeant John Horner had asked me to send the Wheelbarrow up an uncleared road to the culvert where he was working on a suspect IED, so that he could attach a pulley point to the Wheelbarrow. I set the machine on remote control and sent it forward. Unfortunately, nearby pylons affected the radio signal, and I lost the picture on my TV monitor. A few minutes later, I also started to lose control of the Wheelbarrow's

movements. Whilst I was worrying about what to do to try and regain control of the rogue machine, it had turned right on top of the culvert, and was now advancing on John Horner. Despite all of my efforts and those of a very irate John, the Wheelbarrow carried on its merry way and crashed into the culvert, dragging a clanking hook and line box down after it.

How John Horner ever managed to get out of the way of the falling Wheelbarrow in such a confined space, wearing an EOD suit, is one of life's mysteries. At the time of the incident, I was in danger of being hit about the head with a Pigstick barrel, but the rest of the team managed to calm things down. It wasn't until we had returned to Fort George and repaired the flattened Wheelbarrow that John forgave my 'little mistake'. As for the suspect IED . . . it was a hoax!

Throughout 321 EOD's history, the boffins have used the full range of their imagination, ingenuity and knowledge to produce the very best weapons and equipment for the operator in the field. Frequently, these have been the result of a 'good idea' from those on the ground. The whole range of kit covers robotic vehicles, protective suits, disruptive weapons, specialist explosive charges for cutting objects open, metal and explosives detectors, torches, radio-controlled device scanners, vehicles and tools for dealing with devices remotely – from the hook and line set to mechanical grabs. Along the way, some inventions have fared better than others. Some have been left on the design shop floor. Others have made it as far as the operational theatre, but, like Marauder, have been quickly discarded.

In the cinema, the operator seems to have much in common with a surgeon performing a particularly tricky operation. In the early days, the equipment designed for the ATO seemed to support this view. For example, he was equipped with a stethoscope to help him detect the presence of a timer and perhaps narrow down its precise location. Consideration was given to providing a range of cutting tools that would enable the operator to gain access to the bomb's electrical circuit. These varied from extremely sharp knives at the simplest end of the equipment spectrum, through to arc-welding equipment and tungsten-tipped pneumatic cutters that could bite into sheet metal. For a brief period, there was a vogue for trying to freeze the working parts of the bomb using liquefied gas. In theory, the operator could then take his time to render the device safe . . . except that he could never be quite sure that everything had seized up. All these tools relied on the operator being able to spend considerable time at the device, just like the surgeon at the operating table, whereas, quite frankly, he wants to be spending as little time there as possible. None of them stood the test of operational service.

If the operator cannot stop the device from functioning, then at least he should have some method at his disposal that minimises its effects. This was the idea behind 'Foaming Pig'. The principle was that an explosion could be muffled using aqueous foam pumped around the bomb from a container mounted on a Pig armoured vehicle. As the blast wave tried to shoot through the foam, it would burst millions of tiny bubbles, thereby losing energy as it went. In experiments, the concept worked. It was shown that a 10lb bomb in a room could be successfully contained to such an extent that, when it exploded, the windows would remain intact. Out on the streets, it was a different matter. For a start, trying to get enough foam to surround a bomb out in the open, especially on a rainy or windy day, proved immensely problematic. Moreover, if the bomb then failed to detonate, the operator was faced with an even more complex situation than that which had existed before he squirted foam all over the place. Apart from the obvious difficulty of simply trying to locate a bomb in a mountain of foam, if the Wheelbarrow was driven into it, its electrics were likely to short-circuit. Once the ATO had done his stuff, he would leave the local authorities with the residual problem of tons of foam blocking one of their streets, which could take an age to disperse.

Perhaps the most testing run-out for Foaming Pig came on an afternoon in May 1974 when a young ATO, Captain J.F.D. Serle, found himself facing the first 1,000lb home-made explosive bomb ever to be encountered in the Province. To add to his problems, the massive device was contained in a van that had been abandoned at a garage off Chichester Street in Belfast, above underground fuel tanks holding some 3,000 gallons of petrol. Captain Serle could not be sure of the size of the bomb until he had effected an entry into the van, but he could see that it was weighing down heavily on its back axle. This is always the sign that there is a large device inside. On this occasion, his initial estimate put it at 200–300lb.

Being pretty certain that the van contained a bomb that was both real and very large, Captain Serle took the decision to use Foaming Pig to minimise the effects of an explosion. The armoured vehicle was duly called forward. At this point the first problem presented itself: the position of the van in the garage, and the narrowness of the side street leading to it, meant that the 1-ton

Humber Pig could not get to within 30 feet. The situation then just grew progressively worse. Initially, the team tried pumping foam into Chichester Street, which is a wide main thoroughfare, in the hope that enough would divert into the side street to do the job. Although this worked to a limited extent, after three hours of pumping the foam had still failed to reach the van. The foam dispenser was then repositioned and the team tried again from a different angle. At last, the foam started to pile up around the vehicle.

With the entire area looking as though every bath in the vicinity had overflowed, Wheelbarrow was eventually sent into the froth, with the aim of attaching a small explosive opening charge to one of the van's front doors. It had barely disappeared from view when the power died as the battery gave out – no doubt short-circuited by the mass of wet bubbles around it. Captain Serle plunged into the slippery suds to drag the incapacitated machine out of the way so that another robot could be sent in. By this time, the mountain of foam had started to dissipate in the cool spring air, so pumping commenced again. This time, plastic bags were filled and dragged down to surround the van. At last, with the front door having been blown open, Captain Serle could get a look inside. It was immediately apparent that the back of the van was a mini-arsenal of terrorist weaponry and explosives.

Using the hook and line set to open the rear doors, the captain then commenced the time-consuming and dangerous task of extracting the deadly items one by one. First, he hauled out two sacks of explosive, to reveal a timing device containing two watches, which he neutralised. Conscious that yet more timers, or indeed booby traps, might be present, he continued the extraction task with infinite caution. As well as bags of home-made explosive, he also encountered commercial gelignite, and even improvised terrorist mortar bombs; the terrorist had clearly intended to make a big bang. With just a few bags remaining in the van, Captain Serle came across what appeared to be one final trap, when he saw wires protruding from the cache, but these proved to be bogus.

At last, after many hours on task, the captain could declare the van clear and the area safe. When the evidence was examined, it was discovered that the explosives weighed over 1,000lb, making this the largest bomb encountered in the Province up until that time. Had it exploded adjacent to the garage's petrol tanks, the devastation would have been colossal. While the foam might have assisted in mitigating the blast, it had also served to hinder the operation by slowing the procedure down, incapacitating the

Wheelbarrow, and making access to the van more difficult for the operator. This tool clearly had its limitations.

Nigel Wylde (Captain, Belfast, June to October 1974) recalls trying to use Foaming Pig on another task in Belfast:

We were given two Foaming Pigs to play with. On only one occasion did we use them together. That was outside the UUUC [United Ulster Unionist Council] offices adjacent to the Europa Hotel and Central Station, where Enoch Powell was holding a press conference announcing that he intended to stand for Parliament representing South Down. So much foam filled the streets that he had to abandon the conference. He then moved on to the Europa, but we foamed him out of there as well!

Not surprisingly, Foaming Pig enjoyed only a short operational life, before being discarded as simply not worth the trouble. It was found that trying to fill up wide city streets with foam, frequently in a stiff breeze, rarely worked well. It was a slow, drawn-out process, and required a cumbersome array of vehicle-mounted equipment to put it into effect. The idea was therefore soon shelved.

Sometimes, the very best ideas came from the operators themselves as they struggled to find better and safer methods of killing a bomb. This was how the use of a shotgun as a weapon of access and disruption had developed. However, not all 'bright ideas' proved to be successful. P.K. Snell was a young soldier working with a Royal Engineers Search Team in the Armagh region during the summer of 1973 when he observed one ATO's bright idea in practice:

The most notable incident during this tour was the stopping of a mail train from Eire which had what appeared to be three milk churns placed in the cab with Cordtex running outside and hanging down towards the track. The operator was as reluctant to approach the device as we were, and decided to try to sever the explosive link by remote means – a 7.62mm high velocity round from a Self Loading Rifle! A suitable volunteer was found from among the infantry cordon troops. He hit the Cordtex on his ninth shot. The resulting explosion took out the diesel fuel tanks and caused large pieces of locomotive to become airborne. The tracks buckled and the wheels were forced down between them.

What was clear about the development of equipment in the early days was the ad hoc, incremental way in which it was brought in. As a WO2, J.F. Woodward served at several locations in the Armagh region over July to November 1974. He comments:

> With regard to new equipment, one tends to remember this as a gradual improvement as a result of operator requirement, dictated by the variety of tasks, rather than the sudden introduction of an entirely new concept. The early fish hooks and twine developed into the 'Allen Hook and Line Set'. The early 'Gamma Bomb' and wet developing X-ray system became the current 'Inspector' lightweight X-ray machine. The early Pigstick, which also necessitated the carrying of two heavy sandbags, was replaced by the current lightweight Pigstick. And, then, of course, there was the Wheelbarrow.
>
> Undoubtedly, the most significant in terms of life saving were the Pigstick and the Wheelbarrow. For the development of the Wheelbarrow, we shall be eternally grateful to Lofty Pattinson, who, in his desire to improve the lot of the operator, probably spent more time on the streets of Belfast than any other operator, and even passed a 'Pre-Ops' course in 1975.

Since 2000 the EOD community has adopted a whole new approach to the procurement of its equipment. The various evolutions of the bombing campaign in Northern Ireland took the Army by surprise, hence equipment developed in reaction to the latest menace. Consequently, responses were frequently rushed, sporadic and on the hoof. Often the results were quite excellent, but it was a trial-and-error process with many failures along the way. After over thirty years of experience, and with every sign of the worldwide terrorist threat growing rather than receding, it was decided that the preferred approach should be to look in advance at how future bomb technology might develop and predict the best methods of countering it. Although it might not be possible to second-guess every possible option, this process would encourage more cohesive and proactive solutions. In future, therefore, new weapons and equipment should be designed and produced as part of a technologically advanced modular system, in which every piece plays its part.

NINE

ON TOUR

O nce an operator has passed his selection and training, his arrival on tour is usually only weeks, if not days, away. Although the early operators took the ferry across from Liverpool to Northern Ireland, frequently driving their own military vehicles laden with equipment, it has long since been routine to arrive by air. My own arrival in theatre is probably typical of most.

I started my first tour of Northern Ireland in December 1983, and I will admit I was scared. I was being detached from a unit in Germany, and Christmas was rapidly approaching. We were based on the outskirts of a small country town, about an hour's drive south from the big British military troop concentrations at Münster and Osnabruck, and the local town centre had already started to sprout a Christmas market. Amid the laughter, jollity, *Glühwein* and Christmas decorations, it seemed almost incredible that, within days, I would be entering a high-risk theatre of operations. Suddenly, the scenery around me seemed so much more beautiful than ever before – there was the gnawing fear that I might never see it again.

The night before deployment, I packed two suitcases and left them on my bed in the Officers' Mess, before going down to the bar to sink a few final pints. When I returned to my room later, I found that one of my friends had slipped into the room in my absence and popped a *Mayfair* magazine into one of the suitcases. Attached to it was a 'Post-It' note, with the scribbled advice 'Keep your head down'. I resolved to do just that.

My diary of the time contains the following entry for Monday 5 December 1983:

Well, last night it really started to sink in. Everyone was being really nice to me. John [a senior major in his fifties, living in the Officers' Mess] came out with the stunning comment: 'Yes, I will have a drink with you, Steve, as it's your *last* one here.' I thought I'd sleep well, but, having gone to bed at 1230, I was still awake at 2 o'clock in the morning. It seemed that I woke up every hour on the hour until 0530, when I just lay there, waiting.

At 8 a.m. the Commanding Officer's personal staff car pulled up at the mess. It was a nice gesture on his part to ensure that I would be conveyed to the military airport at Gütersloh in style. I sat in the departures lounge, my emotions a mixture of excited anticipation, apprehension and sorrow at leaving familiar surroundings at Christmas. Within thirty minutes, my reverie was broken by the sight of Staff Sergeant Bastable arriving at the lounge and saying his goodbyes to his wife and children. Only a year before, he had been one of my instructors on the ATO course. For the entire month of November, we had shared the delights of the pre-operational Northern Ireland course, and now, here we both were, ready to fly out. Spotting me, he made his way across. I felt sorry for him leaving his family at Christmas, and the fact that he seemed to be in good humour regardless soon caused my own spirits to lift.

We flew out in a Hercules transport aircraft, courtesy of the Royal Air Force. Hardly luxurious, these are the sort of aeroplanes that are used to drop paratroopers. There were few windows, the lighting was murky, and the seats were arranged lengthways along the sides and down the centre. The lavatory consisted of little more than a bucket behind a curtain screen. Conversation was limited – not because we had nothing to say, but because the sound of the engines was so loud that all passengers had to wear foam earplugs throughout the flight.

As we flew in for the final approach to Belfast, I managed to get a glimpse out of the porthole-style window. It was already dark, and the city seemed to stretch out for miles below me. With only three teams to cover Belfast, I immediately assumed that we would be constantly on the go, racing from bomb to bomb for the entire tour. I also assumed that the IRA would take advantage of the run-up to Christmas to inflict some major devastation. In short, I was anticipating a pretty hot time.

We landed at Aldergrove airport. Then, as now, the airport was divided into separate civilian and military sectors. We disembarked and were shown towards some stark Nissen-style huts. It was cold, dark and spitting with rain, and at any moment, I expected mortar rounds to come crashing down onto the tarmac all around us. Once inside, we queued against a long counter for a cursory check by Customs. My suitcases were opened. 'Staying for a while, are we sir?' was the question. 'The usual,' I replied.

I was glad that I had arrived by military aircraft. I had heard stories from the 1970s of individuals turning up on the ferry and waiting about anxiously outside the port to be picked up. As a sergeant operator deploying to the Province for the first time in 1972, John Lawrence recalls: 'I went out to Northern Ireland on the normal civvy ferry. I was as nervous as hell. As far as I was concerned, everyone else on board was an IRA terrorist. I was sure they would spot me by my accent. I had no idea what would happen at the other end, or who would be meeting me.'

By contrast, at least I was safe in a military enclave. Almost immediately, two individuals made their way forward to greet Staff Sergeant Bastable and myself. In their early twenties, with close-cropped hair, they were obviously 'junior ranks' – corporals or privates. As we made our way outside to the car, I wondered which one had the gun. The drive from the airport to Headquarters Northern Ireland at Lisburn takes about thirty minutes. It is across relatively benign countryside. But, racing down the rural roads at night, I began to wonder about the possibility of running into an IRA illegal roadblock, and became even more concerned about my own lack of a weapon.

I would be staying at Lisburn for two days for 'Induction', after which I would join my team in Belfast. I was first shown to my room in the Officers' Mess Annexe – a typically functional 1970s building with lots of glass windows and paper-thin walls. In the corridor, I bumped into an old friend from my very first posting in the Army, Lieutenant Tim Woodman, who was now serving a two-year tour in the Province. He greeted me with: 'Well, blow me down, what are you doing here?' As Tim was in the Royal Corps of Transport, I knew that, almost by definition, he would be doing a rather safer job than the one that I was about to undertake. So, with far more nonchalant bravado than I really felt, I replied, 'Oh, I'm the new ATO.' Tim's jaw dropped. 'Blimey,' he said, 'rather you than me!'

With Tim's reassuring words echoing in my ears, I dumped my suitcases and made my way up to the Mess bar. It was crowded. I slipped up to the counter and ordered a pint. Within minutes I had been spotted by two experienced ATO captains, Alex and Jim, who, despite my relatively junior status, recognised me as a fellow member of the 'community'. They had both completed operational tours some time previously, and were now using their

ATO skills and experience in specialist appointments, Alex being the ATO attached to 22 SAS and Jim being with the Weapons Intelligence Section. Feeling sorry for the newest arrival, they took me under their wing and proceeded to feed me pints, pointing out that these would be the last I would be having for some time.

Within half an hour, I noticed an urbane-looking, silver-haired man in a light grey suit come sauntering in. He quickly gained a small audience and started to produce a collection of black-and-white photographs. 'You'd better come and meet the Colonel – he's 'Top Cat' – the Chief ATO,' said Jim, and ushered me across into the presence. The Colonel greeted me airily; my arrival was clearly nothing special. 'Hi,' he said. 'I've just got these photos back from a job. Ulster Polytechnic. They blew up a classroom of policemen last month. Two dead. See that on the back of the chair. That's brains.'

'Mmm,' I thought, 'I hope mine don't end up like that.' With a 'See you tomorrow then', the Colonel turned away.

'I think we'd better take you down town,' said Jim. I hesitated for about one nano-second. In the lead-up to the tour, I had faithfully promised all those dear to me that I would never go outside an Army base unless it was in the performance of my duties. I certainly would not be going into any pubs. My resolve had lasted all of two hours, and in no time we were heading out to a pub in nearby Hillsborough, with me again wondering who, if anyone, was carrying the gun.

The next two days were interesting enough. Staff Sergeant Bastable and I found ourselves being briefed by every agency that had a connection with our business. We had intelligence and operations briefs in Headquarters Northern Ireland, and met the watchkeepers who would be sending us out to our tasks. We were introduced to the RUC, who showed us their extensive collection of captured weapons, and to the staff of the Northern Ireland Forensic Science Labs. The briefings were hugely beneficial in bringing me up to date, but to my mind they served a more practical purpose – so long as I was safe in a building being briefed, I was not out on the streets being blown up!

Not every operator had the luxury of taking his time to settle in. Just over a year before my own arrival, in October 1982, Staff Sergeant P.T. Myring had flown in at very short notice to be the operator in Magherafelt. He soon found himself out on the ground: 'I may hold the record for being the fastest tasked operator in the Province. Upon arrival, I was driven to Magherafelt, via

Lisburn (for a quick briefing), and was tasked upon arrival at base, still in civvies and carrying my suitcases. The operator I was replacing had been flown home a few days previously with a flea in his ear. Also, this first task turned out to be a booby trap IED.'

While Myring's experience might have been somewhat startling, it was not typical of that of most operators. Myring was taking over an empty slot from an operator who had been sacked. It was far more usual for the new arrival to spend a few days with his predecessor, getting to know the team and the 'patch'. There is much to learn during this time, and the new operator's mind is inevitably buzzing with questions. Who makes up his team, and how long have they been in post? How many devices have there been recently, and where have they been planted? Which infantry units are operating within the local area? What communications are there? Where is all the team's equipment housed and how is it maintained? What is the team's daily routine and how are administrative responsibilities divided up? Who are the local personalities in the chain of command? As the operator being replaced drives out of the camp gates for the last time, his successor will still be thinking up more questions.

Over and above the endless questions, every brand-new operator inevitably harbours a wish that he will get a chance to see his predecessor out on a task during the handover/takeover period. The pre-deployment training will certainly have been as realistic as possible, but there is no substitute for seeing how things really happen 'out on the ground'. Suddenly, one is confronted with an array of characters and situations that have been only 'notional' in training: police inspectors, fire chiefs, infantry company commanders, cordon troops, crowds of spectators, the media, rush-hour traffic being brought to a halt, and so on.

I did not have the luxury of having a spectator's seat at somebody else's job. Two days passed with nothing happening, and then my predecessor wished me luck and departed for the airport. Two more days dragged past, and still the patch remained quiet . . . although apprehension was my constant companion. By mid-afternoon on Day Four I had just started to relax when news began to filter in of a 'thousand-pound vehicle bomb' in Belfast city centre. For an hour, I paced about in our small Operations Room with my heart racing, waiting for the tasking message to come in. The team members could barely contain their enthusiasm. 'Wow, sir, a thousand-pounder for your first job! Wouldn't that be great?' 'Mmm . . . yes,' I replied rather less enthusiastically. Then we got the word that it had all been a hoax and that we should stand down. I tried to disguise my immense relief.

But it had to happen sooner or later, and one morning I was woken by a phone call from the Brigade Watchkeeper to give me advance warning that there had been an explosion in the city centre, and that we were about to be tasked. There was no time to get nervous. By the time I had donned my flak jacket, pistol and helmet, the tasking message was already coming in. Then it was into the armoured vehicles for the race into town, sirens wailing and blue lights flashing.

It was 17 December 1983, and there had been an explosion at one of the entrance gates into Belfast city centre. By this stage of the Troubles vehicular access into the central shopping area was strictly limited, and the entire area was surrounded by a series of security fences. By nightfall most of the pedestrian gates were locked shut, and not opened until the next morning at seven o'clock. Predictable timings always make the terrorist's job easier when it comes to selecting potential victims, and, on this occasion, it had been a patrol from the UDR that had been the intended target. They had been moving down to open the gates situated alongside the Hercules Bar, and were about 100 metres away when the device exploded.

I arrived, and tried my best to look confident in front of the police inspector who was running the incident. My problem was that the device had all the appearances of being command detonated by the terrorist lying in wait, rather than being a time bomb. After all, it seemed quite likely that the bomber had simply pushed the button too early on an ambush device. This meant that there might well be a command wire, which would have to be recovered. The standing operating procedures dictated that it was not my job to go blundering about in the rubble looking for a command wire, which might have a booby trap concealed somewhere along its length; that was the task of a Royal Engineers Search Team (REST). With my mind made up, I called for the REST to be tasked.

Some ten minutes later, I was facing an experienced Royal Engineers sergeant, who, as the Search Adviser, was the leader of the REST. 'What have you called us out for then, sir?' he asked in a slightly challenging tone. I explained my predicament. 'Well, that's the first time a REST has ever been called out in the city for something like that.' He knew I was new.

In the manner of building workers who have been told to knock down a wall they have just put up and re-erect it 2 yards away, the REST carried out a

360-degree sweep of the area. As the Search Adviser had predicted, there was no command wire, and it had almost certainly been a time bomb. Never mind, at least I had completed my first task, nobody had died, and we were back inside the barracks for breakfast. With the first job under my belt, my confidence got an immediate boost. This was not so hard after all. It was just like training, and, so long as I stuck to the rules, everything would be all right.

While the constant nagging threat of death or injury never quite leaves the back of one's mind, it can be eclipsed on a day-to-day basis by the simple fear of 'getting it wrong'. For example, any failure to comply with mandatory standing operating procedures, if discovered, will inevitably lead to a swift verbal reprimand from the Senior ATO, if not an early flight home. If one takes an unnecessarily long time to deal with a device, it will expose the cordon troops to greater danger, and therefore attract harsh criticism. At worst, one might have declared the area safe, only to find that there is still a further, concealed, live device *in situ*.

Frank Steer, who, as a captain, was a Lurgan operator over the period February to May 1971, recalls an incident that befell one of his sergeants, where he certainly thought that he had 'got it wrong':

One amusing incident involved Sergeant Sanders, who was doing a car clearance in Newry. In those days, it was necessary to search the car doing as little damage as possible and, at the end of the exercise, to hand the owner back his keys, should he be there to accept them, using the words: 'In my opinion the car has been cleared, and there are no explosive devices in it.' This Sanders did, after an operation which typically took some three to four hours. As he drove out of Newry, less than two minutes after having left the scene of the incident, there was an enormous explosion. As you can imagine, he went absolutely white, certain that he had made a hash of it, and that the owner of the car, whose keys he had recently returned to him, was at that moment in a state of acute distress. Imagine his relief when he returned to the scene of the incident to find that in fact the explosion had come from a time bomb, which had been in a bank some 300 yards from where the car search had taken place.

One embarrassing incident, where the operator inadvertently got it wrong, was witnessed by Corporal Tepielow, the Armagh team's signals operator from June to December 1979:

We were called to a butcher's shop in Keady market square, where a suspicious parcel had been left on the counter. The shop itself, plus the immediate scene, had been evacuated. Sergeant Jim Collins decided to send in the Wheelbarrow and use the shotgun to dislodge and disrupt any device that might be in the parcel. Four rounds were fired into the package, knocking it off the counter onto the floor, with no obvious ill effects. The Wheelbarrow was then reversed out of the shop onto the square. At this point, Corporal Nick Dawson, the No. 2, pointed out that there was still a cartridge in the shotgun, and that it would have to be fired off for safety reasons. The butcher was called forward and the problem explained. He gave his permission for the Wheelbarrow to go back into the shop to fire the remaining cartridge. We allowed the butcher to watch the events on the remote TV monitor. Back in the shop, the parcel was relocated and the button pressed to fire the shotgun. There followed a huge explosion and the butcher's shop virtually disappeared. As the butcher stood open-mouthed all we could do was offer our apologies . . . and a claim form.

Although most operators quickly lose the overwhelming sense of terror that dogs their footsteps in the first few days, no matter how experienced, brave or well trained, they will still experience a residual sense of unease every time a call-out comes. Therefore, any errors on the part of the terrorist that make the ATO's task easier will always be hugely welcomed. As a captain, J.D. Ross was a Belfast operator from July to October 1972. He remembers two such incidents: 'In the tour before mine, a tipper truck was used to mount an IRA attack on a police station. When the truck stalled, the driver pulled the wrong lever, and the gunmen and sandbags were dumped in the road outside the station. The truck, with the back raised, subsequently got stuck under a bridge.' On another occasion: 'Three IRA blast bombers were taken to hospital minus one hand each, having "run out" of safety fuse. They were using *milli*second delay detonators, thinking they were *seconds* of delay!'

At the scene of one incident in Donaghmore, on 16 July 1973, WO1 Barwell of the Lurgan team found the incompetence of the IRA bombers so difficult to believe that he thought the whole situation must be a set-up:

I was called to an incident involving a portakabin telephone exchange in the Donaghmore area. Apparently, two GPO engineers, working on the maintenance of the exchange, had been held up by two armed men while a bomb of about 30lb was planted inside. The bombers then asked the engineers for matches to light the bomb.

On arrival, an hour or so later, I was immediately suspicious because I could not conceive of the terrorists planning such an operation and then not having the means to initiate it. I therefore considered it to be a 'set up' to nail the EOD operator. Eventually, the bomb was neutralised and the means of initiation was found to be igniferous, but fortunately the safety fuse had not burnt. Clearly, the terrorists had not considered the possibility of the engineers being non-smokers!

R. Noutch was a staff sergeant based in Ballykinler from July 1973 to July 1974. He recalls an incident in which the terrorist was inadvertently deprived of his bomb:

On one occasion, a bomber carried a bomb across some playing fields in Newcastle, left the bomb in the council toilets, and went on to carry out a reconnaissance on the target, which was a hotel backing onto the playing fields. He returned to pick up the device for planting in the hotel, and found that the toilets had been locked for the night. I was tasked to deal with the bomb following a rather embarrassed call from the IRA.

Such seemingly idiotic mistakes were not uncommon. Former WO1 G.A. Smith (Londonderry, September 1975 to January 1976) describes an incident when a mistake by a pair of terrorist bombers resulted in one of them being captured and persuaded to assist in making the device safe.

A Mother's Pride bread van was hijacked and two dustbins of explosives, plus one terrorist, loaded into the rear. Doors were shut, and a second terrorist climbed into the front and forced the driver to take the van to a military vehicle checkpoint. One hundred metres short of the target, the terrorist in the front ordered the van to stop to let his mate out of the back. Finding himself face to face with a vehicle full of soldiers, which had been following on behind, he legged it, leaving his colleague inside with the ticking bomb. The remaining terrorist was quickly released, and, after some persuasion, accompanied the ATO back to the van, where the bomb was neutralised.

However, it was not just the terrorist who was capable of making apparently ridiculous errors when it came to bombs. D.J. Leadbetter, a staff sergeant with the Londonderry team, recalls one embarrassing incident:

Sometime in March 1977, I was called to the Sports Centre in Londonderry at about 2100 hours. I was told by the RUC and the Incident Commander that there was a large metal drum visible through the glass doors of the Centre, and that this was ticking loudly. On further questioning, they admitted actually going up to the doors, opening them (they had not been locked), and very definitely hearing a loud ticking. I asked to see the last person to have left the building. This turned out to be the caretaker. In the meantime, all the usual precautions of evacuation, and ensuring that the Fire Brigade and ambulance were in attendance, had been completed. When the caretaker arrived, he casually informed me that he put the oil drum out in the foyer every night to catch the drips from the leaky roof and, as it had been raining earlier in the day, this was what the RUC had heard. Big red faces all round from the RUC and Incident Commander. Hoots of laughter from assembled multitude. Sighs of resignation from the ATO, who then retired to the comforts of Ebrington Barracks.

The relationships with the 'Teeth Arm' units with which the ATs and ATOs had to work can be variable. More often than not, the operators are treated with enormous respect because of the perception of the terrifying nature of the job. Some non-operators even want to share in the excitement of the moment, as former Staff Sergeant R. Noutch describes:

I remember with affection Lieutenant David Bowes-Lyon, a well-connected officer in the 14th/20th Royal Hussars, who was based with the troops at the Newcastle RUC Station. He was the Incident Commander on a number of occasions. He wore combat kit with brown shoes, and carried his pistol in his combat jacket pocket. I don't think he ever wore a flak jacket. When questioned by me about the devices, he would often volunteer to 'go and have another look'. And if I had let him, he would have done!

Sometimes, the operators are regarded with suspicion as being part of some lunatic fringe organisation, which no sane man would want to have anything to do with. On occasions, their own actions may do little to dispel this view. Simon Scourfield-Evans was a captain in Lurgan from December 1971 to April 1972. He recalls an incident at Headquarters 3 Infantry Brigade:

> I was asked by Commander 3 Infantry Brigade, Brigadier Bush, to show one or two items at the daily morning conference, for the benefit of the other officers. So I produced an IRA stick grenade with its striker mechanism intact. I pulled the striker and, with the bomb fizzing, placed it on the conference table. All the other staff officers ducked for cover, and the Brigadier, looking very apprehensive, sat as far back in his chair as possible. Momentarily, it did cross my mind whether I had picked up the correct (inert) grenade. Subsequently, the Brigadier preferred the items of ammunition to be of a less dynamic nature.

Occasionally, there are units that seem determined not to give the operators any degree of elevated status. Given the tensions of an operational tour, this could result in inevitable friction. WO2 Bob Harvey was temporarily assigned to a rather pukkah cavalry regiment in Armagh:

> I had to go to Armagh to take over from the resident AT who worked in the Enniskillen area. I was put in my place by the Regimental Sergeant Major, Mr Christmas. I did not have with me the normal accoutrements that the well-dressed cavalry warrant officer would carry with them – such oddments as Number 2 [Parade] Dress, Mess Kit, suit and tie. My remonstrations about there being a war on were to no avail, and I was not allowed into the mess bar after 7.00 p.m., being relegated to the TV room and the good offices of mess members if I required a drink.

Former Corporal W. Davies (No. 2, Belfast, August–December 1979) also recalls becoming involved in a dispute over military dress, this time on the streets during an actual task:

> My team was called out when we were on Alpha Shift (the first team out on the day). We arrived to find the area being patrolled by 25 Field Regiment Royal Artillery. We established our Incident Control Point (ICP) and set about the task. About twenty minutes into the job, two soldiers plus entourage came into my ICP and started shouting at the team

members about their poor standards of dress and the need for haircuts. In fact, they were wrecking my ICP! I turned around, listened, and then told my escort to remove the interlopers from the ICP. So he attempted to frog march the Commanding Officer and Regimental Sergeant Major of 25 Field Regiment out of the area. Well, you can imagine what was said! Of course, the RSM went ballistic. I told him that anyone coming into my ICP asks my permission. At that, he promptly asked me, and I said 'No'. He then started screaming at me, 'Do you know who you're talking to?' I replied, 'No, and I'm not bothered.' He announced that he was going to report me to my Commanding Officer. Just then, a gentleman in civilian clothes tapped him on the shoulder and politely asked him to leave. That gentleman was Lieutenant-Colonel Peter Forshaw, the Chief Ammunition Technical Officer. Turning to me, he said, 'Hope that will help a bit.'

Of course, it is easy to understand why the CO and RSM of a gunner regiment might become just a little agitated if spoken to in such a disrespectful manner by a corporal. That said, the ATO's Incident Control Point during a bomb-disposal task is sacrosanct. The last thing the operator needs is to have somebody throwing his weight about and increasing the stress level when he is trying to concentrate on the job in hand. Even if these were the scruffiest soldiers in the entire British Army, there would probably have been a better time to address the issue.

This lack of appreciation of the dangers and constraints surrounding an EOD task is a common source of concern or even frustration for the operators. Sometimes it will even prove life-threatening, as the following incident demonstrates. At sometime on 25 March 1982 an armed IRA gang took over a house in Cavendish Street, Belfast. The house was close to the Springfield Road RUC Station. Holding an 81-year-old woman, her daughter and son-in-law captive, the gang laid in wait for the first opportune Security Force target to move along the road. That target turned out to be a patrol from the Royal Green Jackets engaged in a routine transit task, conveying an RAF sergeant from the RUC Station to the Army base at North Howard Street Mill, less than a mile away.

Minutes after turning out of the police station and heading down Cavendish Street, the two-vehicle patrol was raked with heavy automatic fire. The first vehicle was hit several times, with one occupant, Rifleman Daniel Holland, being killed, and the RAF sergeant being seriously wounded. The driver was unscathed and managed to speed away out of the killing area. As he moved out of range, the terrorists switched their fire to the second Land Rover, which was brought to a halt. In trying to exit the vehicle and assault the firing point, two more riflemen, Anthony Rapley and Nicholas Malakos, were hit, both dying later in hospital.

The terrorists made their escape only when the corporal driving the lead vehicle ran back to the house in a brave attempt to silence the machine gun (for which he was later awarded the Military Medal). In the follow-up, a suspicious object was spotted by troops sealing off the crime scene. The rest of the story is taken up by former Corporal K. France, the No. 2 with the Belfast team:

Around dinner time one day, there was a shooting incident near Springfield Road, resulting in three Greenjackets being killed. Some twelve hours later, we were tasked to clear the firing point. A major reported to the No. 1 that one of his patrols had located a suspect package, and would like us to deal with it. My No. 1, WO2 Davies, asked if he could see the package. They started to walk away, so I asked if I could accompany them to see exactly where the Wheelbarrow would have to go.

We went through the house the terrorists had used as the firing point and into the back yard. From there, we went through a gate into a long alleyway. Both myself and the No. 1 were expecting the Major to say something like: 'Seventh bin down on your left, the package is behind it.' But no! Instead, he eventually stopped and pointed to a package at our feet, with a dowel rod sticking out of it. Then he proceeded to rock it from side to side. My No. 1's jaw hit the ground and, for a change, he was speechless. After both of us had recovered from the shock, it was a controlled panic race to see who could get back through the house fastest. When the device had been cleared, it turned out to contain 10lb of commercial explosive in some sort of large ice cream container, with spent cartridge cases on top. The plan was to lure the Security Forces to pick up the cartridge cases and set off the bomb.

Such lack of understanding by the troops providing the security back-up will inevitably increase the degree of stress being faced by the operator. EOD tasks can take several hours to complete safely, and (as described in Chapter Two) there is often pressure to wrap things up as quickly as possible, whether to get the cordon troops out of harm's way, or to open up a major traffic route. Former Corporal D. Aynsley, a Belfast No. 2 from May to September 1983, describes an occasion when his own No. 1 was placed in this difficult position:

After two small explosions in a hotel, Sergeant Swainland, my No. 1, decided to impose a soak time before continuing his render-safe procedure. This annoyed an already impatient infantry major, who wanted to get away for an officers' mess dinner. He even threatened to contact 'higher command' to 'get things sorted out'. Sergeant Swainland had none of this, and duly put the officer in his place. A while later, there were two explosions, completely destroying the hotel and most of the surrounding area. The officer grunted, 'Good decision, ATO.'

As a sergeant, John Lawrence encountered a similar problem when dealing with a bomb in a shop doorway in Portadown:

We had been on the go since eight o'clock that morning, and hadn't had the chance to get back to base. By the time we were called to this particular job, it was dark, and my 'Lonsborough Lamp' was still on charge at base. The bomb, inside a duffel bag, was placed inside the deep front doorway of a shop. I really wanted to be able to stand across the other side of the road and shine a light onto it before I walked up to it. It was quite a wide road, so I thought I'd be pretty safe from there. My plan was to keep the light pointing right at it all the way.

The incident commander was a young infantry lieutenant. His men had been standing around for some time, and he was keen to get the job over and done with. He asked me what I was doing, so I told him that I would apply a soak time until 11 o'clock, then I'd walk up to it. In the meantime, I sent a vehicle back to the base at Lurgan to pick up the torch, thinking that it would be back in time.

Well 11 o'clock passed, and the young lieutenant came walking up to me asking why I hadn't got on with it. I told him about the torch. As he turned away, I heard him make a disparaging comment which implied that I was too scared to do my job and *that* was the real reason I hadn't gone forward.

I decided to stick it out until the torch arrived. Eventually, it turned up, and I showed the lieutenant what it did and how important it was. I think he got the point, although there was no apology for his earlier comment. I switched on the torch, and started to walk forward from the ICP. Just at that moment there was a most almighty explosion, and the entire building alongside the bomb was brought down. If the torch hadn't turned up late, I'd almost certainly have been standing over the device when it went off.

These problems on the ground are not always limited to the lower-ranking operators. As a lieutenant-colonel, Major-General Peter Istead was CATO Northern Ireland from August 1977 to August 1978. He also recalls becoming involved in a difference of opinion concerning cordon troops:

An amusing incident in Derry concerned a bar which had been bombed. The IRA informed the police that there was another bomb in the building. The local commanding officer did not believe it, and was very loath to put his troops out to maintain a cordon around the bar for us. Eventually, he was ordered to do so, and we searched the building from top to bottom. A very large ATO entered the building through a very small attic window and found a bomb. We dealt with it. The CO acknowledged that he had been wrong and, to show his appreciation, produced, in the centre of Derry square, on a Sunday lunchtime, a table, with a white cloth. The Mess Sergeant, in monkey jacket, served a steak dinner with champagne, to ourselves and, of course, the CO. I thought it a nice touch.

On some occasions, it can be members of the public who unwittingly place themselves in the way of a bomb-disposal operation, as Bob Harvey remembers:

It appeared that there had been a raid across the border that day and the vehicle used had been abandoned on the Strabane Bridge. The police were anxious to recover the vehicle as evidence, and I was invited to the 'ball'. The plan was quite simple: dash onto the bridge; I would search for bombs and sundry devices, then, with assorted escorts, we would return triumphant. Piece of cake. If we got a move on we could all be back in time for tea. I pointed out that, as one of the principal players in this, I was not keen on doing my thing in broad daylight only 100 yards from the IRA's front door. It was agreed that I had made a point which the OC was willing to go along with, subject to me and escort doing the initial recce. This we duly did, under cover of darkness, and, having declared the bridge clear of nasties, were considering the vehicle when a rather inebriated gentleman strolled across the bridge from Southern Ireland and boarded it.

Under the bridge, consternation reigned. Suggestions, such as shooting the guy, were freely bandied about. The plan of action eventually centred on a concerted sibilant hissing to attract his attention. Eventually, he homed in on the noise, jocularly saying that he thought he had a puncture. Such witticism was impatiently dismissed, and it was pointed out to him that we were there first, and that it was now our vehicle. He apologised, and went back to the south. We were by now sure that the next event would be an attack, but, in the nick of time, the Company arrived to escort us out.

When an EOD operator arrives at the scene of an incident, the protection of the public is his highest priority, and one of his first tasks will be to ascertain what degree of evacuation has been accomplished. Given the difficulties of establishing a watertight cordon in an urban area, it is not unknown for members of the public to emerge unexpectedly alongside the device just as Wheelbarrow is about to fire one of its weapons. Perhaps the worst incident of this sort that I ever encountered happened in Belfast outside a strongly Republican drinking den known as the Shamrock Club, in the Ardoyne district. The device appeared to be a fire extinguisher, potentially stuffed with explosives, and with batteries and a timer strapped to the outside. Having used Wheelbarrow to shoot the timing mechanism to bits, I went forward to place a cutting charge that would slice the fire extinguisher neatly in half, thereby emptying any explosive contents harmlessly into the street. Returning to my ICP, I took cover and set off the charge. There was an almighty bang, and the windows at the front of the club, including those in the front door, disintegrated. I then went forward again to inspect the results of my action. The scattered parts of the device were lying in an area just in front of the entrance door, which, having lost its glass, now consisted of little more than a steel security grill. I knelt down and started to examine the evidence, quickly concluding that the bomb had been an elaborate hoax. Suddenly, my inspection was interrupted by a voice speaking to me from the other side of the grill, about four feet away. I looked up to see an inebriated Irishman swaying slightly as he surveyed the damage. He had clearly been in the club, watching my various antics and explosions from close range, throughout. 'Sure, an' we thought it were a hoax,' he said. Given the loss of the club's windows, I didn't like to confirm that it had been.

Despite the high priority placed on evacuating the general public, during the late 1970s and early 1980s, one individual would always be allowed through – an employee of the Ulsterbus Company, known colloquially as 'Herman the German'. W.J. Hillman (Private, No. 2, Lisburn, October 1980 to March 1981) describes his first encounter:

At one incident, we were called to a bus that had been abandoned in a country road at around 2 a.m. This is a highly suspect situation because, in this circumstance, there is a high risk of an ambush bomb (miles of open fields).

The team had got to within 70 metres of the bus. Suddenly, a small man in baggy trousers and wellies wandered past us. I yelled at him, but the Boss shouted over to me that it was okay.

This little guy got onto the bus, turned on all the lights and had a look around. Then he shouted out: 'It's okay. Someone take my Jag home,' and drove off in the bus. I later heard that this guy was called 'Herman the German', and he apparently worked for the Ulsterbus Company. If there was a device on a bus, he would take it off and drive the bus away, leaving the bomb team to deal with the device.

While it is easy to assume that the greatest threat to the life of an EOD operator is a bomb, whenever he is out on the streets or deployed into the countryside, he faces exactly the same dangers as any other member of the Security Forces. At any moment, he may find himself at the centre of an ambush, sniper attack, grenade attack or riot. At the lowest end of the scale might be a petrol-bomb attack, as experienced by former Private R.W. Warren, who served as a Belfast No. 2 in 1976:

In Belfast we were always on the go – one incident after another. From one device we were called to an incendiary in a pub. En route, our Pig was petrol bombed by a young boy 10–11 years old. He came out of a house and just threw it at us. When we'd cleared the device in the pub, we couldn't get out for one or two hours as too many youths were running riot. In the end we had to make a run for it as we'd been called to yet another incident.

During the 1970s, and even into the 1980s, it was not unusual for the operators to be trying to deal with devices in the middle of riot conditions. The following situation, described by G.R. Henderson (Signaller, Belfast and Londonderry, November 1976–April 1977), is not untypical:

A car with two men went through a snap vehicle checkpoint (VCP). The Parachute Regiment were on the VCP and opened fire, killing the driver. The car went through a fence and stopped in a school playing field. My team was called out to clear the car. We went out in Saracens and Pigs. All seemed quiet for a while as we went about our job. Then, as if by magic, we were surrounded by a hoard of screaming and chanting women, who lay down in the road and blocked our exit from the area. The cordon troops from the Parachute Regiment tried to move the women, but as fast as they dragged one away, another took her place. Having completed our task, the order to mount up was given and we were bricked as we drove down the road. As we moved round the corner there was a loud clanging as a complete bicycle landed on the bonnet of my Pig. This, I think, was one of the most frightening incidents I was involved in.

One of the worst attacks on an EOD team happened on 2 August 1979. The team was returning to base having been involved in the EOD clearance of a terrorist's getaway car. Earlier in the day, this vehicle had been used by gunmen from the Irish National Liberation Army (INLA), who had murdered Police Constable George Walsh as he sat in his Ford Escort outside Armagh Courthouse. They had opened fire with an Armalite rifle on automatic as they drove past, and Constable Walsh's car was riddled with bullets. The getaway vehicle had then been abandoned on the outskirts of Armagh and set alight.

Despite the fact that the car was burnt out, bitter experience had taught the Security Forces never to trust a vehicle that had been in terrorist hands. An ATO was therefore summoned. The terrorists would have been expecting this. They would have known where the team would have been called out from, and the likely route that it would have to take, both out and back. A two-step ambush operation was therefore easy to put in place. With the car having been cleared, the team was returning to barracks in a three-vehicle convoy, along the road between Armagh and Moy, when a 400lb culvert bomb was detonated. The blast smashed into the middle vehicle, killing Signaller Paul Reece and Gunner Richard Furminger, both serving with the

Armagh team, instantly. A UDR escort Land Rover following up behind ploughed straight into the 10-foot crater that had been left in the road, resulting in further injuries. Amid these scenes of carnage, at least three gunmen then opened fire, trying to finish off the survivors. The team returned fire, but the gunmen escaped across fields to two waiting cars.

Over and above the routine risks that face all members of the Security Forces on an operational tour, the EOD operator must live with the knowledge that he faces a personal daily battle with the bombers of one of the most sophisticated terrorist organisations in the world. Sometimes their bombs will be aimed at the general public, commercial premises, other soldiers or policemen or even members of rival terrorist groups. But, on occasions, the bomb-maker will be seeking deliberately to target and kill an operator. Every operator knows this. He realises that his every action at a bomb scene is likely to be observed and noted. Any weaknesses in his drills, perhaps the product of laziness, carelessness or inexperience, will be identified for future exploitation.

Right from the outset of his tour, this was certainly made abundantly clear to B.J. Mitchell, a staff sergeant in Londonderry from February to June 1972:

My first call out was to an electrical sub-station on a river bank in Strabane early evening time. As I approached a vantage point with a company commander of 1 Royal Anglian, a loud hailer blared out from the opposite bank, welcoming me to Strabane on my first job, with a promise to look after me. I hoped the ground would swallow me up. Bramley [the Army School of Ammunition] had not prepared me for this! The Officer Commanding, sensing my discomfort, called the job off, and, after 99 coffees in Strabane Company Base, we went in around midnight with no trouble – hoax.

In his book *Fetch Felix*, Lieutenant-Colonel Derrick Patrick (Chief ATO Northern Ireland, August 1976–August 1977) describes the dawning terror as he realises that a bomb placed inside a petrol tanker is almost certainly booby-trapped, and that he is its intended victim. The events that led up to this moment of truth began with the hijack of a Shell petrol tanker in the Crumlin Road area of Belfast at about 11.30 a.m. on 18 April 1977. Some three hours later, the hijackers ordered the driver to deliver it to the front gates of the Flax Street Mill Army base. On arriving at the base, the driver obeyed the sentry's instructions to move the vehicle away from the base and abandon it. When Lieutenant-Colonel Patrick arrived, the driver was being held at the scene as a witness. He was able to reveal that the terrorists had placed one suspected device in the front tank of the vehicle, and another in the cab.

By this stage of his tour, Lieutenant-Colonel Patrick had already dealt with two similar situations involving petrol tankers. However, his most recent outing had received considerable media coverage, and he knew that his techniques had been closely observed. On that occasion, he had used a hook and line to extract the device through the hatch at the top of the bulk fuel tank. This time, the bomb was contained in a plastic putty bucket dangling by its handle from a length of wood wedged across the aperture. He initially attached a hook and line, but when he tried to pull the device out from a distance, he found that the wood was too tightly jammed in place. The only option was to position himself alongside the hatch and, with extreme care, dislodge the length of wood, then lift both it and the bucket out by hand.

As he reached out to start manœuvring the bucket, he was faced with the chilling realisation that this bomb was designed for him. The terrorists would, of course, have known precisely how the previous devices were made up. Watching from the edge of the cordon, and seeing the action played back on TV, they would have been able to work out with a fair degree of certainty what measures the ATO would have taken to make them safe. And now they had a chance to catch him out.

Balanced precariously on the top of the tanker, Lieutenant-Colonel Patrick twisted the wooden support, loosening it so that he could lift it out of the aperture. In the meantime, he had to support the bucket with his other hand. By now, he had deduced that the most likely threat against him was that of a tilt switch concealed in the bucket. To drop it, tilt it or jar it in any way would, therefore, almost certainly prove fatal. Having freed the stick, he took the weight of the bucket, and lifted it gently out, resting it on top of the tanker.

With the bucket out in the open, Lieutenant-Colonel Patrick was once again able to attach the hook and line, with a view to pulling the device clear of the tanker. Retreating behind cover, he yanked the cord. The bucket fell from the top of the tanker. As it started to tumble there was an almighty blast, and a rush of hot air sought out Lieutenant-Colonel Patrick in his hiding place. All around him, glass came crashing from windows, as, in his words, he 'stood crouching stupidly with a bit of slack line in my hand'.

As a lieutenant-colonel, Chris Hendy was Chief ATO Northern Ireland from August 1980 to August 1981. He also recalls one task where the operator had been targeted:

My first recollection of a significant device was the milk churn lorry at Newtownhamilton. This incident started with the driver of the lorry, who was a part-time member of the UDR, delivering empty milk churns and collecting full ones from the local area around Newtownhamilton. The lorry was ambushed by terrorists at a road junction, the driver shot dead and removed from the scene. The RUC tasked the EOD team to clear the lorry. The team tasked was the Bessbrook team, under the leadership of WO2 Boscott. Initial recce of the lorry revealed nothing conspicuous, except, of course, 25–30 full and empty milk churns on the back. Remote clearing of the churns was not possible, and a manual approach was decided upon.

Before any manual approach was made, it was decided to tow the lorry away from the immediate scene. This was achieved by the attachment of a tow rope and, with the aid of Saracen, the lorry was moved approximately 100 yards up the road. The manual approach was then made by the No. 1, who lightly tapped each churn and identified the full churns from the empty ones. Full churns then had a rope attached and were pulled off the vehicle individually and by remote control from within the Saracen. During this procedure, one churn was pulled which immediately blew up, destroying the whole lorry. Clearly, that particular churn contained a large amount of explosive and some form of tilt or anti-handling device.

Lieutenant-Colonel Hendy's successor as Chief ATO was Lieutenant-Colonel Keith Ridley (August 1982–August 1983). He clearly remembers several 'attacks on ATOs – close shaves when members of the IRA's South Armagh Brigade were determined to kill an ATO'. Specifically:

A booby-trapped petrol tanker was placed on the border in South Armagh. During the clearance of this, a command wire was discovered by the cordon troops, which led to a large bomb at the side of the approach road.

A few weeks after this incident, during the clearance of an IRA mortar used to attack the Crossmaglen Security Force base, a house on the only approach exploded and collapsed across the road, almost killing the ATO.

The fuse from the bomb was recovered from the house remains. It showed that the initiator had been 'held off' by mains electric power. The IRA had triggered it as they watched the ATO by engineering a power cut to the whole of Crossmaglen.

It is hardly surprising that, given the constant stresses of their job, most operators are quick to derive as much humour as possible out of any given situation – anything to relieve the unremitting tension. Hardly surprisingly, such humour more often than not has a 'gallows' quality to it. Kevin Goad (Captain, Lisburn, March 1970–1) recalls:

On 17 March GOC Northern Ireland, Lieutenant-General Erskine-Crum, died during his handover. Prior to his body leaving the Military Hospital for transfer to UK, his coffin and body had to be 'swept'. I attended with WO2 Glover. Prior to entering the morgue, which we knew contained only his coffin and body, innate and instilled courtesy made me knock. In the ensuing silence, WO2 Glover looked at me and said, 'We'll get a shock, sir, if he says come in.'

Former Signaller G.R. Henderson describes an incident in which he managed to see the funny side during a potentially tense situation:

We had just been called out of the Mill in Belfast and were heading towards the incident when the leading Saracen broke down. I leaned out of my Pig and shouted to the No. 2, who was in the Saracen, 'What's the matter?' Back came the reply, 'My Saracen's broken down.'

We informed ops, who tasked another team to the incident we were supposed to be going to. We were then told to leave the vehicles and drivers with a Para patrol for recovery later, and the No. 1, No. 2 and myself were to join onto another patrol heading back to the Mill.

We tagged onto the patrol, which was a foot patrol, and headed back. The patrol acted in a very professional manner and, as we carried pistols, we decided to do our bit too. So there we were, running along the street with pistols drawn. I was having trouble stopping myself from laughing at the team No. 2, who was waving his pistol in every direction.

The patrol commander stopped the patrol after a few hundred yards and said to the No. 2, 'For fuck's sake stop waving that pistol around before you kill somebody!' Whereupon the No. 2 replied, 'Don't worry, I never load it with a magazine because I leave it under my pillow so I don't lose any bullets.'

J.J. Gordon (Captain, Belfast, November 1972–March 1973) even saw the funny side of being blown up: 'My tour's extended by two weeks, during which time I get injured by a bomb in a jeweller's shop in Castle Street. Throws me 30 metres. All clothes blown off, with exception of underpants. Joke is that my name is to appear in Guinness Book of Records for longest jump from a standing start.'

J.A. Anderson, a sergeant in Omagh from October 1979 to February 1980, tells an amusing story about two soldiers who were 'blown up' (fortunately without tragic consequences):

During the attempted RSP [render-safe procedure] of a car in Omagh, the device, estimated at 200lb, functioned. The RUC had cleared all buildings in the street, including the pub directly opposite the car. However, two Army Catering Corps Junior NCOs in the pub ignored the warning and remained to drink the beer that was lying about. The pub doors had been left open, and they observed the attempted RSP by Wheelbarrow. When the device functioned, the building was demolished around them, and they were blown to the rear of the pub. They had no injuries to speak of – just cuts. On release from hospital a day later, they were reduced [in rank] to privates and sent to outstations.

A few weeks later, while feeding at a small military base, I discovered the cook was one of those involved. At the end of our subsequent conversation, I asked him what the experience had been like (he had been no more than 15 metres from the device). His reply was: 'Well, Sarge, all I can say is, those blast waves don't half hurt!'

One of the luckiest men alive!

One product of the ever-present humour within 321 EOD was 'Felix' – which must rate as one of the most unlikely, but highly regarded, military emblems ever. Prior to the Troubles, the Army already had a list of nicknames, representing specific military appointments, for quick use over the radio. For example, commanders at all levels were known as 'Sunray'. With the involvement in internal security operations, the list grew. If one was referring to a member of the RUC, the code name was 'Rucksack', while a female member of the UDR was called a 'Greenfinch'. It soon became apparent that there would have to be a specific code name for the EOD operator.

The first suggestion, 'Jelly Baby', did not go down well, as Alan Clouter (Captain, Lisburn, March 1971–March 1972) observes: 'It was decided that this would be embarrassing if someone was hurt.' The next suggestion, 'Phoenix', at least had a degree of logic behind it, as the ATOs would frequently find themselves 'arising from the ashes'. However, the tale, possibly apocryphal, goes that there was a mix-up in translation when the new name was passed down the phone line to a soldier. Instead of 'Phoenix', the new title was hastily scribbled down as 'Felix' – the cat with nine lives – and Felix it remained.

Initially drawn in a style similar to the well-known American cartoon cat, Felix was quickly adopted as 321 EOD Unit's logo, as well as being the ATOs' radio appointment title. Indeed, as referred to briefly in Chapter Eight, Felix was greeted with such enthusiasm that he was soon featuring on a tie awarded to every operator to commemorate his first live bomb successfully rendered safe in the Province. The award of the 'Felix tie' remains in practice to this day.

In 1974 the logo based on 'Felix the Cat' from the movies underwent a transformation when a couple of ATs turned their imaginations to producing an unofficial cartoon strip. WO1 G.E. Barrow was one of the operators in the Londonderry Section at the time: 'As a feature of my Section, I introduced a means to relieve tension and stress by producing cartoons of daily events of operators and their crews. These cartoons were ably drawn by Staff Sergeant Shepherd and Staff Sergeant Baker (once a commercial artist). Staff Sergeant Shepherd also designed the Felix crest for 321 EOD Unit.'

The logo that was to remain with the unit for the next thirty-plus years became a Disney-style orange and white cat, with pop eyes and a permanently startled expression on his face, wearing a visored helmet, flak jacket and pistol. His place in history was sealed by the prolific flood of cartoons that poured out of Londonderry, and that so accurately caught the mood of the time. Felix was shown emerging sheepishly, but usually unscathed, from endless life-threatening or embarrassing situations, no doubt causing operators to think, 'That looks familiar . . .'.

But, despite the outward appearance of calm professionalism and good humour that all operators try to maintain, the stresses of the tour inevitably start to take their toll. It is at this stage that the risks become greatest. Not only is one tired, and therefore more prone to making careless mistakes, but a sense of invulnerability starts to creep in. Risks and shortcuts are taken that would have been unthinkable in the early weeks of the tour. A typical example is cited by former WO1 R.M. Barwell of the Lurgan Section (June–August 1973):

A car bomb was discovered outside a women's prison in the centre of Armagh on the day that our Wheelbarrows were being exchanged at HQ 321 in Lisburn. Because of the pressures on the Security Forces at the time (political, publicity and media coverage) I, foolishly perhaps, attempted to defuse the bomb manually. Having spent five minutes opening up the car – a Hillman Imp – and exposing the bomb in the boot, I was returning with the equipment to neutralise it when it exploded. Although I was only about 20–30 feet away, I was uninjured, apart from cuts to the face and a damaged watch. However, an RUC constable behind me received leg wounds.

Bob Harvey sums up the typical feelings endured by many, if not most, operators very well:

Towards the end of my tour I felt that as a team member I was in bad shape. I was now sleeping all the hours I could; I felt exhausted. It seemed never ending. The senses seemed to become more perceptive and every noise and bang awoke me. The fact that we could hear the activity in the city did not help.

The drivers were magnificent at protecting us from some barmy onlookers and taking on as much of the burden as they possibly could. As No. 2's they were without parallel, always providing a steadying influence to us nutty lot who sometimes became absorbed in the technicalities to the detriment of other important matters.

Incidents mounted, but by now it was the old business of surviving until the time came to go home. Some incidents come to mind: a hoax in the ladies' loo at the railway station, an old Castlerobin in the GPO Londonderry, the Brickworks at the top of the Creggan, listening in disbelief to radio Free Londonderry, who used to broadcast all the Security Forces' movements in the city. When the time came to go home, I knew that I had had enough.

For my own part, the end of my tour in Belfast equally could not come soon enough. As I boarded the military flight taking me back to my parent unit in Germany, all I could think was 'I'm alive!' I arrived back in the Officers' Mess on the last day of the Easter break, and found myself to be the only occupant. That night I settled down in front of the TV in the mess bar, determined to make up for lost time as far as alcohol intake was concerned. Glad to be back on safe ground in Germany, I selected an attractive looking bottle bearing the brand name *Clausthaller*. Before long a small ring of empty *Clausthaller* bottles adorned one of the circular coffee tables close to the TV.

The next morning I arose with a surprisingly clear head. Making my way down to breakfast, I found that John (the senior major who had kindly had a 'last' drink with me on the night I left Germany) had arrived back at some stage during the early hours. He greeted me enthusiastically across the breakfast table. It soon became apparent that he had taken note of the debris left behind by me in the bar from the night before: 'So you *like* that *alcohol-free Clausthaller*, do you, Steve?'

TEN

WHEN IT ALL GOES WRONG

'It's okay, nobody died' is an expression commonly used nowadays, in all walks of life, to shrug off a minor disaster or mishap. When an EOD operator uses it, he probably does so with a palpable sense of relief, because he lives in a world where there is every chance that someone could die. It could be him. Perhaps even worse, if he makes a mistake, it could be someone else. A professional footballer, earning thousands of pounds a week, is allowed, even expected, to make mistakes. Not so the ATO. His errors have life or death implications. When he makes the declaration that the area, house, weapon or vehicle is 'clear', there can be no room for doubt. Sadly, there have been occasions where precisely that mistake has been made. Sometimes it has caused death or injury to others conducting the follow-up, at other times, to the ATO himself.

One such tragic incident occurred at Moybane, near Crossmaglen, on 5 May 1973. Earlier in the day, a Company Sergeant Major from 2nd Battalion, The Parachute Regiment, 36-year-old WO2 William Vines, had been killed by a command-wire IED concealed in a roadside wall. It had been detonated as he walked towards it. A follow-up operation was mounted. The ATO carefully investigated the scene of the original explosion. Having ascertained that the explosive charge had fully detonated, and that the immediate area of the ambush site was now safe, he gave instructions for the command wire to be recovered. Two soldiers, Corporal Terence Williams (2 PARA) and Trooper John Gibbons (17th/21st Lancers), began walking back along the line of the electrical flex, reeling it in as they went. Unknown to them, a booby trap had been concealed in a nearby ditch, through which the command wire passed. As they crossed over the ditch, one of them triggered the secondary device. The ensuing massive blast killed both soldiers instantly, scattering debris over 100 yards and leaving a crater 12 feet wide. Thus was learnt an early hard lesson about how to conduct follow-up operations in the countryside. In future, operators would always look beyond the obvious to see what further nasty tricks the terrorist might have up his sleeve.

Vehicles present a particular problem in this respect. There are so many places that a small booby-trap device might be hidden that, almost inevitably, there have been occasions when they have been missed. The first time this happened was on 8 October 1976. A stolen car had been located at Gortnacrene, Co. Londonderry. An ATO had been tasked to ensure that it was free from booby traps. The vehicle had been examined at some length, and a controlled explosion used to check out one particularly suspect area. With the vehicle having been declared safe, 43-year-old Reserve Constable Arthur McKay slipped into the driver's seat, in order to steer it as it was towed back to the police station. As the car moved off, a pressure switch, cunningly concealed under the wheel, initiated a booby-trap device, killing Constable McKay instantly and injuring five soldiers.

One staff sergeant operator, who served in Bessbrook in the late 1970s, describes being involved in a similar incident:

In January or February 1978 there was a mortar attack on Forkhill SF base. Mark 9 mortars were successfully launched and caused damage in the base. The lorry from which the bombs were launched was subsequently searched during the render-safe procedure, but I failed to find a booby trap, which was concealed in the windscreen washer bottle. Presumably there was a time-delay switch between it and the ignition circuit of the vehicle. The vehicle was eventually started up by the RUC, and the booby trap exploded, causing severe injuries to the two RUC officers. I believe this was the first time that a vehicle carrying mortars had been booby-trapped in this way.

Sixteen years later, the incident was to be replayed, with almost identical results. This time, the serious casualty was to be the ATO. At 5.21 p.m. on 10 January 1994 a single Mark 15 'Barrack Buster' mortar round struck and destroyed the generator building inside the Crossmaglen Security Force base. Within twenty minutes the firing point had been identified as a blue Toyota HiAce van, and the area was cordoned off. The ATO based at Bessbrook was tasked, but movement into Crossmaglen could be carried out only by helicopter, owing to the risk of ambush on the roads. Bad weather prevented the helicopter taking off until 8.22 p.m., and, consequently, the team was not in position and ready to commence operations until nearly half past ten that night.

For the next hour and a half, the ATO, an experienced Warrant Officer, carried out his clearance of the mortar firing point. During this period, he managed to recover two battery packs, a 'timing and power unit' (for initiating the mortar remotely by timer), and a standard Mark 15 mortar tube from the HiAce van. He then started to drive the vehicle inside the Crossmaglen base, where it was planned that it should be garaged in a hangar overnight pending further forensic examination.

The ATO started up the van without incident, switched on the headlights, and began to drive it into the base. It was necessary to apply the brakes several times during the short journey, but the jarring motion had no adverse effect. For a short period, the vehicle idled while the road ahead was cleared of barricades. The route involved driving over some pitted ground and up a short, sharp incline, during which the maximum speed attained was 20 mph.

Entering the base, the ATO was directed towards the designated parking area by a lance-corporal from the Grenadier Guards. Once the van had arrived at the hangar, a young craftsman (private soldier) from the REME took over the task of guiding it into its slot, taking up a position in front of the cab with a torch in his hand. The van eased into place and the Warrant Officer applied the brakes. The vehicle immediately exploded.

The Company Sergeant Major of the Queen's Company, 1st Battalion, Grenadier Guards, was one of the first on the scene. He immediately tried to assist with applying first aid to the ATO. He could see the REME craftsman, lying on his back approximately 5 metres in front of the demolished vehicle. It looked like he had been blown backwards by the blast and was now lying unconscious.

The Sergeant Major was joined by the company medic, a private in the Royal Army Medical Corps. The medic moved to the unconscious man on the ground and started to administer first aid. It then became apparent that the ATO, although terribly wounded, was still conscious, so the Sergeant Major tried to gain his attention: 'I called to him by name, and he said, "What a fuck up." I kept talking to him throughout, and he kept saying, "What's the score?" I took this as a reference to his injuries. He was dripping blood from the top of his head, so I applied a field dressing.'

Meanwhile, the medic had managed to assist the REME craftsman to regain consciousness. Not sure where he was or what was happening, the casualty immediately started to scream and wriggle around. He had to be restrained so that morphine could be administered. Stretchers then arrived on the scene. Once the casualties had been stabilised, they were ferried by Saxon armoured ambulance to a pick-up point for subsequent evacuation by helicopter. With the helipad inside the base still out of action following the earlier attack, a landing spot was found for a Puma helicopter in a field some 250 metres away.

The injuries to the two soldiers were serious. The ATO had received blast injuries, lacerations and a penetrating wound to his neck. His left eye had been badly damaged by the blast, muscles had been torn away from his lower left leg, and his left foot was lacerated. The REME craftsman had received a blast injury of such severity that it had caused one of his lungs to collapse (subsequently reinflated). He had also suffered three serious fractures to the right arm, as well as broken fingertips. Both soldiers survived.

A second ATO, this time a young captain, was called out to the scene of the explosion. In addition to the items recovered by the Warrant Officer, he was able to detect the remains of a second timing and power unit, which had undoubtedly been responsible for triggering the booby trap. The seat of the explosion appeared to have been to the front and left of the driver, in the area of the dashboard, which had been destroyed, along with most of the front of the vehicle. The windscreen had been ripped from its mounts and thrown further into the hangar. The hangar's supporting beams closest to the seat of the explosion were severely damaged, causing the roof partially to collapse onto the cab. It was assessed that the overall damage to the van and the injuries sustained by the casualties were consistent with a device containing less than half a kilogram of military explosives. Further investigation failed to find the precise means of initiation of the booby trap.

The Warrant Officer was lucky. As we have already seen, others have been less so. Throughout the course of the Troubles, seventeen operators have met their deaths in Northern Ireland, along with three other EOD team members. Patterns are difficult to detect in determining how or why they died. The eight deaths in 1971–2 occurred before the widespread introduction of a tracked and multi-capable Wheelbarrow, and most of them before Pigstick was on general issue. Of these, four (Davies, Butcher, Cracknell and Calladene) were the direct result of operators walking up to a time bomb while it was still ticking, three (Stewardson, Young and Clark) were almost certainly caused by anti-handling mechanisms, and one (Hills) happened when the operator made a fatal error while trying to dismantle an improvised mortar bomb (see Chapter Three).

Beyond 1972, seven of the remaining nine deaths resulted from operators being caught out by anti-handling devices, one was caused by a time device and one was a command-wire ambush. A closer examination of these will highlight in no uncertain terms the stresses under which an operator must function in the field.

Television and films almost invariably show the bomb-disposal operator crouched, concentrating, over his device, with only the sound of droplets of sweat splashing from his forehead onto the ground to break the silence. The reality will often be vastly different. Captain Barry Gritten found himself trying to deal with a potentially booby-trapped find under far from ideal conditions. He had been in the Province for 109 days, and was coming towards the end of his tour, when, on 20 June 1973, he was called out to a find of explosives in a Nissen hut at the back of Lecky Road in Londonderry.

During the late evening, a foot patrol had come across three men working in a corrugated-iron motor workshop. At the appearance of the soldiers, the three had immediately run off. A cursory search had revealed a large quantity of explosives and other bomb-making materials. While the search was in progress, a volatile crowd had begun to gather outside. Reinforcements were despatched to secure the area, and an ATO was summoned. By unhappy chance, the duty team had already been called out to another job, so the task defaulted to Captain Gritten. He had only just started his rest period, having recently come off duty, and was therefore likely to be tired. By the time he arrived at the scene, the cordon troops were under sustained pressure from the crowd, which had started bombarding them with rocks and bricks. It was already dark, and Captain Gritten commenced work by the light of a torch. It was clear that this was going to be a valuable haul, and the young captain could barely contain his excitement. 'What a wonderful find,' he was heard to say, before a booby trap functioned and ended his life in an instant. An angry crowd, time pressure, tiredness and poor light – all of these undoubtedly played their part in Captain Gritten's death.

Two months later, on 30 August 1973, Sergeant Ron Beckett was called to the aftermath of an armed robbery and bomb attack in the border village of Tullyhommon, near Pettigoe. It had been a terrifying incident. Two groups of IRA men had driven across the border from Co. Donegal. One group had placed bombs in the Customs Station and the Post Office, stealing cash and postal orders in the process. The other carload had gone to a garage that had already been bombed once before. There, they had herded the garage staff outside at gunpoint and began to take names and addresses. When the owner gave his name, the gunmen immediately realised that he was a member of the UDR and tried to shoot him on the spot. With bullets flying after him, he had managed to make his escape, running the 100 yards to his house, where his self-protection weapon was concealed. He had then returned fire from the house. A 13-year-old boy took a bullet in the arm in the crossfire. Having failed to kill the garage owner, both groups of IRA men had made their escape back across the border. With ticking bombs still in place, Sergeant Beckett's team was tasked to the scene.

Beckett's signals operator, Signaller Loveridge, recounts what happened next:

> Our team was tasked to Pettigoe, a small village straddling the border. Staff Sergeant Ron Beckett went into the Post Office, and returned after placing the Pigstick. He then fired it and waited. After a few minutes, he went back into the building, which then exploded. He died instantly. This incident totally devastated the team, as Ron was a good man and the nicest person you could wish to meet.

On this occasion, probably the greatest factor in Staff Sergeant Beckett's death was his eagerness to re-enter the Post Office to see the effects of his controlled explosion. Without Wheelbarrow inside the building, he would not have had a camera trained on the device, so there was no possibility of seeing what the effects of Pigstick had been before he risked going back in. There is always the chance that, rather than inflicting a killer blow, Pigstick might merely have succeeded in making the beast angry. That is almost certainly what happened here.

The next to die was Staff Sergeant Alan Brammah. During the late afternoon of 17 February 1974 some explosions were heard out in the countryside near Crossmaglen. Staff Sergeant Alan Brammah, an operator based at Bessbrook, was tasked to check them out. Having completed 103 days in the Province, he was already well into his tour and was, by that stage, within a month of going home. By the time the tasking message had been received, darkness was imminent, so the decision was made to delay deployment until the next morning.

On the morning of 18 February an infantry cordon was put in place, and Staff Sergeant Brammah flew in by helicopter, taking a good look at the scene from the air before landing. It was apparent that there were six craters where the explosions from the night before had gone off. These formed a rough circle, but left a gap, as if for a seventh device that had failed to function. The impression was that the IRA had been conducting test firings.

After a brief search, Staff Sergeant Brammah discovered a wire running towards the craters. Accompanied by two other soldiers (an officer and a sergeant), he started to follow it, keeping a wary eye open for any booby traps. The wire crossed two fields, at one stage passing through a pond, and led towards a road. Here, it passed through a dry stone wall, emerging onto the grass verge by the roadside. The wire was visible for a very short distance, before it disappeared beneath a turf cut out of the surrounding grass. The grass on the turf had already started to die off and discolour, causing it to stand out from its surroundings.

With his two colleagues standing a short distance away, Staff Sergeant Brammah stepped forward and lifted one corner of the turf. Beneath it, a neat white package was visible. Gently replacing the turf, he and the others turned to walk away. However, something persuaded him to go back and take a closer look. Kneeling down, he reached forward to lift a different corner of the sod, saying something along the lines of: 'This must be one of the new remote-controlled ones.' They were his last words. As he leaned further forward, the device detonated, obliterating his life in an instant. The other two soldiers escaped uninjured, but it was a close run thing. One cannot help thinking: 'If only . . . Why did he just have to have one more peek?'

It was another rural clearance operation, this time just outside Stewartstown, that caused the death of Staff Sergeant Vernon Rose on 7 November 1974. During the previous night, an explosion had been heard in the vicinity of an electricity sub-station. The next morning, a mixed party of police, soldiers and civilians attended the scene to ascertain what had happened. During this process, Staff Sergeant Rose discovered what appeared to be further items of bomb-making equipment – in this case, two bags of a fertiliser mixture, commonly used in home-made explosives, and some black tape. These items would undoubtedly have proved useful to the police for forensic evidence purposes. Still surrounded by other soldiers and some civilian workers who had come to clear up after the overnight explosion, Staff Sergeant Rose leaned forward to investigate further. There was an almighty blast. The operator was killed instantly, along with Staff Sergeant Charles Simpson of the Royal Hussars. An RUC constable was blinded and three civilians injured. The explosion was sufficient to leave a crater 4 feet deep and 10 feet across.

WO2 John Maddocks had been examining a milk churn packed with explosives when it blew up on him at Gortmullen, near the border with Monaghan, on 2 December 1974. Unfortunately, he made the classic mistake of taking a course of action that seemed straightforward on the basis of the evidence presented. Sticking out of the explosive appeared to be a strand of detonating cord, looking just like a length of washing line. As this would normally provide the explosive link from the detonator into the main charge, cutting it would virtually render the device safe . . . so long as it *was* detonating cord. Taking out his pliers, WO2 Maddocks cut into the plastic coating. But, instead of snipping through what he assumed would be an explosive filling, his pliers severed a coaxial cable cunningly concealed inside. It was a collapsing circuit. As WO2 Maddocks interrupted the current flow, it rerouted to the next best alternative – straight to a concealed detonator. The effect was immediate, devastating and fatal. His No. 2 was Corporal D.S. McAdam, who recollects:

I know there have been many tragic incidents in Northern Ireland since the Troubles started, but for me, the most tragic was the loss of WO2 John Maddocks. As his No. 2, I was 30 yards from John when the bomb he was working on blew up. We had been called to the area at 6 a.m. on that fateful day. I do remember that it was midnight before I got back to our base in Omagh – a long and sad day for me.

Bessbrook operator WO2 Edward 'Gus' Garside met his death on the sixty-fifth day of his tour. On 17 July 1975 he was investigating suspicious milk churns in a field near Ford's Cross, some 3 miles from Forkhill. They were a decoy. The real device, containing 70lb of explosive, was hidden beneath a gap in a hedgerow. It had been placed a fortnight before by members of the Crossmaglen unit of the Provisional IRA, who had dug a trench to conceal a command wire that led to a firing point some 400 yards away. Garside was one of a party of four, all of whom were killed as they passed through the gap. The others were the Incident Commander, Major Peter Willis, of the Green Howards (whose brother, coincidentally, was an ATO), the Royal

Engineers Search Adviser, Sergeant Samuel McCarter, and Garside's No. 2, Corporal Calvert Brown.

Clive Evans was a 25-year-old soldier attached to the EOD team, who was caught in the explosion that killed his colleagues. His recollection of events is given in *The British Army in Ulster, Volume 2*, by David Barzilay:

A company of the Green Howards on patrol at the bridge noticed a suspicious device. In fact several things didn't look quite right. They went back to Crossmaglen, reported, and an operation was planned to go in and clear the devices. There was a five gallon oil drum, a milk churn and a white object set back off the road. We were told there was going to be an operation to deal with the suspect objects and that the date would be given to us. A couple of days before we were told that the operation was on. I think that it was July 15th.

So on July 17th, the ATO, Gus Garside, his No. 2, and the Royal Engineer search adviser, Sammy McCarter, and myself, left Bessbrook at about 9 a.m. by helicopter and flew down to the area where the troops were on the ground, and had staked it out. We landed and the helicopter set off back to Bessbrook. We had a quick Orders Group with the Officer Commanding.

It was pointed out where we were on the ground and where the devices were. The ATO planned to move forward with his No. 2, the RE search adviser and myself and one rifleman for covering fire. Then the ATO would have gone forward by himself to check on the device. We went along the inside of a hedgerow. In a field the other side of the hedgerow was the road and a little bit further up the road was where the device was. We went along and then stopped to do a sweep. Without going into detail we were using a piece of equipment which will detonate any radio controlled devices in the area. The sweep was carried out, but nothing went bang, so we felt safe to assume that there were no radio controlled devices in the area.

The line of order setting off again to get onto the road was the OC, Gus Garside, Sammy McCarter, Brown and myself at the rear. We went a further 10 yards until we came to a gap in the hedge and decided to go through it and onto the road. Now all I remember really is that the OC and Gus Garside went down this bank. We were just coming out on to the road from the hedgerow. Sammy McCarter was at the bottom of the bank inside the hedgerow. Brown was just about to go down on the right and I was about two feet behind him.

Then the explosion occurred. I must have been blown backwards by the blast and I landed face downwards in the field. The next thing I remember is lying in the field face down with my hands over my head and feeling all the mud dropping on my back, and I could hear stuff falling out of the sky. Then I realised that there had been an explosion. My ears, God, terrible. It's hard to describe the sound in your ears. And my eyes they just stung like hell. I didn't remember any flash. It's hard to say whether you remember the flash. When I was lying down I can't remember whether I experienced the flash or whether it was when I was lying down that I thought Christ, there has been an explosion. I will never be able to say that I knew there was a flash. Apart from my ears and my eyes one hand was quite painful. I could open my left eye after a little while and I stood up and I could see a bloody great hole and a body nearly next to me.

I heard someone running towards me and I felt pretty giddy at that point, and sick, and I sat down again. Then I felt someone picking me up and I heard a voice saying 'this one is dead', and I was just dragged off across the field to the corner of the field. By that time my other eye, the eye I could see out of, was stinging again so I closed both of them. In fact someone, one of the soldiers put a field dressing on the bad eye. I knew it was bleeding, I could feel the blood. But he put the bandage over both eyes so I couldn't see anything.

I just lay there and I could hear people on the radio requesting a helicopter and telling them exactly what had happened and I still just lay there. I think I realised what had happened when I first stood up and I saw Brown lying there. I realised what had happened and I think that at the time I knew there wasn't much chance for them.

As it happened, luck had really stacked up against Corporal Brown that day, as Corporal C.A. Miller, a fellow AT, recalls: 'Corporal Calvert Brown, one of my AT course, was killed on his last day in Northern Ireland, with members of his team. I got mumps on a home visit at the end of the EOD course. I spent my Northern Ireland flight day travelling to the British Military Hospital at Munster in the back of a Land Rover. Corporal Brown took my place . . .'.

It was to be seventeen months before another ATO was caught out. The date was 9 January 1977. On this occasion, a booby-trapped milk churn device was to kill Sergeant Martin Walsh near Newtownbutler. Lieutenant-Colonel Derrick Patrick was Chief ATO Northern Ireland at the time. In his book *Fetch Felix* he describes the incident in some detail. WO2 Walsh had been tasked to clear the milk churn, which had been discovered in suspicious circumstances adjacent to a general store and garage, near Newtownbutler in Co. Fermanagh. The occupiers had already been the subject of serious IRA intimidation. Walsh managed to use his hook and line to extract the milk churn to a convenient piece of open ground, where he could get a better look at it. Having discovered what appeared to be a quantity of explosive with detonating cord running through it, the operator placed his hands inside the churn and started to rummage about, watched by his team escort. His last words were: 'Oh Christ, what've I got here?'

With the perfect vision of hindsight, a combination of several unhappy factors becomes apparent. He had returned from R&R only one full day before, so had probably not yet fully readjusted to his operational surroundings. When his team members were later interviewed, it became apparent that he had used a hammer to knock the lid off a milk churn during a clearance on a previous occasion. Because of the risk of booby traps, this was strictly against standing operating procedures; indeed, it was specifically forbidden, yet he had got away with it unscathed. He had been up late on the night before the clearance, and may therefore have been more tired than he should have been for such a task. When he approached the device, he had not worn the protective bomb suit. While this would not have saved his life in such close proximity to the bomb, it is perhaps an indication of his relaxed, but potentially overconfident, approach to the task. Notwithstanding these contributory factors, one fundamental oversight secured his fate. WO2 Walsh's death occurred on 9 January 1977. Only sixteen days earlier, on Christmas Eve, his boss, Lieutenant-Colonel Patrick, had defused an identical booby-trapped milk churn. The description had immediately been circulated to all operators, and a drawing of the device was actually on the wall of Walsh's office. Despite this, he had still been caught out.

As the equipment, training and operating procedures continued to develop through hard-earned experience, deaths mercifully became far less frequent. Given the casualty rate during the first half of the 1970s, amazingly, six years were to pass before the next ATO fatality was to occur.

It is rarely just one mistake that kills an operator. When one looks back at the circumstances leading inexorably towards the fatal moment, the warning signs start to appear early. This is certainly very apparent in the death of

WO2 Mick O'Neill. His final task, on 31 May 1981, involved the clearance of a Ford Cortina estate car, abandoned on the southern outskirts of Newry. It was thought to have been used by gunmen who had killed RUC Constable Mervyn Robinson in Whitecross, South Armagh, four days earlier.

Everything surrounding the vehicle was suspicious. The police first became aware of its appearance when, on 30 May, they received a tip-off on their confidential telephone line by an anonymous caller, who stated that two armed men had abandoned the car by the roadside at the junction of Hillhead Road and Drumalane Road near Newry. A covert reconnaissance was then carried out by an RUC patrol wearing civilian clothes. It reported back that the car's registration number was EIB 9462. A quick check on the computer showed that this number plate, which was allocated to an identical pale-blue Ford Cortina estate, was registered to a man living in Crossmaglen. However, a telephone call to the registered owner revealed that his car was, at that very moment, parked outside his house. Further police enquiries discovered that the abandoned vehicle was actually a similar car, hired from a firm in Taunton, Devon, which had been hijacked in Northern Ireland on 6 May 1981, and which had since been resprayed.

The Army was requested to undertake a clearance operation, and WO2 Mick O'Neill was to be the ATO for the job. After taking an initial look at the car on the ground, he reported back to his Officer Commanding in Lisburn that he planned to tackle it in slow time over the next couple of days. This conversation happened at 8.30 p.m. on 30 May. We then find the team inexplicably departing for the clearance at 4.20 a.m. the next day. We do not know what discussions took place in the meantime with the local infantry commander, who would have been running the operation. Maybe there was some pressure from the police to get the car moved. Possibly the police wished to get their hands on it quickly so that they could start to gather forensic evidence to assist in the pursuit of Constable Robinson's killers. Perhaps its location was inhibiting military patrol movements. Whatever the reason, the plan seems to have changed at relatively short notice, and, in the early hours of the morning, the team began making its way out to commence the operation.

Once on the ground, the series of unfortunate events continued to mount up. An attempt to open the boot using Wheelbarrow served only to jam it shut. Then the robot's camera picture started to break up, eventually rendering the machine unusable. The bad luck carried on when O'Neill's first attempt to open the driver's door remotely failed; he was successful only on the second attempt.

With all of the obvious areas declared clear, he ordered the team to start packing up. At some stage during his manual approaches, WO2 O'Neill expressed surprise to his team that the car appeared to have had a poor respray. The very fact that the car was assessed to have been in terrorist hands for such a long time, from 6 to 30 May, should have caused the alarm bells to ring. Indeed, on previous occasions where such efforts had been made to disguise a car, the vehicle had almost always been rigged with explosives.

With the team starting to collect up its gear, WO2 O'Neill told his No. 2 that he was just going back to check on one last thing. He was no longer wearing his helmet, having taken it off earlier because it was impeding his vision. Perhaps it was at this stage that he realised that the glove compartment remained shut, and might therefore still be concealing a booby trap. The team busied themselves with the clearing-up process, and nobody was really observing their 'boss'. One soldier noticed that O'Neill had knelt down by the front passenger door and was about to lean inside.

At 7.45 a.m., as WO2 O'Neill was leaning across the front passenger seat, there was a large explosion, which completely destroyed the car. He was killed instantly, his body being hurled over a fence and down a nearby embankment.

Subsequent tests and reconstructions indicated that the bomb had consisted of some 10–15lb of commercial explosives. The destruction to the car was so extensive that it was difficult to determine the precise make-up of the device. Possible options included a pressure pad concealed in the front passenger foot well, or a booby trap hidden in, or close to, the fascia, which would have been initiated by the action of opening the glove box.

WO2 O'Neill had been detached from the Base Ammunition Depot at Bracht in Germany for his Northern Ireland tour, and his wife and children had remained behind in their Army married quarter. As a WO1, John Lawrence was the Depot's Senior Ammunition Technician (SAT) when the message of O'Neill's death came through:

I was summoned to the Depot Headquarters to take a telephone call from Lieutenant-Colonel Chris Hendy, CATO Northern Ireland. It was early on a Sunday morning. By the time I got to the phone, I'd already decided what it was all about, and that Mick O'Neill was dead. There was no other reason why CATO would be calling on a Sunday morning, and, if Mick had only been injured, then they would have been trying to get the message through by the fastest possible means, rather than going through the formality of summoning the SAT.

When I picked up the phone, I was asked to identify myself. Having done so, Colonel Hendy then spoke very formally to me – almost as if he was giving orders down the phone: 'Mr Lawrence, I regret to inform you that at 0745 hours this morning, WO2 (SQMS) M. O'Neill was killed whilst conducting operational EOD duties.' He finished by saying that I must now tell my commanding officer.

When I got to the CO's house, he was still in his pyjamas and dressing gown. He obviously thought that I'd come round on some sort of social call, because he threw the door open with a hearty welcome: 'Mr Lawrence, do come in.' I stood on the doorstep and broke the dreadful news in the same manner that Lt-Col Hendy had used with me.

Once the CO was dressed, we started off towards Mick's married quarter to inform his wife. Although we were the only ones who had been told at that stage, I felt that all eyes were upon us, as if everyone just knew what we were on our way to do.

At the time, a story went round that WO2 O'Neill had developed an uncanny premonition about his death. He had already served a previous tour as an operator in Lurgan in 1974, and, as was the case with many operators, had been required back as a witness in a court case against a suspected terrorist. As he was leaving the foyer of the court, having been identified as a soldier, one local woman rounded on him with words to the effect of: 'Next time you come back, we'll get you.' Furthermore, only a short time before his deployment, a firework banger had been pushed through the letter box of his married quarter as a prank, setting light to his curtain. It seems that Mick had taken this as a bad omen.

Seven years after the death of WO2 Mick O'Neill, it was to be a pressure pad submerged under a puddle of water that would kill WO2 John Howard. At about 5 p.m. on 7 July 1988 an IRA gang assumed control of the Falls Road Public Baths, which incorporated a leisure centre. The staff were held hostage, and a female member of the gang took over the reception desk. Over the next two hours, the terrorists set up an ambush device in one of the exterior walls of the Baths, with the intention of taking out an unsuspecting Army foot patrol. Shortly after 7 p.m., a telephone call was made to the reception desk. It was the signal to detonate the bomb – and for some reason the signal went badly wrong. No troops were in the vicinity of the device; two Catholic civilians were. Sixty-year-old Elizabeth Hamill had only popped out to buy some milk; she would never return home. Fate would put her in that part of the street, at that time of the day, with Eamon 'Regy' Gilroy, a 24-year-old man who had just dropped off his baby daughter at his girlfriend's house. Both took the full force of the blast, dying later in hospital. Troops immediately deployed onto the ground to seal the area off and bring aid to the victims, although jeering, taunting and hostile crowds initially hindered the medical teams getting through.

As control was regained over the situation, it became necessary to task one of 321 EOD Company's teams to the scene. The Belfast team was called out from Girdwood Park Barracks, less than five minutes' drive away. The team would have been expecting the call. The shock wave from the explosion would almost certainly have rattled the windows of the self-contained team bungalow inside the barracks, and news flashes would have started to appear on the radio and TV. Quite probably, the junior officer acting as watchkeeper at Headquarters 39 Infantry Brigade, based in Lisburn, would have been on the telephone to give the team a 'heads up' that something was going on before the formal tasking message was sent. Inside the bungalow, troops would have been pulling their 'flak' jackets on over their heads, then zipping up their combat jackets, while the operator and his No. 2 checked out the precise grid reference on the wall map.

WO2 John Howard, a 29-year-old married man, was the team's No. 1 operator. The scene at the Falls Road Public Baths was still one of chaos and devastation when he arrived. Rubble and glass were strewn across the street where a large part of the outside wall had been blown out. The peculiar acrid smell that follows an explosion hung in the night air, and pools of blood from the casualties stained the road. Here in the IRA's heartland of urban West Belfast, the security troops on the cordon were still on the receiving end of a certain amount of 'aggro' from the locals. The pressure would have been mounting for the ATO to declare the area clear of further explosives, so that the Police Scenes of Crime Officer could get on with his job of collecting forensic evidence. The sooner that was done, the sooner the vulnerable infantry cordon troops could be pulled in off the ground.

It must have seemed a straightforward task. The bomb had fully functioned, the casualties had been removed, and, in the process, many people had swarmed all over the site before being pulled back from the potential danger area. It was now just a case of giving the area a once-over to ensure that it was clear. WO2 Howard quickly detected the command wire that had initiated the device. From the firing point in the leisure centre, it snaked down a set of stairs and through a cellar, which was being used to store sports equipment, before emerging at the scene of the explosion – the cellar wall adjacent to the road. A water pipe in the cellar had fractured, and the room was now some 2 inches deep in water. A stack of gym mats was stored in a space under the stairs. Others had been used to tamp the back of the device. Fragments of them had been blown back into the cellar when the bomb went off.

WO2 Howard cleared the explosion site and the command wire, before allowing a female member of the Northern Ireland Forensic Science Laboratories (NIFSL) into the crime scene. She descended into the cellar and noticed the command wire snaking behind the pile of mats under the stairs. Tentatively pulling one mat back, she was surprised to see a duffel bag secreted behind the stack. She left the cellar, sought out WO2 Howard, and told him what she had seen. On the face of it, it sounded like the sort of normal everyday item that one might expect to encounter in a leisure-centre storeroom, but an operator cannot be too careful. WO2 Howard decided to take a closer look. He ordered people to stay clear of the scene and re-entered the cellar.

Several of the mats were lying on the floor, now soaking wet from the water that had flooded the cellar. As WO2 Howard stepped onto one of them, his foot depressed the top plate of a concealed pressure pad. The contact was made and the booby trap detonated. The blast ripped through the close confines of the cellar and killed him instantly. This two-step operation was a classic example of an IRA 'come-on' – an ambush device, followed up by a booby trap. At the time of writing, no further operators have been killed in the Province.

In trying to determine a common theme running through the fatalities, it would seem that the operator's level of experience, his length of time in the Province and his team's base location had little bearing on his chances of survival. Some of the deceased were young captains, having only recently graduated from their ATO courses. Others were experienced warrant officers, with many years in the ammunition trade. That said, it is notable that only the last two fatalities, O'Neill and Howard, had served an operational tour in the Province before. The main reason for this is that the Troubles were into their second decade by that time, so second tours were becoming routine. These days, it would be common for most non-commissioned operators at least to have served as a team No. 2 before progressing to No. 1's duties, as a sergeant or above, several years later. Those being assigned to the more high-risk areas might also have served a previous tour as a No. 1 as well.

The length of time served in the Province before the fatal incidents occurred covers a wide spread, and is almost evenly distributed, from a low of only eight days (Stewardson) to a high of 141 days (Calladene). There is a significant grouping around the late point of 55–75 days into a tour – about the time R&R was either imminently due, or had just been taken. In terms of team location, four operators were based in Lurgan, three each in Belfast and Bessbrook, and two in each of Lisburn, Londonderry and Omagh. While this again seems like an even dispersion, it is noted that only one death (Howard's) occurred in either Belfast or Londonderry after mid-1973. This points to the possible conclusion that, although the rural areas have always been quieter than the cities, the operator is actually at greater danger when he is out in the country. Here, the terrorist is better able to dominate the ground, and has more time to employ his cunning and ingenuity to the maximum.

The sad fact is that, at the critical moment, almost all the deceased made a fatal error that led to their deaths. This is hardly surprising. The pressures placed upon the operator are enormous. He knows that he is tying up large numbers of troops on the ground, who themselves are at risk, until he has got the job done. His brain is buzzing with thoughts about the likely threat, secondary hazards, the security of the cordon, time constraints, liaising with the emergency services and picking over the details given by any available witnesses. It takes only one omission or short cut on his part, and it could be his last. The situation is akin to that faced by expert mountaineers. They too must remain calm under the most testing circumstances. They will occasionally make mistakes that are within a hair's breadth of being fatal. And, every once in a while, even the best will die.

As the campaign in Northern Ireland has continued, the operators' training, procedures and equipment have improved beyond all recognition. No longer do students spend time manufacturing and defusing each other's 'bombs' in a classroom. Instead, they face realistic scenarios played out in a purpose-built mock village, complete with its own shops, farm, bank and railway. With each death, injury or narrow escape, procedures have been reviewed and adapted to prevent a repetition. Likewise, equipment has been the subject of a constant development programme, often being designed at very short notice to counter a new emerging threat. The immediate reduction in fatalities following the introduction of Wheelbarrow and Pigstick in 1972 is tangible proof of the life-saving benefits of these particular items.

Nevertheless, even with the very best training, procedures and equipment, operator error remains the most likely cause of death, and this could happen at any time. In the heat of the moment, he may miss something – perhaps while he is distracted by a nearby hostile crowd. Perhaps he has got away with a short cut on several previous occasions, so becomes accustomed to cutting corners. Perhaps a run of false alarms or hoax devices serves to convince him that the terrorists have slackened their efforts. Maybe he bows to pressure from the police or the incident commander to get the task over with as quickly as possible. These are just some of the mistakes that most operators will make at some time, which they will survive for the most part, yet which will prove deadly when luck runs out.

In 2002 the Felix Memorial Garden was opened in Thiepval Barracks, Lisburn, home of Headquarters 321 EOD Squadron RLC, by the General Officer Commanding Northern Ireland, Lieutenant-General Sir Alistair Irwin, and the Chief Constable of the RUC, Sir Ronnie Flanagan. The ceremony was attended by many relatives and friends of the deceased. The landscaped garden provides a quiet place for reflection. The seventeen operators and three additional team members who died are each commemorated by a small headstone. One side of the garden is lined by a wall, onto which has been painted a dramatic mural, depicting a busy street scene in Belfast city centre. The intention is to depict the return to normality, for which so many members of 321 EOD have risked, and in some cases given, their lives. In the bottom right-hand corner, hunched alone over a terrorist device, is an operator dressed in his bomb suit. Beneath him are the compelling and hugely appropriate words from John Bunyan's hymn 'To Be a Pilgrim':

> Who would true valour see,
> Let him come hither.

EPILOGUE

INTO THE TWENTY-FIRST CENTURY: WHATEVER NEXT?

The Good Friday Agreement of April 1998 should, perhaps, have marked the beginning of the end for 321 EOD Squadron. To all intents and purposes, the Provisional IRA (PIRA) had declared an end to all 'military' operations and accepted the need for the decommissioning of its weapons stockpile. Despite huge cynicism on both sides of the sectarian divide, the Agreement promised to set the conditions for real progress at the negotiating table. As far as the general public was concerned, support appeared to be overwhelming. A referendum, held shortly after the Agreement was signed, revealed that just over 71 per cent in the north and 94 per cent in the south of Ireland were in favour. At this stage, it seemed that the scaling-down of 321 EOD Squadron as part of the 'peace dividend' must be imminent.

However, the democratic wishes of the majority have never meant a great deal to hardline terrorists. After all, if they could achieve their aims through the legitimate mechanism of the ballot box, they would have no need to intimidate and kill innocent members of the public. Unable to move with the times, and vehemently opposed to the peace process, a number of disaffected individuals split from PIRA in late 1997. Led by former PIRA 'Quartermaster General' Mickey McKevitt, the new group labelled itself the 'Real' IRA (RIRA). Denouncing the PIRA leadership for 'betraying Republicanism', the group released a statement saying that the ceasefire was over and that it would return to 'military' operations.

RIRA immediately gained a number of disaffected, skilled bomb-makers and picked up the terror campaign where PIRA had left off. For 321 EOD Squadron, without even pausing to draw breath, it was back to 'business as usual'. From September 1997 onwards, vehicle bombs and mortar attacks became RIRA's stock-in-trade. Car bombs exploded in Moira, Portadown and Newtownhamilton, and RUC stations were mortared in Armagh and Newry. On 2 August 1998 a 500lb car bomb ripped apart the main shopping area of Banbridge, Co. Down, injuring thirty-three civilians and two police officers. But it was with the Omagh bombing, less than two weeks later, that RIRA came to international prominence. As described in Chapter Four, 29 people were killed and over 200 injured in the worst atrocity of the Troubles.

The attack was met with worldwide revulsion. The backlash of condemnation emanated from all communities across the Province. Mainstream Republicans, such as Gerry Adams and Martin McGuinness, denounced the dissidents. Even RIRA's leaders, hardened and brutalised though they were from years of terrorist warfare, could not overlook the fact that the indiscriminate murder of innocent civilians was hardly likely to gain popular support for the movement. Three days after the Omagh bomb, RIRA announced its own ceasefire, and, for a while, went quiet.

So did this mean that 321 EOD Squadron could relax its efforts? Not a bit of it. The temporary withdrawal of RIRA from the fray left two remaining Republican dissident groups prepared to kill (rather than die) for their cause. These were the Irish National Liberation Army (INLA) and the 'Continuity' IRA (CIRA).

INLA had been formed in 1975 by disaffected members of PIRA who had rebelled against a temporary ceasefire prevailing at the time. Despite being small in number, it quickly gained a reputation for extremism, even among other Republican groups. What it lacked in weapons and explosives, it made up for with sheer inhuman savagery. Its notoriety was established in 1979 with the murder of Rt Hon Airey Neave MP, the Conservatives' shadow Northern Ireland Secretary. He had been killed by an under-car booby trap on a Friday afternoon, as he drove his Vauxhall Cavalier up a ramp from the House of Commons underground car park. It had also been INLA that had conducted the no-warning bombing of the Droppin Well discothèque on 7 December 1982. While this had killed eleven soldiers, it had also caused the deaths of six innocent female civilians – no doubt justified as 'legitimate targets' or the 'collateral casualties of war'. By 1998 INLA's efforts to secure a better Ireland had accounted for the deaths of 140 people. Nevertheless, in the face of Omagh, even this cadre of hardliners wavered, and a ceasefire was called.

With PIRA, RIRA and INLA all declaring either long- or short-term cessations of violence, CIRA meanwhile announced that it would continue to mount terrorist attacks. This further breakaway group had come into being in 1986, when it had split from PIRA for ideological reasons. Like RIRA, its aim had always been to drive the British out of Ireland. At a time when closer links with an increasingly federal Europe seemed inevitable, CIRA was apparently stuck in a time warp in which the English were still synonymous with Oliver Cromwell's army of occupation. It was one of those many terrorist groups around the world that seemed intent on refighting wars that were centuries old. Luckily, the organisation's small size and limited access to weapons and explosives hindered its ability to launch frequent attacks, but it remained an occasional source of work for 321 EOD's operators.

Omagh might well have sounded the death knell for RIRA, but, despite overwhelming international revulsion, the group somehow managed to survive. Initially, it maintained a low profile, but, within two years, it was starting to reassert itself, commencing a steady stream of attacks. From the style of those attacks, it became clear that Omagh had taught RIRA one particular lesson: that large devices placed in busy shopping areas in daylight, and over which the terrorist has no control once the timer is running, are far too risky. Instead, the dissidents turned their attention to targets that might gain a better propaganda response in certain circles. That is, to try to kill members of the Security Forces, ideally on duty, in uniform.

After 2000 RIRA demonstrated that, in terms of cunning, ingenuity and technical capability, it could match the Provisionals at the height of the Troubles. This was hardly surprising, given that up to thirty experienced PIRA operatives were believed to have joined its ranks.

Often, sheer luck seemed to take a hand in defeating RIRA's efforts. On 31 June 2000 a bomb exploded on the Belfast-to-Dublin railway line between Newry and Dundalk at a place called Meigh in Co. Armagh. The Security Forces staked out the area and began a cautious investigation. During an over-flight by helicopter, it was noticed that the shingle alongside the tracks appeared to have been displaced in one particular area just feet away from the seat of the earlier explosion. This was apparent because the stones in that spot had not been weathered and discoloured in the same way as those around them. Sure enough, a closer look revealed a secondary device set to take out members of the Security Forces responding to the initial blast. This consisted of 108kg of home-made explosive in plastic fertiliser drums, and would have been set off by radio control as soon as a soldier – possibly the ATO – entered the killing area.

Luck once again played a part on 17 January 2001. A van, supposedly containing a bomb, was delivered to the front of Claudy RUC Station. The immediate action in such a situation should have been for the police to evacuate out of the back gate onto an area of wasteland. On this occasion, however, they had lost the key to the back gate, so they had no choice but to exit via the front gate, running past the suspect device as they did so. A team from 321 EOD Squadron attended, dealt with the van, and declared the incident a hoax. Over the next two days, a number of telephone calls were received from the terrorists stating that a device was still in the vicinity of the RUC Station. A subsequent search revealed a victim-operated tripwire device connected to the back gate. Had the police found the key, and used that escape route, they would undoubtedly have suffered serious casualties. A young captain, Matthew Middleditch, from 321 EOD Squadron attended the scene and spent several hair-raising hours dismantling the device. During this process, while he was actually alongside the main charge, a black bin liner, which had been caught up in the tripwire, was being flapped about by a strong breeze. He just had to hope that the resistance on the wire was sufficient for the device not to function. For this, and several other difficult tasks performed during his tour, Captain Middleditch was awarded the Queen's Gallantry Medal.

Within days, this same young officer was to be personally thankful for RIRA's run of bad luck. Just after midnight on 23 January 2001 a blue Isuzu van was driven to the rear of Ebrington Barracks in Londonderry. Some 10 minutes later, a Mark 15 'Barrackbuster' mortar bomb, containing approximately 160lb of home-made explosive, was launched through a cut-out panel in the van's roof. It struck the Officers' Mess inside the camp, approximately 40 metres from the firing point, but failed to function. It was assessed that the bomb hit the wall sideways on with such force that the fuse broke off, rendering it inoperable. As it happened, Captain Middleditch was asleep in his room only a few metres from where the device landed. He was then called out to make it safe. He could almost have completed the task by simply leaning out of his window while still wearing his pyjamas!

Just like PIRA before, one of RIRA's favourite tricks was to use some fake incident to lure the Security Forces into an ambush situation – the so-called come-on. Sometime after midnight on 17 July 2002, shots were heard in the area of the New Model Farm estate, Downpatrick. Police were despatched to investigate. At 1.50 a.m., as officers were driving along the Killough Road, an explosion occurred adjacent to their patrol car. They witnessed a flash, heard a muffled report, and felt an object striking the nearside front wing of their vehicle. There were no casualties. This time, the device had been fired by command wire from an elevated position in a field just 50 metres away. Only a fraction of a second's difference in the time that the terrorist pressed the firing button would have turned this near miss to tragedy. Once more, lady luck favoured the Security Forces.

Unfortunately, not all RIRA's deadly schemes failed, but when they did get lucky, it always seemed to be against 'soft targets'. Just before lunchtime on 8 February 2002 a black military-style water bottle was spotted lying next to the perimeter fence of the Magilligan military training camp in Co. Londonderry. It was reported to the civilian security guards, and a guard was despatched by Land Rover to investigate. He pulled up next to the water bottle, stooped down and picked it up. A nearby sangar sentry heard an explosion at 11.40 a.m., followed by the sight of the guard staggering along the road towards him. The victim had lost both arms below the elbow and suffered serious abdominal injuries. The explosion had also stripped the clothing from the upper half of his body. His injuries were made worse by the fact that a large quantity of change, which he had been carrying in a trouser pocket, had been driven into his body by the blast. Surprisingly, the guard had only recently retired from the Army after twenty-two years' service, having attained the rank of warrant officer. This incident shows that basic lessons, such as 'never pick up discarded military equipment', can easily be forgotten on the spur of the moment.

A similar incident occurred on 1 August 2002. Caw Camp is a Territorial Army centre near Eglinton, Co. Londonderry, which was being refurbished at the time. Under cover of darkness, a Tupperware lunchbox was left near the front gates of the camp. Early the next morning, one of the civilian building contractors, David Caldwell, arrived for work. Seeing the Tupperware box, he picked it up and carried it inside the camp to a former 'Band Block', which was being used as a contractors' hut. At 7.25 a.m. a civilian living adjacent to the camp heard an explosion from the direction of the Band Block. Scaling the fence, he rushed to the scene, where he found David Caldwell with severe injuries to his face and hands, and puncture wounds to his chest and abdomen. The victim was admitted to Altnagelvin Hospital, but died within two hours of the explosion. The device had almost certainly been an anti-open booby trap.

Despite the prospect of peace emerging from the Good Friday Agreement, and the much-vaunted IRA ceasefire, it can be seen that the workload continued at a steady rate for the operators of 321 EOD Squadron. The Provisionals may have confined their activities to fuel, alcohol and cigarette smuggling, counterfeiting, punishment beatings, extortion and armed robbery, but the war against Republican terrorist bombers continued – they just operated under a different name. Fortunately, the impact of Omagh was to put an end to large car bombs in public places. Hence, the mass slaughter of innocent civilians, for the time being, ceased. This still left the operator having to deal with the remaining panoply of terrorist explosive devices: command-wire and radio-controlled IEDs, anti-armour weapons, booby traps, secondary devices and incendiaries.

Meanwhile, the Loyalist paramilitaries remained at work. In comparing the two sides of the sectarian divide, it became very much a case of quality versus quantity. While the Republican dissidents continued to manufacture technically sophisticated devices that were deployed with cunning and ingenuity, but in relatively small numbers, the Loyalists employed simple blast bombs in large quantities.

The Ulster Defence Association (also known by its 'cover name' as the 'Ulster Freedom Fighters') began toying with a ceasefire from October 1994. By January 1998, however, it had to admit to numerous breaches, and in July 2001, disillusioned, it withdrew its support for the Good Friday Agreement altogether. By October of the same year, the British Government stated that it no longer recognised a UDA ceasefire, but in February 2003 the UDA announced a twelve-month period of 'military inactivity'. The so-called ceasefire observed by the Protestant paramilitaries therefore tended to come and go.

Whatever the state of the ceasefire as far as the UDA/UFF was concerned, Loyalist terrorists continued to wage a campaign of violence and intimidation against the Catholic community. This frequently involved the use of explosive devices, usually in the form of 'pipe bombs'. Loyalist dissatisfaction and disillusionment with the Good Friday Agreement also brought about numerous incidents of large-scale public disorder, during which pipe bombs again proved to be the weapon of choice. Over and above this, internal feuding between Loyalist factions led to the use of explosive devices against each other.

One report that appeared in the *Observer* on 29 July 2001 stated:

On average once every four days, improvised explosive devices constructed from materials found in any household's garage, kitchen or garden shed are being thrown at houses belonging to Catholics in predominantly Protestant areas: a cheap but nasty form of ethnic cleansing.

Since last summer, the Royal Ulster Constabulary says, more than 100 so-called pipe bombs have been hurled at Catholic homes in the northern part of the Province. Given the number of incidents that go unreported, the figure might even be higher.

Pipe bombs are among the simplest forms of IED. In their most basic state, they will consist of little more than a length of plumbing pipe, filled with home-made explosive, with a burning fuse inserted into one end, and a detonator to set the whole thing off. Such simple devices may be enhanced by the inclusion of an electrical circuit, perhaps containing a timer, such as a modified watch or clock, or an anti-handling mechanism, such as a mercury tilt switch.

Between 2000 and 2005 the number of pipe-bomb attacks made by Loyalist terrorists vastly outweighed those by Republicans. Initially, the attacks were claimed by dissident Loyalist groups, such as the 'Red Hand Defenders' or 'Orange Volunteers', but later bombings bore the mark of the mainstream organisations – the UDA and the UVF. Since the Good Friday Agreement, pipe bombs have made up by far the largest part of 321 EOD Squadron's workload of genuine devices in Northern Ireland. As an indication of the proliferation of these crude but potentially deadly weapons, the statistics over just one quarter, from December 2000 to the end of February 2001, show thirty-nine pipe-bomb incidents. Of these, eighteen involved explosions, twenty concerned pipe bombs that had failed to function being recovered by ATOs, and one was a 'find'. Despite the very large number of attacks, pipe bombs inflict few casualties – they are prone to failure, contain relatively small quantities of explosive, inflict damage over a limited radius, and can often be avoided if they are seen coming. Their greatest value seems to lie in their effect as weapons of intimidation.

As was often the case in the early days of the Troubles, most of the very serious injuries caused by pipe bombs have been as a result of 'own goals'. For example, on the afternoon of 11 November 2001, sectarian civil disorder broke out following a Remembrance Day parade in Belfast. Police moved in to separate two crowds of rioters at the sectarian interface between New Lodge and Tiger Bay. As the Loyalist crowd was pushed back down North Queen Street, a police officer saw a hooded youth light an object and advance towards the police riot squad's 'base line'. As he held the object in the air, it exploded, causing the immediate traumatic amputation of his arm and a severe head injury. The youth died from his injuries and two people in the vicinity were injured.

Another such incident occurred on 3 January 2002 at Coleraine in Co. Antrim. Just before midnight, an explosion was heard from an alleyway to the rear of a street in the town known as Winston Way. A passer-by went to investigate and found a body lying on the ground. The victim, who had been kneeling over the device when it functioned, sustained blast and fragment injuries to the left ankle, right knee, face, throat and upper-chest area. From the remains recovered, the ATO was able to assess that the bomb had been constructed from a mechanical alarm clock and a PP9 battery, attached to a steel pipe wrapped in a plastic bin liner. The pipe contained 30–50g of shotgun propellant.

For all the reasons outlined above, and despite the Good Friday Agreement, after 2000 the level of tasking for 321 EOD Squadron continued at a high level. As an example, throughout 2002, its teams were called out to 1,003 incidents. Of these, 132 resulted in an explosive device being made safe, 68 were to explosions, 188 involved finds of weapons and bomb-making equipment, 103 were to assist with 'forensic clearances', and most of the remainder arose from deliberate hoaxes or false alarms. The average number of taskings across the Province in 2005 remained at just under 300 per month.

What changed, however, was the whole tenor of operations. Although RIRA, CIRA and INLA might have proved themselves capable of producing deadly devices that matched the worst of those made by PIRA, they did not do so in anywhere near the same quantities. And, although Protestant paramilitary pipe bombs may have accounted for a high proportion of overall 'real' tasks (as distinct from hoaxes and false alarms), they are comparatively easy to deal with. The theatre certainly grew less hazardous for the EOD operator, but he had constantly to be on his guard and certainly could not afford to become complacent.

Meanwhile, during the time since the British Army had become involved in Northern Ireland, there was a staggering proliferation of terrorist bombings worldwide. The spread of IED technology matched the expansion of the

Internet. Knowledge that was previously gained by painful trial and error could be picked up in minutes from the World Wide Web. In the first eleven years of the Troubles, the IRA lost ninety bombers due to own goals. In most cases, simple safety errors were to blame. By 2005, terrorist groups could exchange the technical information to prevent such errors at the touch of a button.

As we move into the twenty-first century, new threats are emerging constantly. Very sensitive, organic peroxide, home-made explosives, which require no detonator to set them off, are being exploited by many terrorist organisations around the globe. With titles such as HMTD (hexamethylene triperoxide diamine) and TATP (triacetone triperoxide), these can be manufactured from a range of simple ingredients – nail polish, hair bleach, solid camping stove tablets and citric acid – and can be used as an effective booster to a much larger, less sensitive, main charge. The organic peroxide explosives are extremely sensitive to friction, shock, heat and flame, even when wet. Exposure to direct sunlight alone may be enough to set them off. It is therefore hardly surprising that, when Muslim fundamentalist 'shoe-bomber' Richard Reid tried to blow up a passenger airliner in December 2001, using a bomb concealed in his shoe, he used TATP as the booster, planning to ignite it with a match. Perhaps what is surprising though is that he walked to the aircraft using shoes loaded with TATP, which might have detonated at any time.

The boom in communications technology has given the bomb-maker new and improved methods of initiating his devices from a distance by radio control. The advantage of this is that there is no requirement for a physical wire link between the bomber and his target. It is therefore quick and easy to deploy an ambush device, less evidence is subsequently left on the ground and the terrorist has a good chance of escaping. Radio-controlled devices are therefore appearing in the hands of terrorists worldwide – from Iraq and Afghanistan to Kosovo and Colombia.

Perhaps the most worrying threat of all is the increasing exploitation of suicide bombers. Whereas terrorists in Northern Ireland would always plan an escape route, this is irrelevant to the suicide bomber. Such attacks are extremely hard to defend against, and, as such, carry a significantly disproportionate perception of fear compared to other terrorist incidents. They are frequently employed against population-rich targets, and the public will feel both vulnerable and impotent in the face of the threat. The suicide bomber's devices may come in all shapes and sizes, from shoe bombs, carefully constructed to eliminate metal components, up to large vehicle-borne IEDs.

On the face of it, there seems little that the EOD operator can do against the suicide bomber. He is up against a moving target, who cares not one jot for survival and to whom collateral casualties just do not matter. A firing button may be pressed as soon as the operator gets anywhere near the target – and initiation may even be effected from some distance away by an observer using radio control. Nevertheless, the operator does have a role. If the terrorist is intercepted and shot dead by the Security Forces, there is still a live device that must be dealt with. The risk becomes even greater if the bomber is only wounded, or is uninjured and being restrained, as he or she may still be trying to detonate the explosives as the operator works.

Al Qaeda has developed the tactic of combining a suicide bomb attack with an integrated, armed, shock assault. This was most clearly demonstrated in the attack on three residential compounds used by western expatriate contract workers in Riyadh on 12 May 2003. At the 'Jedawal Compound', occupied by employees of such companies as Lockheed and Boeing, armed terrorists drove up to the back gate in a Ford saloon car and shot dead the gate guard. They then fired and threw grenades at other security guards responding to the assault. When they failed to force an entry, the main device, contained in a GMC truck, was diverted to a second gate, where it was detonated. The blast killed two terrorists in the truck and three others standing outside with IEDs strapped to their waists. The attackers also killed two security guards as they approached the gate, but no residents died.

Meanwhile, at the 'Cordoba Compound', housing members of the US Vinnel Corporation, an initial assault was made by terrorists driving a Ford Crown Victoria saloon into the main gates. All the gate guards were quickly killed by small-arms fire or grenades. The ramming attempt failed, but the terrorists were able to gain access to the gate control switches. With the front gates open, the terrorists fought their way through two further layers of security and drove a Dodge pick-up truck, containing some 400kg of explosive, up to 'High Rise No. 1', the main accommodation building. The device was detonated, but, mercifully, casualties were few as many of the contractors were away from the compound at the time. After the explosion, the three surviving attackers fought their way out, escaping over a wall.

The third target was the 'Al Hamra Compound', where over 70 per cent of the residents were Saudis. This was the most lightly guarded of the three, with only one unarmed guard, who was shot and wounded. It was attacked by terrorists in a Toyota Camry, with a suicide bomb in a GMC Suburban truck. They drove into the centre of the compound, where they detonated the device. It is possible that the explosion was initiated prematurely, since the accompanying Toyota was also hit by the blast and four terrorists inside killed. The recreation centre was reportedly holding a party for a large group of Saudis at the time, and many of the casualties were believed to be at the function. The fatalities across all three attacks were officially given as 35 or 36, although some estimates were closer to 100.

One particularly harrowing development, which is becoming more common, is where a person is wired up to a bomb, or held in close proximity to it, under duress or by force. This is becoming increasingly prevalent in hostage situations as a means of deterring offensive action by counterterrorist teams. After all, terrorists prepared to blow themselves up for their cause will have little compunction over inflicting the same fate on their chosen victims, innocent or not.

In Colombia, on 15 May 2000, terrorists from the FARC (Revolutionary Armed Forces of Colombia) broke into the rural village home of 52-year-old Elvira Cortes Gil. She was refusing to pay an 'extortion tax' that the terrorists had been demanding. They used a silicon-based adhesive to glue a square-shaped pipe bomb around her neck. She was told that the bomb contained anti-handling switches, which would set it off if it was tilted or tampered with. In addition, there was a timer, which would eventually run down and cause the bomb to explode unless the terrorists' demands were met. Police and bomb-disposal operators were called out, and a desperate battle began to remove the 'necklace' bomb. After six hours, the device exploded, killing the woman instantly. Two bomb-squad officers both lost their left arms in the blast, one of whom bled to death at the scene.

While it would have been vastly preferable not to have had to wage a counterterrorist war in Northern Ireland for more than three decades, the experience has put the British Army ahead of the game when it comes to dealing with improvised explosive devices. As a consequence, lessons learnt in Northern Ireland are proving of immeasurable value in the 'Global War against Terror'. Most major countries are nowadays equipped with robotic vehicles that owe their antecedents directly to Lieutenant-Colonel (Retd) Peter

Miller's remote-controlled lawnmower. Disruptive weapons, using the same principles as Pigstick, are a routine part of the EOD operator's arsenal worldwide. Protective bomb suits tend to share the same basic designs as those used for decades in Ulster.

International terrorism is a growth industry, and, sadly, this is not a problem that is going to go away. As far as the British Army is concerned, its ATOs and ATs are unlikely ever to go back to simply looking after ammunition. Although the Troubles in Northern Ireland may finally be moving towards resolution, the Army's EOD operators have never been in greater demand. Since the 2003 war in Iraq, and the subsequent outbreak of terrorist activity there, that theatre has already been designated 'High Threat', alongside Northern Ireland, and training courses have been shaped accordingly. A new generation of operators is learning how to deal with command-initiated devices, booby traps and come-ons, but in the sun-baked deserts and towns of Iraq.

The terrorist atrocities in America on 11 September 2001, when passenger airliners were used as flying bombs, emphasised the danger posed to civilised, democratic societies by weapons of mass destruction. Accordingly, even greater effort has gone into hitherto highly secret plans to deal with chemical, biological, nuclear or radioactive terrorist devices planted in one of the UK's major cities. All of these ultimately rely on one man taking the long walk to 'do the business' – the ATO.

The Northern Ireland experience may have put the British Army at the cutting edge of the EOD business, but there is no room for complacency. As the threat grows, so does the technology available to the terrorist with which to prosecute it. Huge efforts are therefore being put into staying ahead of the game. Wheelbarrow has reached the end of the line as far as 'bolt-on' enhancements are concerned, and is likely to be replaced by 2010 by a revolutionary new machine. This will be armed with advanced manipulator arms, enhanced weaponry and sharper cameras. It will be faster and more manœuvrable than its predecessors. In the meantime, research has been going on into a new and better bomb suit. The aim is to achieve much better flexibility and comfort while improving the level of protection.

Such is the demand for EOD operators that requests from foreign countries to be taught by the UK's experts are at an all-time high. Frequently, ATOs will also be requested to fly out to trouble spots around the world to advise on EOD equipment, organisation, procedures and training. As operational lessons filter back to the training school, courses are constantly being reviewed to ensure that what is being taught gives the operator the very best chance of survival in the field.

Counterterrorist bomb disposal has been an enormous success story for the British Army. As a result of its experiences in Northern Ireland, it has a capability that is the envy of the world, and to which many nations turn for training or advice. Things have come a long way from the days when a young captain, armed with just a Stanley knife and a hook and line, took calls to his married quarter to go out and deal with something nasty. In the intervening years, the numbers of lives saved, property rescued, devices rendered safe and explosives recovered by the operators of 321 EOD Squadron have all reached astronomical proportions. Gallantry awards have numbered 2 George Crosses, 29 George Medals and nearly 300 other medals for outstanding gallantry, along with innumerable Mentions in Despatches and other commendations.

As we have seen, these achievements were not without cost. Seventeen operators and three other team members lost their lives on operations in Northern Ireland. The Ammunition Technical Officers and Ammunition Technicians of the Royal Logistic Corps continue to face increasingly sophisticated threats as the menace of international terrorism grows. Regrettably, but almost inevitably, more stand to lose their lives in the process. But, with the situation in Northern Ireland finally reaching a degree of calm, it is an ideal time to salute them, and all the officers and soldiers who have served with 321 EOD Squadron.

GLOSSARY

ANFO home-made explosive

battalion a unit of the British Army usually consisting of some 600–800 soldiers

black powder a mix of potassium nitrate and sulphur

Bramley Central Ammunition Depot, and the home of the Army School of Ammunition from 1922 to 1974

Bramley Shadow Unit a unit made up of soldiers who routinely worked at the Bramley Central Ammunition Depot, but who could be deployed into the field to perform a more active role in time of war

brigade an Army formation consisting of several battalions, and usually in the region of 5,000+ strong

Claymore a directional, command-detonated, anti-personnel mine that fires a huge number of small metal fragments

collapsing circuit in a collapsing circuit, the terrorist lures the ATO into cutting an obvious wire; when he does so, the electrical current re-routes into an alternative circuit, which fires the detonator, causing the device to function

come-on a term used to describe a situation in which the security forces are lured into a trap – for example, a second device at the scene of an explosion

company an Army sub-unit of 100+ soldiers, commanded by a major; each battalion will consist of a number of companies

controlled explosion the application of an explosion under controlled conditions to disrupt or destroy a terrorist device

Co-op mix nickname for home-made explosive, stemming from the fact that all ingredients could be bought at the local Co-op store

Cordtex trade name for a brand of detonating cord that is applied generically, in the same way as Biro or Hoover (see detonating cord, below)

Craftsman term used in the REME for a private soldier

detonating cord plastic-coated demolition item, resembling a washing line in appearance, shape and flexibility, but filled with high explosive; it may be used as a link, either between several main charges, or between a detonator and the main charge; it may also be used for explosive cutting – for example, to slice a metal container in half

Eager Beaver a radio-controlled, military fork-lift truck, with a cross-country capability

false an innocent object, such as an abandoned shopping bag, which has mistakenly been reported as a possible terrorist bomb

Felix radio nickname for EOD operators in Northern Ireland; logo for 321 EOD Unit

Ferret Scout Car light, four-wheeled, armoured vehicle, mounting a Browning machine gun

find a hidden cache of terrorist weapons and/or ammunition that has been discovered by the Security Forces.

forensic clearance action carried out to ensure that an object, such as a weapon or vehicle, is free from booby traps

Garda police force of the Republic of Ireland

Gelamex commercial explosive

high order complete detonation of the device

hoax a deliberate attempt to mislead the Security Forces with a dummy or bogus device

Humber Pig armoured personnel carrier used extensively in Northern Ireland

Jack Horner first nickname for the disruptive weapon usually referred to as Pigstick

junior rank non-commissioned ranks of corporal and below

manual approach when the operator walks up to the IED to carry out his render-safe procedure rather than deploying a robot to do it remotely

own goal term used when a terrorist blows himself up

Pig 1-ton Humber armoured car, principally used as an armoured personnel carrier, but also employed as an EOD team vehicle for some teams

Pigstick a disruptive weapon that fires water and gas into a bomb to disable it

platoon an Army unit of around thirty strong, commanded by a lieutenant; a company will be made up of several platoons

ring-main several explosive charges linked by detonating cord

sangar a military observation post, protected against shots and explosions by concrete or sandbags.

Sapper nickname for a member of the Royal Engineers

Saracen a six-wheeled armoured personnel carrier

Saxon a wheeled, armoured, troop-carrying vehicle that replaced the Pig and Saracen in the early 1990s

Self Loading Rifle standard issue, 7.62mm, British Army rifle used throughout the 1960s, 1970s and most of the 1980s.

senior rank non-commissioned ranks from sergeant to WO1 inclusive

Sterling sub-machine gun a short, light, 9mm, automatic weapon, used by some soldiers and members of the RUC

subaltern junior officer of the rank of lieutenant or second lieutenant

Top Cat radio nickname for the Chief Ammunition Technical Officer (CATO), a lieutenant-colonel on the staff of Headquarters Northern Ireland

BIBLIOGRAPHY

PRIMARY SOURCES

Unpublished Private Memoirs, Letters and Interviews

J.A. Anderson GM
D. Aynsley
G.E. Barrow QGM
R.M. Barwell
S. Brazier GM
M. Chapman
A.I. Clouter GM
J.M. Coldrick MBE, GM
P.H. Dandy GM
W. Davies
K. France
S.R. Futcher
A. Gaiger-Booth
K. Goad
J.J. Gordon
D.H. Green
R.W. Harvey
F. Haley
H.G. Heap OBE
G.R. Henderson
C.M.G. Hendy OBE
W.J. Hillman
P. Istead OBE, GM
G.J. Lawrence
D.J. Leadbetter
R.J. Loveridge
D.S. McAdam

M. Medcalf
M.J.F. Middleditch QGM
P. Miller
B.J. Mitchell GM
A.J. Modd GM
P.T. Myring
K.W. Nash GM
R. Noutch
G.A. O'Sullivan MBE, QGM
D. Pickford
B.M. Raine
T.C.K. Ridley OBE
J.D. Ross
S.H. Scourfield-Evans
F.W.R. Smith QGM
G.A. Smith
P.K. Snell
M. Snelson
W.B. Squires
F. Steer MBE
G. Thomas
A.D. Thorogood
R.W. Warren
R. Willcox
J.F. Woodward
A.J. Wright
N.N. Wylde

Military Records

321 EOD Unit Operational Log Book, August 1971–December 1972

Conference Address

Stewart, Brigadier D.C.V., Director of Army Psychiatry, *The Psychometric Assessment of EOD Operators*, Deepcut, March 1977

Gallantry Citations

WO2 J.M. Coldrick GM
WO2 P.H. Dandy GM
Lieutenant-Colonel J.M. Gaff GM
WO1 B. Johnson GC
Captain D. Markham GM
Captain R.F. Mendham GM
Major S.G. Styles GC

Newspapers and Periodicals

Belfast Telegraph (Belfast)
Daily Mail (London)
Irish Times
Newtownards Chronicle
Sunday Times (London)
The Times (London)

SECONDARY SOURCES

Books

Arthur, Max, *Northern Ireland Soldiers Talking, 1969 to Today* (London, Sidgwick & Jackson, 1987)

Barzilay, David, *The British Army in Ulster, 1973–1981*, 4 vols (Belfast, Century Books, 1981)

Birchall, Peter, *The Longest Walk: The World of Bomb Disposal* (London, Arms & Armour Press, 1985)

Coogan, Tim Pat, *The IRA* (London, Fontana, 1980)

——, *The Troubles* (London, Hutchinson, 1995)

De Baroid, Ciaran, *Ballymurphy and the Irish War* (Dublin, Aisling Publishers, 1989)

Dewar, Col Michael, *The British Army in Northern Ireland* (London, Arms & Armour Press, 1985)

Geraghty, Tony, *The Irish War: The Military History of a Domestic Conflict* (London, HarperCollins, 1998)

Hamill, Desmond, *Pig in the Middle: The Army in Northern Ireland, 1969–1984* (London, Methuen, 1985)

Harnden, Toby, *Bandit Country: The IRA and South Armagh* (London, Coronet Books, Hodder & Stoughton, 1999)

Hogben, Maj Arthur, *Designed to Kill* (Yeovil, Patrick Stephens Ltd, 1987)

Holroyd, Fred, and Burbridge, Nick, *War without Honour* (Hull, Medium, 1989)

McCreary, Alf, *Survivors* (Belfast, Century Books, 1976)

Macdonald, Peter G., *Stopping the Clock* (London, Robert Hale, 1977)

McKittrick, David, *Despatches from Belfast* (Belfast, Blackstaff Press, 1989)

——, *Endgame* (Belfast, Blackstaff Press, 1994)

——, Kelters, Seamus, Feeney, Brian, and Thornton, Chris, *Lost Lives* (Edinburgh, Mainstream Publishing, 1999)

MacStiofan, Sean, *A Revolutionary in Ireland* (Dublin, Free Ireland Book Club, 1979)

Maguire, Maria, *To Take Arms: A Year in the Provisional IRA* (London, Macmillan, 1973)

O'Brien, Brendan, *The Long War: The IRA and Sinn Fein, 1985 to Today* (Dublin, O'Brien Press, 1993)

O'Neill, Terence, *The Autobiography of Terence O'Neill* (London, Rupert Hart-Davis, 1973)

Patrick, Lt-Col Derrick, *Fetch Felix: The Fight Against the Ulster Bombers 1976–77* (London, Hamish Hamilton, 1981)

Phelps, Maj-Gen L.T.H., *A History of the Royal Army Ordnance Corps 1945–1982* (Deepcut, Trustees of the RAOC, 1991)

Ryder, Chris, *The Ulster Defence Regiment: An Instrument of Peace?* (London, Methuen, 1991)

Shepherd, Ben, *A War of Nerves: Soldiers and Psychiatrists 1914–1994* (London, Jonathan Cape, 2000)

Styles, Lt-Col George, GC, *Bombs Have No Pity: My War against Terrorism* (London, William Luscombe, 1975)

Taylor, Peter, *Families at War: Voices from the Troubles* (London, BBC Books, 1989)

——, *Provos: The IRA and Sinn Fein* (London, Bloomsbury Publishing, 1997)

Urban, Mark, *Big Boys' Rules: The Secret Struggle Against the IRA* (London, Faber & Faber, 1992)

Watson, Peter, *War on the Mind: The Military Uses and Abuses of Psychology* (Harmondsworth, Penguin Books, 1978)

Academic and Professional Papers

Hallam, R.S., BA Ph.D., and Rachman, S.J., MA Ph.D., 'Courageous Acts or Courageous Actors?', Psychology Department, Institute of Psychiatry, 1980

Scientific Adviser HQNI, 'A Study into Factors which May Influence Performance on the EOD (IEDD) RLC No. 1 Course', October 1997

Thompson, Lt-Col G.W., RAMC, 'A Report on the Selection of EOD Operators', Tidworth, March 1977

Williamson, Paul, 'Psychometric Testing and Selection Procedures for Ammunition Technical Personnel', Cranfield University, October 1994

Website

www.wesleyjohnston.com/users/ireland/past/omagh/event_victim.html
The victims describe the Omagh bomb; recollections by Dorothy Boyle and John King

INDEX